MYSTERIOUS MIDWEST

Unwrapping Urban Legends and Ghostly Tales from the Dead

ADRIAN LEE

[signature]

Wisdom Editions

Minneapolis, Minnesota

Minneapolis

FIRST EDITION OCTOBER 2016
MYSTERIOUS MINNESOTA: Unwrapping Urban Legends and
Ghostly Tales from the Dead.
Copyright © 2016 by Adrian Lee.
All rights reserved.

Printed in the United States of America.
10 9 8 7 6 5 4 3 2 1
ISBN: 978-1-939548-57-3
Cover and interior design: Gary Lindberg

Front cover: Loon Lake Cemetery, Jackson County, MN

Back cover photographs in descending order:
Vaclav Soukup with his family, Jackson, MN
Edith Christie's doll, the Christie House, Long Prairie, MN
The Christie House c1901 with Edith standing on the lawn, Long Prairie, MN
Shadow figure captured on the stairwell of the Kemp Opera House Block,
Long Prairie, MN

Where humanity leaves its footprints, paranormal activity will follow.

I cannot even imagine where I would be today were it not for that handful of family and friends who have given me a heart full of joy. Let's face it, family and friends make life a lot more fun; so imagine the fun we can all have when we're all dead!

CONTENTS

"The most beautiful thing we can experience is the mysterious. It is the source of all true art and science." —Albert Einstein.

Also by Adrian Lee

How to be a Christian Psychic: What the Bible Says about Mediums, Healers and Paranormal Investigators

Mysterious Minnesota

MYSTERIOUS MIDWEST

Unwrapping Urban Legends and
Ghostly Tales from the Dead

ADRIAN LEE

FOREWORD

"From the earth up through the trees... I can hear her calling me. Her voice rides on the breeze... Oh, it's haunting me."

Megadeth – "Mary Jane"

I am a native of Jackson, Minnesota, a lovely, yet industrious, farm community nestled around the Des Moines River in southwestern Minnesota. Located just a few miles north of the Iowa border, and only an hour's drive from the eastern edge of South Dakota, with open skies, clean air, and 10,000 lakes of gracious and plentiful water, it truly is God's country.

Settled in the 1800s, Jackson is the quintessential Midwest farm setting, designed for families whose ancestry was all about raising crops, livestock, and enjoying the simpler things in life. Two of the things I loved the most about growing up there, before moving to Hollywood in 1983 to pursue my dream of rock stardom with Megadeth, were the friendliness of the people and the feeling that one is far from big city danger. On the farm, we left our houses unlocked with the keys in the car with nary a concern for theft or illicit behavior. Neighbors dropped in frequently to spend hours a day just chatting about the current affairs of the area, usually over a cup of coffee and 'bars' (those tasty desserts handed down from local recipes of neighbors, harnessed within the pages of the church recipe cookbook). Everybody knows everybody, and never does a need go unnoticed without a helping hand from a friendly neighbor, always at the ready to pitch in and help.

These are centennial farms and villages, founded by ancestors from the early migration of the 1800s into these regions, almost all of European descent, built firmly on the traditions and superstitions of their European homelands.

But, like most quaint villages, there brews a disturbing mixture of rumor and hearsay, left over from bygone generations, of 'things that go bump in the night.' Just a few miles south of Jackson lies Loon Lake Cemetery, filled with the headstones and memorials of the founding generations of pioneering families in southern Minnesota. From this one rural cemetery unfolded haunting tales of tragedy and hardships—tales those who playfully violated these graves believed, as if the witchcraft buried within them was actually true. As a curious teenager, the morbid fascination with these tall tales ran deep in me, and these sometimes frightening local fables took on a life all their own.

As daring teenagers without much else to do, my generation of youngsters would often sneak into Loon Lake to taunt these gravesites, knowing that no deed would go unpunished. We would creep around amongst ominous graves by moonlight, with irrational fear building in our guts. The threat of being caught by the cops was always a consideration, but that ran a distant second to the supernatural wrath we feared we were about to unleash; yet we persisted.

Seemingly, the spirit of one of those local 'Urban Legends' followed me all the way to Hollywood and would go on to establish itself firmly into heavy metal lore through a song called "Mary Jane." Fast forward many years, and MEGADETH was putting together songs for our third album, *So Far, So Good... So What!* which would be released by Capitol Records in 1988.

After we finished the *Peace Sells* album, Dave Mustaine and I flew back to the farm in Minnesota where I grew up. I took Dave down to Loon Lake and showed him a grave that lies on top of a hill out in the middle of a field. The wind was blowing, and it was very haunting. Dave really caught the spirit of it.

So together we wrote "Mary Jane," which would go on to become not only a single, but a classic song in the Megadeth repertoire, further propagating the myth of the young girl buried alive in the Loon Lake Cemetery. And, like most things heavy metal, "Mary Jane" took on a life of its own, giving birth to new generations of fans intrigued by this macabre tale.

Is it folklore, or is it truth? Could these horrifying stories be real, or are they just fiction? Are they just tall tales blown out of proportion to keep teenagers out of graveyards?

The book you now hold unwraps the tales that have so delightfully gripped us natives for decades. Author Adrian Lee has masterfully brought his inquisitive light to the darkest side of quaint farm life while uncovering the truths and dispelling sordid myths across the mysterious Midwest.

So sit back and enjoy these intriguing and intense tales of the paranormal, which have over time become persistent 'Urban Legends.'

David Ellefson
Megadeth Bassist

PREFACE

Here we are again—four years after my first book *Mysterious Min-nesota*—with a whole new collection of previously unseen para-normal evidence and social history. Read about first-hand, real-life ghosts and hauntings recorded and documented across the historic Midwest. Hear tales of executions, grisly murders, witches, strange masonic practices, curses, ghostly children, and headless spirits. These are all played out in front of a backdrop of creepy disused schools, magnificent mansions, abandoned cemeteries, soul-filled ships, resplendent theaters, libraries, banks, and grand masonic tem-ples. So let me take you by the hand and lead you into the damp, dark world of the haunted mysterious Midwest—and don't forget your flashlight.

After dedicating so many years of my life to researching my last historical paranormal guidebook, I vowed that I would never at-tempt a second text on the same subject. This was due to the amount of work required in organizing so many high-profile investigations, from liaising with all of the other investigators geographically spread throughout the Midwest, to the considerable amount of time invested in transporting the necessary equipment. Then there was the number of miles and extended journey times I had to consider when traversing this wide and sprawling part of America—and al-ways it seemed in the harshest and most exacting of climatic con-ditions.

I also remembered spending endless hours consuming histori-cal research in musty antediluvian library vaults or dusty historical societies, long after the investigations had finished, where one week of searching could leave me with nothing more than a single usable sentence. But was this exhausting process completely inspiring, exciting, ridiculously addicting, morbidly fascinating, and oddly intriguing? Absolutely!

So this book eventually wrote itself. The process of annotating and documenting the investigations and historical researching generated the text one investigation at a time. This has now left me with a document that can be proudly added to the canon of Midwestern social history and a book that will hopefully lead to having a better understanding of the spirit world. With nerve jangling chapters crammed with photographs, haunting history, vivid descriptions, and the very best of paranormal investigating, I guess you just can't keep an enthusiastic historian down.

INTRODUCTION

In this book I wanted to raise an awareness of the smaller towns and homesteads that are scattered throughout the plains of the Midwest, the less familiar locations. I wanted a new and refreshing road trip throughout the states of Iowa, Minnesota, and Wisconsin; one that would be pushing me into areas and buildings that no one had ever investigated before. I wanted to be the very first to discover and write about those ghostly results and findings.

Throughout this book I want to explore what happens when we die and to prove that an afterlife exists. During my research, I discovered that many of the locations were haunted by multiple entities open to engaging in communication. They remained present for many reasons. Some believe they still have a job to do and stay perhaps out of a sense of duty or an obligation. Some have messages to give, or unfinished work to complete. Others are just curious and like frequenting the buildings they once loved. Some turned up because I simply asked for them by name.

I found that the deceased actively want you to document their names and achievements, as many of those details have been lost to time. It appears that if you have an ounce of humanity in your spirit, you will want your name spelled right in a book containing elements of your life. This strengthens my belief that ghosts are there to remind us of our past, and as any historian will tell you, we can only judge the present by what is left to us from the past. It also means that many traits we would consider to be part of the human psyche continue into the afterlife, including our ego. It was a rare occurrence to *not* find some form of paranormal activity in these locations. It can truly be said that wherever humanity leaves its footprints, paranormal activity will follow—and humanity leaves its footprints all over this planet.

Everything paranormal that I have documented in this book is 100 percent factual. As a qualified, practicing historian, and an experienced paranormal investigator, it would be detrimental to my reputation to elaborate upon anything other than the facts. In actuality, such a wealth of paranormal evidence presented itself in every location that I had the difficult task of editing my findings down into manageable chapters. An entire book could have been solely written about the Christie House or Fairlawn, for example.

All of the paranormal phenomena I have highlighted were witnessed not only by myself, but by the professional and experienced members of The International Paranormal Society who assisted in the investigations. The evidence presented exists as video footage, photographs, documented measurable data, and audio files—and most incidents were recorded on multiple devices. The paranormal activity was also witnessed and experienced by the owners and workers of each property as they accompanied me on the vigils. Many were skeptical and had little interest in the workings of the paranormal until they made sharp contact with it. They can verify that everything documented in this book happened and was genuine.

It was important to inform my version and understanding of the historical events described in this book through the use of primary source material. These included newspaper articles, photographs, period documents, banking details, letters, and interviews. I was then able to uniquely add to this methodology the facts presented to me by the dead. As a historian I would be dismissed by my peers if this book was nothing more than a collection of conversations I had experienced with spirits via my psychic skills or equipment. But as I began to research the details presented to me by the dead, I found them to be true. So the spirits focused and narrowed my research and directed me to new historical or lost information. It was the catalyst for my work, and the result is now in your hands.

This combination of historical research and paranormal investigating creates a very powerful tool, especially if you can utter the name of a person who was intrinsic to the fabric of a building, usually one who has long since been forgotten. On this journey I have spoken with entities, been touched, seen apparitions, and witnessed events that I cannot rationally understand—so by default they are paranormal—above and beyond normality in that they cannot be explained by known science. I cannot always give a reason for the nature of these experiences I have encountered, but they are all documented here for readers to form their own opinions. Some of the ghosts and spirits were good and some were bad; this is just a reflection of society in general. But in all circumstances respect was shown to those we encountered. This project was not about provoking innocent, kind, deceased people into performing parlor tricks. It was about recording their lives and thoughts to give us a better understanding of our history.

The International Paranormal Society

I am the founder of The International Paranormal Society and a member of the Luton Paranormal Society in England. I have comprehensively investigated ghosts and paranormal activity all over the globe. I first became interested in the paranormal after experiencing several events in my childhood home. In adult life the idea progressively intrigued me to interface with the dead from a historical perspective. I first came to Minnesota early in 2008 to work on several paranormal video productions and spent two years working in Minneapolis as the national and international news correspondent for a live paranormal talk radio show on 100.3 KTLK. I currently host the only weekly paranormal news quiz show *More Questions than Answers*, live every Friday on the Dark Matter Digital Radio Network.

My paranormal investigations are informed by my clairvoyance. I see detailed pictures in my third eye, presented by the deceased. This allows me to have a very precise communication with the spirits. I also have the skill of remote viewing and clairsentience. In my youth my psychic sensitivities were dormant for some time. It was only through my work with other 'sensitives' and through being exposed to various kinds of paranormal contact—coupled with my own personal psychic development—that I developed to where I can now utilize those skills freely. Like any other ability, my clairvoyance continues to evolve and is becoming stronger through the implementing of a design for life, critical introspection, and practice.

I have also written the following books: *Mysterious Minnesota: Digging up the Ghostly Past at 13 Haunted Sites*; *How to be Christian Psychic: What the Bible says about Mediums, Healers and Paranormal Investigators*; and Tale*s of a Pioneer Town: the Earliest Stories of Sauk Centre, Minnesota*. I currently lecture on all aspects of the paranormal, including ghosts, UFOs, psychic development, and angels.

My journey through the haunting world of the mysterious, strange, and bizarre was undertaken with the members of The International Paranormal Society. Their input, support, comradeship, evidence, and professionalism runs through this book like a meta-narrative and is recorded in every sentence and vigil. Let me introduce them to you:

Heather is my most experienced paranormal investigator and has been intrinsic to the majority of the audio evidence presented here. She is a leading expert on Electronic Voice Phenomena (EVP), the audio recording of disembodied voices. Heather also participated in investigations for the *Mysterious Minnesota* book. Before joining The International Paranormal Society, she was the founder of Hellhound Investigations.

Lorna was the Minnesota State Director for the Mutual UFO Network (MUFON) for many years. MUFON is a global nonprofit organization that investigates and records UFO sightings and activity. She is very analytical and was once employed as a Death Investigator. She is an accomplished and experienced team leader of the highest caliber. She is also responsible for the team's websites and products. She is the founder of the *Lakes Area Paranormal Interest Group* based in St. Cloud.

Scott is an experienced paranormal investigator and team leader who originally participated with the team at the Chase on the Lake Resort in Walker and the St. James Hotel in Red Wing, where he impressed the team with his knowledge and technical skills. Scott also excels at reviewing evidence.

Kim has a very skeptical and analytical mind. She does her best work behind the scenes and in the shadows when our team is delivering lectures, holding events, or preparing to investigate.

Greg is one of our technical experts. He is often found running vast lengths of cabling through old buildings and basements for our infrared cameras. He is also responsible for towing our trailer/command center to each investigation. He is the studio engineer for all of our media work and is skilled in using the thermal imaging devices and video cameras. He is married to Kim.

Paul is a technical expert who builds his own paranormal equipment. He is one of our most reliable investigators and has been with the team for many years. He brings a wealth of invaluable knowledge and know-how.

Karen is an active member of MUFON and a member of the *Lakes Area Paranormal Interest Group*. She has also been a long serving member of the team.

Ashley is a seasoned team leader and brings a down-to-earth attitude and knowledge to the paranormal. Ashley participated in several investigations for the *Mysterious Minnesota* book and is Heather's sister.

Jordan is new to the field of paranormal investigating and is the youngest member of our team.

Many other investigators have contributed to this book throughout its long journey. They include team members Kris, Gloria, Caroline, Pat, Brian, Sarah, Adam, and the members of *S.E.E. Paranormal* in Iowa.

Equipment

Throughout this book I will refer to various tools and devices that I have employed during the paranormal investigations. I have listed below a glossary of that equipment, and I will expand upon their use in more detail as they are mentioned.

Digital Voice Recorders (DVRs) are used by the paranormal investigator to document the vigils and ghost box sessions. It has been my experience that when listening to disembodied voices only a small percentage of the conversation is heard in real time, with the majority being documented via the recording. It is believed that some dialogues are only picked up on these devices because they are capable of recording at wider frequencies than our own hearing. DVRs are also used to record Electronic Voice Phenomena (EVP). This is when you are able to hear a voice without any other equipment being used—as if the spirit is standing next to you and whispering in your ear. I use very advanced DVRs that have twin tubular condensing microphones as well as the cheaper models, since these older devices do not filter out background noise, the audio information we are actually seeking to record.

Ghost Box devices scan radio frequencies at various speeds and can generate words and sentences believed to be from those in spirit. Sometimes called a *shack-hack,* they can be modified radios or purpose-built devices for use in the paranormal field, like the P-SB 7. Spirits can use the words that are presented to them on the radio so they can communicate, like piecing together a ransom note where each word is taken from a different newspaper headline to create a sentence. They also generate white noise that allows voices to be heard under the static. Due to this process, the words uttered by disembodied voices can be hard to hear or distinguish. The recording of these sessions with a DVR allows me to listen retrospectively in a quiet, controlled environment with earbuds. More of the conversation then becomes apparent as audio information can be missed at the time. I also ask spirits to restate words and sentences to confirm the dialogue during the vigil. This allows me to make sure I have heard correctly and to remove the element of coincidence. These tools have been likened to electronic Ouija boards, but this would be a misrepresentation since the communication is via the machine and not through me or any other individual.

Electrical Magnetic Field (EMF) Meters are used to measure the amount of ambient electrical magnetic energy in a location. It is believed that ghosts need energy to be able to manifest and be physical. This is said to be EMF energy and can be recorded. A K2 EMF meter is a handheld device that registers electrical energy in a series of colored LEDs—EMF is measured in a unit of energy called a gauss. The Melmeter is a tool that also measures EMF but has a calibrated and more accurate numbered digital display. It is possible to have a very basic dialogue with a spirit using these meters if the entity moves back and forth over the device to register a reading in response to a question asked. Fuse boxes, electrical sockets, and electric poles will register an EMF reading.

Full Spectrum Cameras take photographs that cover part of the electromagnetic spectrum, from infrared to ultraviolet. This is a useful tool since we can see more through the viewing screen than we can with our own eyes.

Infrared Cameras are used to film in dark locations. They are devices that form an image using infrared radiation—similar to a normal camera that forms an image using visible light. Infrared cameras operate in wavelengths as long as 14,000 nm (14 μm). They can be handheld or positioned statically with a tripod, so that empty rooms can be monitored from a central command area or for recording the vigils.

Thermal Imaging Cameras are devices that record and take photographs in a full range of temperatures. This camera can detect radiation in a way similar to how an ordinary camera detects visible light. It works in complete darkness because an ambient light level is not required as the higher the object's temperature the more infrared radiation is emitted. This makes the device useful for rescue operations in smoke-filled buildings and in earthquake situations—as well as for the paranormal investigator.

Trigger Objects are items placed in strategic locations to document interference or physical activity. They can range from the simplicity of drawing around a coin on a piece of paper to the more advanced electronic motion sensors. I have an equipment case full of circular, red and white fishing bobbers. These can be balanced on their ends so they become top-heavy and are light enough to react to the smallest tremor, touch, or breeze. They will then fall and bounce around to notify me of any physical activity—even if I am investigating in another room. I set them up in doorways, on door handles, stairs, the edges of chairs and tables, and anywhere there appears to be a thoroughfare, or next to an object that held significance for the deceased.

We used many other devices during our investigations, including static meters, the Ovilus, laser thermometers, Electro-Magnetic pumps, oscilloscopes, and laser grid pens. I will highlight and explain their function within the text when they are used.

THE CHRISTIE HOUSE

LONG PRAIRIE, MINNESOTA

The face of a ghostly man haunts the house that time forgot.

When I first saw the elaborately designed and historic Christie House I knew it would be haunted—and I was not disappointed. Long Prairie resident and team leader Lorna had originally introduced me to the property, and I approached the Christie Home Historical Society with a proposal to investigate. The house is open to the public during the summer season and is closed during the rest of the year. Before its annual opening the dust covers are removed, and the house is cleaned and made ready for visitors. It was during this week-long window of opportunity that I gained permission to take a small and experienced team into the house that time forgot.

Long Prairie residents have long claimed that the building is haunted. They have described seeing a ghostly figure looking down at them through the north-side attic window. Volunteers have also experienced the sensation of being watched as they entered certain rooms. It was also a common occurrence to find cupboard doors mysteriously opened during the night when the house was left empty.

The Christie House was donated to the city of Long Prairie in 1976 following the death of its final occupant, Dr. Robert L. Christie. The Christie Home Historical Society was then founded as a non-profit organization to preserve the building. The property is now regarded as historically significant by the Minnesota Historical Society as it has remained uniquely unchanged since its construction. Only the Christie family resided here, and the furnishings and artifacts displayed are original to them. The Christie Home Historical Society also possesses extensive historical resources and documentation. I accessed additional information from period newspapers and obituaries at the Todd County Historical Society. The house volunteers were also very knowledgeable and informative.

The History

Long Prairie was first occupied from 1845-1855 when the United States government selected the land to use as a Native American reservation for the displaced Winnebago tribes. After 1855 the area was largely unpopulated until the 1860s when settlers began to build farmsteads and reside in the area, attracted by the rich soil and easy river access. During the 1880s the town became the local county seat, and a courthouse and railroad were constructed. This transformed Long Prairie into a successful commercial and farming community.

Margaret and Andrew Christie came over from Scotland on the Glasgow registered ship *Alsatia* to start a new life. They landed in New York harbor and entered onto American soil on April 23, 1855. Andrew was a mason by trade but looked to find work as a tailor in this burgeoning country. Their first son, George Ralph Christie, was born on January 19, 1858 in Berlin, Wisconsin and was later joined by his younger brother Robert in 1860.

George grew up with ambitions to be a medical practitioner and was a good student. He subsequently graduated from Rush Medical College in Chicago at the age of twenty-four. It is believed that Dr. Edwin Sinclair from Sauk Centre (Sinclair Lewis' father) then encouraged Dr. Christie to relocate to Long Prairie, having met him at the same college. The first record of Dr. Christie practicing in Long Prairie came on February 22, 1884 in an advertisement placed in the *Todd County Argus*. Dr. Christie stated that he could be found for consultation at the Canfield Drug Store and the American House, a local hotel. It was common during this era for doctors and dentists to move from town to town. They would practice in hotel rooms and use the local newspaper to highlight their presence. Many hotels actually doubled as infirmaries as exhausted travelers and businessmen often became unwell during their stay. Dr. George Christie set up a purpose built office on Central Avenue in 1884 and operated from that location until 1895.

Dr. Christie settled permanently in the town on May 5, 1886 when he bought a simple farmhouse-styled home close to the current Christie House location. Dr. Christie then married Susan West on September 1, 1887 in Milwaukee, Wisconsin, and the family soon began to grow. Land was subsequently purchased at a cost of $800 with a view to building a larger home. The Christies had four children: George West Christie (1890-1956), a newspaper editor in Red Lake Falls who married Eva Lindbergh (the half-sister of Charles Lindbergh); Dr. Robert L. Christie (1892-1976), the last resident of the Christie House; Edith Lisle Christie (1894-1902); and Donald R. Christie (1896-1985), a banker who settled in Perham.

The Christie House c1901 with Edith standing on the lawn

The architect employed to design the Christie's new abode was a local resident named C. W. Smith. His hand-drawn, white linen blueprints for the 3,100-square-foot building are currently on display in the carriage house. The two-foot-thick foundations were completed first, from local split bedrock and brick. The wood for the house construction was then purchased from Mr. Dinkel for $800 and was cut at the Schomaker Mill on the west side of town at Venewitz Creek. The interior's decorative panels and intricate woodwork were constructed of straight-cut oak. After two years of work, the house was finally completed in 1901 at a cost of $5000.

The exterior of the Christie House perfectly reflects the synergy of Richardson neo-gothic architecture with the classical colonial vernacular. It also boasts many Richard Norman Shaw architectural influences with flashes of Queen Anne inspired features and trim. Built during the height of the Arts and Crafts period, the house presents the movement's philosophy perfectly—with its individually handcrafted furniture and décor. The Arts and Crafts influence can be recognized further in the nature-themed, William Morris inspired wallpaper, especially in the parlor and entranceway with its tessellating pineapple motif—a Victorian symbol that represents hospitality. The design manifesto is also reflected in the one-of-a-kind stained glass windows, signed New York Tiffany patrician light fixtures, oriental rugs, curtains, and quilts.

The whole house has a splendid collection of themed stained glass throughout. This glass would have been created and installed at a great cost to the Christie family. Stained glass was so expensive during this era that some families even had it removed when they went on vacation so it would not be stolen. The glass in the Christie House has become irreplaceable since many of the colored dyes used for their production are no longer available.

Gas lighting, plumbing, and electricity were installed as the town evolved. Added to the Christie's new home was a carriage house large enough for a cow and a horse and buggy. The buggy was an important vehicle for the practicing of medicine in a sprawling rural community. A ramp allowed livestock to be kept in the basement below ground level to allow easier access to the buggy and to keep the animals cool in the summer.

Tragedy first hit the Christie family in 1902 when Edith Lisle Christie died at the age of eight. Edith became ill with stomach pains and was operated on by her father on November 21. Unfortunately, he soon realized that he needed help with her treatment. Dr. Christie, Susan, and Edith then made the painful overnight carriage journey to Sauk Centre to catch the train to Minneapolis. Sadly, Edith passed away on November 22 from peritonitis and septicemia caused by a bowel obstruction. Dr. Christie documented the depressing incident in his ledger for that day: *Trip to Mpls Thursday night with "my little sweetheart" Edith who died Nov. 22, 1902. "Peritonitis with septicaemia" at Asbury Hospital.* The grief-stricken doctor could not save his only daughter. Tragedy then struck for a second time in 1905 when Dr. Christie's wife Susan suddenly fell ill, suffering from stomach ulcers. She died on March 28, 1910 at the age of fifty-one. Dr. Christie then married his childhood friend Ida Lewis Mason the following year.

Dr. Christie's son Robert (Bob) followed in his father's footsteps and started studying medicine at the University of Wisconsin, Madison, in 1910. He transferred to the University of Minnesota in the Twin Cities to complete his studies and graduated in 1917. The *Todd County Argus* documents that Dr. Robert then joined the US Navy on May 31, 1917 during the First World War, assuming the rank of Lieutenant Assistant Surgeon. According to his medical naval diaries he served on the USS *Utah* (BB-31), a Florida class dreadnought battleship. This ship was later torpedoed and sunk during the Japanese attack on Pearl Harbor during the Second World War with the loss of sixty-four men. Dr. Robert Christie also served on the Clemson-class destroyer USS *Smith Thompson* (DD-212).

Dr. Robert Christie rejoined his father in Long Prairie in 1921, and both doctors held their medical practice in the home. The library became their office and consulting room, and the kitchen served as a reception area. They even performed surgeries on the kitchen table. Both doctors practiced at Asbury Hospital in Minneapolis, and Dr. Robert became a well-known skin specialist and consultant for the Mayo Clinic. Dr. George Christie was Todd County's oldest physician and surgeon until his death in 1947. Dr. Robert Christie proceeded to live in the house alone after his father's passing and continued to see patients up until his own death in 1976, bringing to an end ninety years of medical care by the Christie family in Long Prairie. Dr. George Christie and Susan are buried in the Long Prairie Cemetery alongside their four children.

The Investigation

Several years before I investigated the Christie House, I attended a charity fundraising luncheon at the property. In 1903 Susan Christie had contributed, with other local ladies, to a cookbook that was published by the Bank of Long Prairie. It included recipes for veal loaf, escalloped oysters, tomato salad, and prune pudding. The food served during this event was taken from this document. I love culinary history and the afternoon was a great success.

A guided tour of the house was given after lunch, and I walked around the elegant and ornate rooms as a guest visitor, rather than a psychic or paranormal investigator, although through curiosity I was open to the idea of seeing what entities frequented the property. Then suddenly, without warning, the spirit of a young woman joined the guided tour in the kitchen. I stepped back, and a chill ran through my body as the dead lady walked among the living unbeknownst to everyone else. As a psychic I am able to see spirits appear in my third eye. This is a concept that refers to an invisible eye that provides perception beyond ordinary sight, so I am not physically seeing the entity in the way that ghosts can appear and present themselves to everybody. I could now see her fully formed and just a few paces away.

I have the ability to control when I see those in spirit. It would be problematic during the course of my average day to see a world filled with dead people. I want to buy my groceries undisturbed. The practice of meditation has given me the ability to quieten and empty my mind. This allows me to differentiate as a clairvoyant between my own thoughts and images and those that are presented to me. Once I could only access the dead psychically after a period of meditation, but with experience and practice I can now plug myself into the spirit world with more ease when required.

As the tour of the house continued, I found a quiet moment away from the group to ask the mysterious woman who she was. She replied she was the housemaid and was checking to make sure the property was left in good condition and that nobody interfered with any of the furnishings or ornaments. She actually appeared a little perturbed when the small crowd filed into her bedroom, as she felt this was an encroachment upon her privacy.

The maid's room was a small, unimpressive space compared to the rest of the house, perhaps befitting of the hired help in a middle-class household. Many of the objects in this room reminded me of the things we now take for granted, including a kerosene lamp and a chamber pot positioned next to the bed. The flushing of a toilet and the flicking of a light switch are now merely reflex actions in today's society. The wallpaper in this room was the original adornment with a decorative printed border. Handmade blue and white bed covers caught my eye in this otherwise sparse room. I had little opportunity to reengage with the maid throughout the tour, since it would have been unfair of me to impose upon the sensibilities and religious beliefs of others—especially when they were there, like me, to just enjoy the house. But this all changed as I entered the dining room.

A long, polished dining table dominated the room and was adorned with the finest porcelain and place settings, all laid out in anticipation of a formal meal. The Limoges French china, with its diaphanous fragility, looked almost too delicate to touch. Cutlery gleamed; napkins were pressed and folded. The dining room had an impressive stained glass window designed with a horn of plenty motif that illuminated the reverential, deep red burlap wall coverings. An ornate, omnipresent, dark wood carved buffet rendered this room into a chapel of dining dedicated to the worship of food.

At that moment the spirit of the maid whispered in my ear. She told me she was sick and tired of Dr. Christie constantly ringing the servant's bell. She complained bitterly of having to run back and forth to the dining room. I'm sure this was in regard to her aching feet and the inability to finish her daily chores due to the frequency of the interruptions. A glimpse into this dining room convention may be gleaned from a book found in the Christie's own collection entitled *Don't,* a text that highlights the complicated etiquette associated with the Victorian middle classes. It includes the insight that servants were required to pass the food at all times during meals—not the diners and guests themselves.

I inspected the dining room vigorously but found no trace of a bell. The maid then informed me that the button was located on the floor and could be pressed with one's foot. This meant the family did not have to leave the dining table to summon her. To the surprise and bewilderment of the visiting party, I proceeded to get down onto my hands and knees to look under the table to see if a bell was visible. Alas, all I witnessed was a large expanse of a decorative antique rug and a flash of polished wooden flooring. As the tour came to an end, I thought about the short interaction I had shared with the maid and wondered if I may have misheard what she was telling me, since no foot-operated bell appeared to exist.

The tour ended back at the visitor's center situated in the carriage house. I was taken aback when the guide introduced me to the other guests as the local psychic and paranormal investigator. I was asked if I had felt or sensed anything paranormal in the house. The only thing I had received psychically in the short time I had ambled around the building was the limited interaction I had shared with the maid. I found myself standing to address the now seated guests, and the event evolved into an impromptu gallery reading. I relayed the limited details of my encounter as everyone listened, enthralled.

Despite the fear of being admonished, I outlined my experience in the dining room when the maid had told me about the bell, despite visual evidence to the contrary. I was glad I had decided to vocalize my experience, because the lady who gave the tour suddenly took an audible intake of breath and blanched. She then proceeded to inform the other guests that the bell on the floor was removed from the dining room nearly twenty years ago—and she was the only person alive who knew the bell had existed. There was a moment of wide-eyed awe and wonder that moved like a wave over the fifty seated visitors.

Those who had been skeptical were suddenly given a lot to ponder. It was this incident that led me to the possibility of gaining entry into the house to undertake the following series of investigations. The maid actually enabled that process, and I thank her for her contribution.

The Walkthrough

The walkthrough of the property was conducted like a giant game of Clue. Jim, the president of the Christie Home Historical Society, took us into the kitchen, then into the dining room, the living room, the study, and finally the hallway—I looked around to see if I could spy a candlestick or some lead piping. What I did discover was a psychic feeling that somebody or something was lurking in the stairwell of the grand staircase looking up at me as I stood outside the master bedroom. It is important to follow your instincts and intuitions. These have been honed over millennia to keep us safe from all kinds of predators during the course of our long existence as hominids, during an era when all manner of mean and nasty animals were intent on making us their dinner. Thus it was important in our evolution to develop a sixth sense to know when we were being tracked. This evolutionary tool obviously worked; there are no saber-toothed tigers around, but humans are still here.

I glanced into the twilight of the grand staircase as my eyes followed my intuition. From the top of the stairs I was privileged to witness the largest of the stained glass windows, but I could not make out the presence of a ghost. I then decided to use my full-spectrum camera and proceeded to take a series of photographs. The full-spectrum camera takes pictures that cover part of the electromagnetic spectrum, from infrared to ultraviolet. Thus one can see more on the viewing screen than through the human eye. As each photograph was briefly presented to me on the back of the camera, I glimpsed a person-sized cloudy shape that looked like a figure forming from what looked like cigar smoke. It seemed to move and drift slowly in front of the window as I saw its locomotion revealed in each passing picture.

A misty form photographed in the stairwell with a
full spectrum camera

I stepped down into the stairwell and looked for any temperature changes or anomalous traces of electrical magnetic energy—I
did not find any. Due to this experience I decided to set up a static
infrared camera in this location and placed a series of trigger objects
on the stairs. This unfortunately provided me with no further evidence. I believe that a spirit was following us around on the walkthrough, and I wondered if this could have been the maid again. This
spirit was not residing permanently in the stairwell.

We decided to use the study as our control area and set out the
equipment. We discussed where the best vantage places might be
for our cameras and where we should focus our vigils and trigger
objects. The study was impressive and had four bookcases that were
filled with medical volumes dating back to the 1880s. Strange and
intriguing surgical devices were scattered around the room, and a

human skull looked on with a scowl. The medical ledger was left open on Dr. Christie's desk and presented the cost of medical care for the early 1900s. Many Long Prairie families were documented in this book, and their histories went back to the earliest pioneer days.

The team moved into the parlor to set up the equipment for the first vigil. The stained glass window to the west illuminated the area with the remnants of the setting sun and draped us in a warm kaleidoscope of colors. I was unsure whether this room should be labeled the parlor or the living room. The Christie House guidebook has it listed as the living room—but this is a fairly recent term. During the nineteenth century and into the early twentieth century, deceased members of the household were laid out for wakes in the parlor as part of the tradition of funerary. I believe Susan and little Edith were laid out in this room. Later, when medical science better understood germs and bacteria, it was determined that keeping corpses in the house in open caskets was unhygienic.

Unfortunately, the tradition had been in place for so long that even when specific buildings were allocated to the task of housing the dead they were not embraced or used. To help with the process and fracture of removing the body of a loved one from the parlor to the possession of a stranger, the buildings were given the names *funeral parlors* and *funeral homes*. Gradually, as bodies were no longer laid out in the parlor, the room was renamed the living room since it was no longer a resting place for the dead.

The Kitchen

The kitchen was situated to the left as I entered the house. This was where the maid first came to me in spirit. It had a large black range with a small white enamel pan that sat on the stovetop. This was used for sterilization—it contained syringes and other medical tools. The older residents of Long Prairie remembered the vaccination needles well—they hurt due to their dullness through overuse. The sturdy, wooden kitchen table was used until 1917 for the purposes of surgery. I believed that a residual energy from the pain and possible suffering undertaken on this table could be present. I would not be surprised if surgically removed body parts were buried on the grounds of the Christie House.

Lorna set up a static infrared camera in the doorway to the kitchen to record any paranormal activity that might take place in this area. It visually covered the table and the laundry room beyond. I had placed a selection of trigger objects on the table including a large, red and white fishing bobber. I also positioned a K2 meter next to the objects in full view of the camera. I turned off the light and shut the room down leaving the camera running for the duration of our investigation throughout the house. This was a controlled area with no access for any of the investigation team. I left the kitchen and positioned myself in the parlor to start the first vigil. Suddenly we heard the bobber bouncing around the kitchen floor, and we hurried back to the kitchen and turned on the light. The bobber had disappeared under the table, and I glimpsed its last motion as it finished rolling around the room. Right then I knew we had caught the whole incident on film.

I played the footage back immediately and witnessed a strange and bizarre series of events unfolding before me on the monitor. After I had turned off the light and left the room, a large number of orbs started to appear in the darkness. An orb is a solid or transparent ball of energy and light. Some parapsychologists believe that orbs are spirits or lingering energy from deceased entities. Orbs can appear in many different shapes and colors with white orbs being the most common. In my experience many of the orbs that appear in photographs can be explained away by the flash reflecting off dust particles, insects, or moisture droplets in the air in front of the camera. Witnessing orbs with your own eyes or with a device that does not emit a light is a better example of paranormal evidence and can remove that element of doubt. This was the case with the camera we positioned in the kitchen.

We continued to observe the scene as an orb then shot from the top, right-hand corner diagonally to the bottom, left-hand corner at high speed. Several other orbs then ran through the kitchen and disappeared into the laundry room. They all emitted their own light, and the camera's autofocus kept adjusting as they appeared and disappeared. Some moved quickly across the screen in an upwards direction and looked like tracer bullets streaming into the ceiling above.

Then a shaft of darkness moved across the room from left to right. It stopped at the pantry door, and we could now see a dark, humanoid-shaped shadow standing and hovering against the white door. Then the bobber was pushed off the table in a single quick motion. Moments later a swirling orb danced around the position the bobber had vacated in a circular, whirlpool motion. Ten seconds after that the camera recorded the team running back into the room and turning on the light to see what was happening.

Before I had a chance to comprehend the phenomena of the orbs, the shadow figure, and the poltergeist activity, I was called back into the parlor. One of our flashlights had just turned on by itself in our absence. I hurried back into the parlor and saw the bright beam of light spreading across the parlor rug. This opening activity reinforced the anticipation I had felt when I first entered the building. We regained our composure after running from room to room in a bid to catch up with the paranormal activity and set up the trigger objects once more, closing down the kitchen for a second time.

The Parlor

When I had first visited the house on my documented guided tour, I could not fail to notice an Edison Victrola that sat resplendently in the corner of the parlor. It emanated its luxuriant presence with its skilled crafted beauty in the haze of a warm, wooden, polished glow. It was bought in 1915 by the Christie family and was insured for the princely sum of $300. It came from Camden, New Jersey, and was soon accompanied by a fine collection of RCA records, mostly of the classical genre. This device is still operational, and the sound of music can be occasionally heard drifting through the house for some lucky visitors.

I decided that it might be beneficial to re-create the sound of the Victrola during our parlor vigil. I believed that it could be a catalyst for grabbing the attention of any spirits that might be present in the house. I have witnessed many positive results when implementing this technique in other historical buildings. In some early Minnesotan theaters, I have even played the sound of the organ music that once accompanied the live action of an old, flickering silent movie.

I recorded several tracks via my laptop onto a compact disc before the investigation and packed a portable stereo with my equipment. I now pressed the play button and waited. The first track was the 1912 hit "By the Light of the Silvery Moon," sung by Ada Jones and accompanied by a male quartet featuring Billy Murray. The track started with the usual crackling, hissing, and clicking that accompanies the beginning of most old gramophone records. Then the Victorian parlor room was filled with the sound and atmosphere of a bygone era, under the questioning gaze of the stoic, sepia-tinted portraits that seemed to look down on me disapprovingly.

The hairs on the back of my neck stood up! This is not a common occurrence for a seasoned paranormal investigator. But as the sound of the record quickened and slowed due to the warped nature of the recording, and the eerie distorted singing started to fill the air, I felt a strong sense of foreboding. It was rapidly becoming a scene from the creepiest horror film and at that very moment I feared for what might happen next if a spirit decided to manifest right there in front of me. I am a tall, well-built guy, and the rough edges created by my East London upbringing sometimes show through the armor of my refined education, but in that moment I gripped the arms on my chair hard. I have been asked many times during my career if I have ever been scared, to which I reply, "No, I have never been scared, but I have been concerned a few times." As I sat there in the dark with the dim glow of my equipment scattered around me, I was concerned.

The concept of trying to encourage spirits to respond by using music from a certain period is called the *Singapore Theory*. It is also known as the *Theory of Familiarization* or *Paranormal Stimuli*.

This concept involves trying to re-create the audio environment of a particular era in an attempt to stimulate paranormal activity. This is achieved by providing a comfortable and familiar environment in which the spirits would be more willing to interact. This theory can also be applied to environmental stimuli in a visual form by filling a building with historical furniture to re-create a period feel, like in a museum tableau or the décor of a historical bed and breakfast, for example. The use of trigger objects from a certain era, or the wearing of period costumes may also be considered a facet of this technique. The re-creation of a traumatic or historic event can also fall into this category. It then comes as no surprise that ghosts and spirits are attracted to reenactors in period costume.

The music did elicit the response I had hoped for, and the K2 meter I had placed on the rug flickered into life. It started to pulse from its neutral green position all the way up to the amber reading of 15 milligauss and back again. Most electrical magnetic field (EMF) activity caused by non-paranormal influences should be displayed as a constant reading as the electrical device activating the reading is either on or off. After the vigil, we inspected the basement directly below to see if anything could have been influencing the meter, but we found nothing. Then the pulsing began to become synchronised to the rhythm of the song we were playing. I placed two additional K2 meters on the floor and watched as all three devices blinked in unison to the beat of the song. I grabbed my full spectrum camera and recorded the entire experience from start to finish.

With Lorna and Scott's help we edged the three K2 meters out from the middle of this concentric circle to see how far the EMF energy would reach. The EMF readings continued to register on each device as we slowly backed away from the centre of the rug. We discovered that the energy dissipated at around the circumference of a hula-hoop. I suggested that a large column of energy could be running through the entire building. I was informed by Lorna that this was the location where the volunteers had said they had felt an uneasy sensation. I had never experienced such a bizarre set of circumstances registered on a K2 meter before. We then placed a thermometer and a trigger object in the circle of energy, but this failed to record any significant results. I also stood within the mapped out circle on the rug but felt no discernible difference from standing outside of the circle—either psychically or physically.

Then as the song finished, a second tune began. We then noticed a discernible decrease in the amount of pulsing energy now being registered. I suspected that whoever was causing this phenomenon was not as enamoured with the second track as they had been with the first. I then played the first song again. The energy immediately picked up and the readings went back to what they were when we started the experiment. This now suggested an element of intelligence to be able to distinguish the difference between each track and respond accordingly. To inform my theory further about the column of energy rising up through the building, we went into the guest bedroom directly above the parlor. We gathered the same readings in exactly the same spot over the bed in the room above and then in the attic above that. If we could have safely got onto the roof, I am sure we would have registered the same readings there too.

In all the excitement of moving the K2 meters around the rug in the parlor like a giant game of chess, and with the volume of the music being played, we had failed to notice that a fishing bobber trigger object placed on the piano had been knocked to the floor. Scott wondered if the process of moving around the rug had caused a vibration that may have dislodged the object. So we placed the bobber in the same spot and walked around the room. Scott even jumped up and down next to the piano, but not a single tremor was felt. These old Victorian houses were built sturdily from thick timbers and the floorboards were as solid as concrete. The piano was also a hefty piece of crafted furniture and would have required a burly team to relocate it. I left the vigil confident that our own locomotion had not interfered with the moving of the trigger object. We had already experienced poltergeist activity in the kitchen, so it would not be unreasonable to suggest that it also occurred in the parlor.

The Attic

The back stairs were primarily used by the maid and were uniquely curved to guide visitors towards the attic in a resplendent ascent of oak wainscoting. This is the attic that every child wants to explore. There was a telescope, old trunks left behind from the days of railroad travel, and the majority of the Christie's book collection. Paintings and prints were strewn around, and hooks were found placed in the rafters for the purpose of a clothesline. Two walnut beds, once used by the Christie children, gave the area the feel of a dormitory. This was where local residents believed they had seen a ghostly face looking down at them from the window.

Before every investigation we take hundreds of photographs of each room. This procedure is part of our baseline tests and acts as the perfect way to document the environments we will be working in. These photographs become an important tool for reference if an object moves during a vigil or a door slams in another part of the house. We can then look back to see how the objects were placed before the paranormal activity occurred. It also acts as a useful *aid memoir* when describing the locations we investigate. With digital photography it is now possible to take multiple photographs that can be deleted if later not required.

The attic with the dresser and mirror

Heather completed this task during the Christie House investigation. In the attic she moved around the space photographing and documenting every aspect of the interior, from the furniture to the decorative objects. She took several photographs of Dr. George Christie's long, buffalo skin coat that was hanging in the middle of the attic room. This would have been an invaluable garment for a nighttime emergency call during a chilling Minnesotan winter. Next to the coat was positioned a small dresser with drawers and a rectangular, wooden-framed mirror. A pencil portrait of Ida's daughter Lucille was resting against the mirror.

The dresser and mirror with the haunting male face reflected above the picture frame

After the investigation Heather uploaded the photographs she had taken of the attic. In the picture she had taken of the coat and dresser, she saw the face of a man looking back at her in the sliver of mirror between the gilded picture frame and the wooden surround. This was a chilling experience for Heather when she realized that the ghost she had captured as a reflection must have been standing next to her without her knowledge. The man's face was flesh colored and looked very real and three-dimensional. He had the look of a more elderly gentleman with slightly drawn eyes and a balding head. There were no men investigating the property that fitted this description and Heather was working by herself when she took the photographs.

This was a remarkable piece of evidence, as capturing the face of an apparition is exceptionally rare. We then looked to ascertain who this ghostly face might belong to. Lorna said he looked exactly like Dr. George Christie, so we compared the image of the ghostly face to a portrait of Dr. Christie hanging in the study. The resemblance was remarkable, and based on the visual evidence presented here I am confident in saying that the ghostly image in the mirror was that of Dr. George Christie who died in 1947. He appeared to still be residing in the house he once built and loved.

The ghostly face of Doctor George Christie appearing in the mirror compared with two portraits of Doctor Christie from the house

The Children's Room

The children's room had a hand-carved and brasswork bed with a lowboy dresser. The furniture set here was the oldest in the house. Edith's doll and Robert's Native American collection were museum quality relics of a bygone childhood and decorated the room in an eerie manner. I started a vigil in this location with Paul and Scott in the hope of making contact with Edith, the daughter of Dr. George Christie, who had died at a young age under tragic circumstances.

The vigil was reflective of much of the work we undertake on paranormal investigations. We sat there in the dark with very little happening. I had tried to tune in psychically but to no avail, and the equipment was not registering anything anomalous in this location. Just as I was about to give up, I received the smallest hint of ghostly activity when I asked the question "Who is here?" In just two repeated words I had the evidence I had been looking for. In response to my question the ghost box replied, "Edith, Edith" in quick succession. Then, as much as I tried for the rest of the vigil, little else took place. I have surmised that the amount of interaction depends on the amount of energy a spirit has. The energy required to sustain a prolonged contact drains the spirits, and they can become flat without warning as the energy is dissipated through the action of being physical or talking.

The Dining Room

After limited results investigating the children's room, I set up a vigil in the dining room. This was an area where the maid had spoken to me. I was confident I could document some kind of activity there. I decided that a better response in the children's room might be forthcoming if I sent a team of women into that location, due to their maternal nature and the affinity a child might have towards them. I wondered if the process of talking to three unknown hairy men was ever going to elicit a strong response from an eight-year-old girl, especially when one of the hairy men had a strange accent.

I set out the equipment on the dining room table trying not to disturb any of the expensive china. Paul and Scott joined me and we sat there like three little boys waiting patiently for our dinner. After experiencing so much activity during our first vigil, I was lulled into believing this would be the norm for the rest of the investigations. Unfortunately, the vigil in the dining room appeared bereft of any incidents. The women came back down from the children's room with a similar tale to tell. I thought this to be odd since we had previously made contact with Edith in that location, be it briefly. I then believed she may have left that area and followed me down to the dining room.

As with the incident involving the photograph of Dr. George Christie, the audio and visual review of each vigil takes place after the investigation. For every hour of investigating a further hour is required for every DVR and camera that is in operation during that vigil. It was several weeks later when Scott contacted me to tell me of an EVP he had picked up in the dining room. He had captured a Grade A EVP during what we thought was the quietest vigil of the night. Halfway through the session you could clearly hear a little girl say, "Mommy, Mommy," with an interval of a second between each word. It reinforced my view that Edith had come down into the dining room with us, thus leaving the women to investigate the children's room without success.

I then listened to my own DVR recording of the dining room vigil and the words *Mommy, Mommy,* can also be heard clearly on this second device. To experience an audio recording of a little girl asking for her mommy in spirit is very disheartening to hear. But I would suggest the tone of her voice made it sound like she was calling her mom like any small child does, indicating that her mother was also in the house in spirit. I do not need to remind any mothers reading this of how many times your child calls out *Mommy* during the course of a day.

Conclusion

The paranormal evidence presented in this location was very impressive in its frequency and diversity, from the filming of the poltergeist activity and the shadow figure in the kitchen, to the way
the entities responded to the period music. The EVP Scott captured
in the dining room was one of the strongest I have heard, and the
photograph of the ghost in the stairwell and the image of Dr. George
Christie's face were unprecedented. Yet none of this evidence would
have been possible without the cooperation and support of the Christie Home Historical Society and the residents of Long Prairie. Their
willingness to embrace my work and my team enabled us to be so
productive.

I can understand why the Christie family still wants to frequent
their home in the afterlife. The Christie House is a location for them
to haunt that presents an enshrined dedication to the beneficent life-
style of the fortunate few during that era; a place where not just
the model of social etiquette was displayed, but also the visible at-
tributes of craftsmanship, pride, and expertise. It is evident on every chair leg, every tablecloth, and every inch of wallpaper. It is
also the place where they lived, loved, laughed, worked, cried, and
grieved—a concentrated microcosm of what humanity is and represents, captured in a decorative time capsule for all to observe and
cherish. Why would their spirits be anywhere else?

The Christie family was born in a period of history where reading, music, and cultural learning were prominent leisure activities
and pastimes, an era where ladies learned the crafts of lace-mak-
ing, piano playing, and culinary excellence, and where gentlemen
opened doors and doffed their hats for those ladies. I suspect there is
a small part in all of us that actually wishes those conventions were
still here. In the Christie House they are.

THE FIRST NATIONAL BANK

LONG PRAIRIE, MINNESOTA

A dead employee now resides where only the bricks and mortar remain.

I have experienced every extreme of cold climatic conditions when investigating in the Midwest, ranging from the bitter interior of a cargo freighter beneath the frozen surface of Lake Superior, to the biting winds of a treeless pioneer cemetery. Yet the investigations at the bank and opera house in Long Prairie, between the months of February and April, were the coldest I can ever recall. In the falling temperatures, our batteries failed and rendered our equipment unusable. We progressively embraced an 'old school' approach, relying more on our senses and a pen and paper—but even that plan foundered as the ink froze!

I had met Rob, the owner of the bank, during the Long Prairie History and Ghost Walk the previous summer. He was in the process of remodeling the building's interior and was open to the suggestion of an investigation. Rob had experienced activity in the bank that he considered paranormal. He was working late on the property on a Sunday evening when the lights suddenly went out. His flashlight then failed when he tried to make his way into the basement to check the fuse box. He proceeded to feel his way in the darkness and located the problem. As soon as the building was reilluminated the flashlight mysteriously worked again. It would appear that the spirits residing at this property were eager to gain his attention.

Team leader Lorna provided me with a wealth of historical documentation via the Todd County Historical Society archives, including period newspapers, obituaries, and photographs. Her contributions to organizing and researching the Long Prairie investigations were invaluable.

History

The First National Bank was constructed in 1909 at a cost of $6,000. Its design perfectly reflects the period taste for neoclassical Greek revivalist architecture that is proudly displayed in every part of its form and features, combining the attributes of symmetry, harmony, balance, and strength. Its reinforced Bedford rock pediment, denticular cornice, Ionic styled columns, and inspired scrollwork reflect this classical vernacular.

In June 1927 the People's National Bank purchased the First National Bank and further building work and redevelopment was undertaken. Moorman and Company were tasked with enlarging and rearranging the building, extending both the front and the rear to create a greater floor space, and introducing a modern steam heating system. The building continued to serve the banking public of Long Prairie up until 1964. It was then donated to the town and used as the city hall. It then became the police headquarters and finally a community corrections office. Despite its dilapidation, the bank clings stubbornly to enough remaining features to make me believe it will once more be one of the finest buildings on Long Prairie's Central Avenue, a potential jewel shining in one of the sporadic gaps created by the closed and disused buildings that now seem to litter every Main Street in every small town.

Investigation

Our investigation represented the last opportunity to explore this great building in its original form. This large, echoing space was now adorned with building debris, exposed wiring, and broken masonry. It made picking my way through the property hazardous. I looked down to find a safe passage through the evidence of dilapidation and noticed a beautiful, mosaic, tessellated floor beyond the dust and dirt. This wonderful tiling drew my attention, but I should have been looking up at the impressive circular, stained glass, domed skylight dominating the high ceiling. I was being visually informed from every angle of the grandiose standing of this property and its success at presenting a pillar of banking within the community.

The interior of the First National Bank with the domed stained glass window

I started the walkthrough in the basement to familiarize myself with the property and to gather baseline data. This area had thick, whitewash-painted river rock walls and was used by the bank to house a walk-in safe. The rooms were located around a turning corridor, and as my flashlight darted into each one I gained a glimpse of long, tall shelving units presented in rows. These repositories once held documents for the bank, city hall, police department, and correction facility.

As the team made its way along the corridor, Kim noticed her K2 meter spiking violently into the red with a measurement of twenty-five milligauss, which is the highest possible reading on this device. It stayed in this position for several minutes before disappearing. It then randomly returned back to this reading after short interludes. Scott brought his K2 meter into the area and the same readings were reflected on his device. I sensed that we were being followed around in spirit as we were undertaking the walkthrough. This would explain the transient nature of the EMF readings. This building had been left unoccupied for some time and no other electrical equipment was present in this vicinity to contaminate our readings.

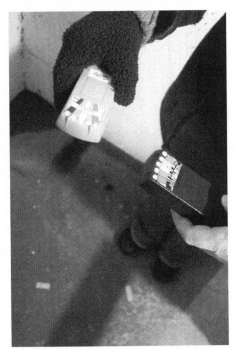

Electrical-magnetic energy recorded on a K2 meter in the basement of the First National Bank

We started our first vigil in the basement and I positioned the investigators in order to obtain the best coverage of the space. Each team member was within verbal contact, even though some individuals were located in other rooms. Scott and Lorna were in the large, walk-in bank safe. Heather was positioned in one of the record rooms, and I went with Greg, Paul, and Karen into the corridor. We placed infrared cameras and DVRs throughout the basement to record any visual and audio evidence. We also utilized several EMF meters, an electro-magnetic (EM) pump, a ghost box, an Ovilus, and several trigger objects including a helium balloon that sat suspended from a string halfway between the floor and ceiling.

The vigil had barely started when I felt the presence of a spirit creating a coldness behind me. I felt a chill on my back as it peered over my right shoulder. My back was confirmed to be colder by a ten-degree drop by using a laser thermometer, compared to the front of my body. We then heard a crash coming from the floor above. We were obviously beginning to stir up paranormal activity and I braced myself for contact.

Without warning, I then psychically saw a gentleman in spirit literally walk through the wall from the basement of the building next door. He was standing in the corridor looking at me. He was an Edwardian looking man with circular, brass-rimmed glasses and a period waxed moustache. He was wearing an apron and sported black elasticated bands on his arms in order to keep his shirtsleeves up. I casually asked the gentleman if he had come from next door. He replied by saying, "Yes." I then asked him for his name. His response was difficult to determine, but I believed he uttered a word similar to "Schrivener" or "Schrader". I asked him what year he thought it was and he produced a newspaper to show me. The headline documented the sinking of the *RMS Titanic*. That would be 1912. I began to notice that our interaction was creating a steady increase in EMF activity. It was rising one increment at a time, starting at 0.2 milligauss, before reaching 0.4 and 0.5, then all the way up to 0.8 and 0.9.

My thoughts were then interrupted by a second spirit that travelled between Lorna and me, leaving goosebumps on my left arm. Seconds later, a flashlight placed on the floor in front of the bank vault started strobing on and off very quickly, filling the room with flickers of bright intermittent light like a nightclub dance floor. The floating balloon trigger object then started spinning slowly around on its own without any external stimulus. I began to wonder what else might ensue during our evening.

Then a sane moment of stillness prevailed. The gentleman in spirit had disappeared and the basement regained its calmness. Everything fell silent. We now listened intently for any sound that might point to a further paranormal presence. Scott then heard a woman whispering in his ear. He quickly recovered his DVR, and we gathered around in the hope of hearing the disembodied voice he had heard moments earlier. Scott pressed the play button as we held our breath.

"Help!" came the message loud and clear.

This was a chilling and startling response as we heard the emotive despair in her voice. We continued with the vigil in an attempt to contact the female spirit. We tried for several hours and used every piece of expertise, experience, and equipment available to us. Yet, despite our intent, the basement remained bereft of any further contact. I wondered if she had used the last trace of her energy in a final bid to contact us through the physicality of the spoken word, and by interacting with the flashlight and balloon trigger object.

I then implemented the Ovilus. This device measures the ambient temperature and electromagnetic fields in the environment and assigns specific words to the changes in those aspects. An extensive lexicon of words is then made available and is verbalized through a pre-programmed mechanical voice. It is believed that a spirit can then find specific words to communicate with by making subtle changes to the atmosphere and surroundings. This device can initially appear random in its results, as the entities experiment with trying to find the right vocabulary. Lorna switched it on as a last throw of the communicative dice. In the darkness the robotic and somewhat sinister voice again split the silence with a single word—"Killed."

Once more, a painfully difficult and slowly achieved piece was added to the mystery of the puzzle. Could the spirit of this woman be trying to tell us she was murdered? Two single words do not indicate irrevocable proof, and it would be easy to place the wrong emphasis on them and then jump to a conclusion. I decided to start investigating in more than just the basement, as we were now investing our valuable time in a location that was delivering little reward. I decided to leave the EM pump running, since this device energizes the space and is believed to be a good way of juicing up an environment in the hope of creating a catalyst for paranormal contact. It would certainly be worth trying in order to give back the energy I felt the female spirit had expended.

The Office

The Edwardian gentleman in the basement demonstrated that spirits can move around freely, so locating to another area within the building would still allow him and the lady to access the team if they so desired. I went to the second floor of the bank where the offices were located. This area should have the residual energy of everyday repetitive work running through it, compared to the relatively unused and unoccupied basement. I had the name Henry come through to me psychically when I asked if any spirits were present and wished to communicate. I felt this to be the same Edwardian looking gentleman who briefly interacted with us in the basement. This hypothesis proved to be correct when I then saw him psychically appear.

He then turned to Lorna and said, "I knew her when I was alive."

This was a remarkable statement as it suggested that Henry had a full understanding that he was now dead. It also informed us that, despite losing our physical form in death, our memories and minds still remained in spirit, as he was able to remember Lorna, a lifelong resident.

In the hope of obtaining a greater dialogue with Henry, I turned on the ghost box and asked once more for his name in the hope of corroborating my psychic work.

"John!" was the surprising response.

I was not expecting a second spirit to come through at this time, so I said hello and asked for his last name.

"Sheets, Sheets, Sheets!" He replied three times in a row.

"So is that John Sheets?" Lorna then enquired.

"Oh, yeah!" he replied. Nothing could be simpler in terms of communication, having just spent the last few hours in the basement with little reward.

"What year is it?" I asked.

"1909," he said in a clear voice.

"How many people were employed here?" I questioned further.

"Eight!" he said.

"How did you make your money?" I continued.

"Through selling," he replied.

I wondered what aspect of banking he was referring to when he spoke of making money from selling, and I continued to ask questions. Unfortunately, the spirits of both John and Henry disappeared as quickly as they had arrived, and no further contact was made with them that evening. We finished the investigation.

Henry W. Schroeder

This location presented such a wealth of paranormal evidence that my historical research for this property became extremely involved and time consuming. I firstly wanted to find Henry, the gentleman who had presented himself to me in the basement wearing an apron. He initially appeared to come from next door, so my research first focused on what this building was originally used for and who owned it.

Henry W. Schroeder director of the First National Bank

Lorna discovered via the Todd County Historical Society that the property in question was the first in Long Prairie to be fire-proofed, which was done when it was reconstructed in brick with a reinforced roof and concrete floors in 1909. Before this it was a wooden structure that was first used as a meat market and was then home to the *Todd County Argus*. An article printed in 1899 actually described a fire starting in the building that had to be brought under control by passing buckets of water up to the attic.

It continued to be the home of the town's first newspaper, es-tablished in 1876 and printed from this location until 1917. An ar-ticle written by the current owner of the *Long Prairie Leader* men-tions that the basement was used for printing and housed a press. I believed the gentleman who appeared wearing the apron with his sleeves held up could easily be involved in the print trade. I also recalled from the first vigil that he had presented a newspaper to me that indicated the year 1912. That would certainly fit with the time frame of when the newspaper was produced there. The *Argus* was sold to the *Leader* in 1917 and moved to a different location in 1919. This building was then used by Chyba Cleaners for dry cleaning and tailoring.

I still had not found Henry, so I concentrated my efforts on re-searching the past employees of the bank. As I glanced through one document that highlighted all of the previous owners and directors of the bank, I saw an old black and white photograph I instantly recognized. A chill ran through my body as I stared into the eyes of the spirit I had come face-to-face with in the basement. He had the same round-rimmed glasses, and his hair was as I remembered. All that was missing was his moustache that I suspected may have come and gone with the whims of changing fashion. I quickly searched for a name to accompany the picture and could barely believe my eyes when I read the text, "Henry W. Schroeder, director of the First National Bank."

Henry W. Schroeder was born on Schroeder farm in Long Prai-rie Township in 1887. He studied at Concordia College in St. Paul and was initially employed by the First National Bank in 1906 as a clerk. In 1908 he was promoted to the position of assistant cashier and in 1915 became one of the bank's directors. He then rose to fill the role of head cashier. He was active in both the social and political life of Long Prairie and was a prominent member of the village council. He lived in Long Prairie all of his life. There were many people who remembered Schroeder issuing personal loans and extending financial support to those considered to be at financial risk during the depression so that families could keep their farms and businesses, sometimes even paying out his own money. He was dedicated throughout his life to the growth and development of the community. He then became president of the bank in 1927.

Several remarkable things had now taken place. I had no knowledge of this gentleman when I entered the building. It was only through interacting with his spirit psychically that I was able to note his personal details. To then historically find this gentleman should prove beyond any doubt that a spirit realm exists and that psychic communication is possible. The only way a skeptic could denigrate this information would be if they didn't believe the words and descriptions I have annotated in this chapter. I would respond to that criticism by saying that everything we encountered was captured on several cameras and audibly recorded on multiple DVRs, as well as being witnessed by all those who had participated in the vigils, including several members of the Long Prairie community.

I had incorrectly assumed that Henry was a printer due to his appearance when he first arrived from the basement next door, but his attire was in fact that of a bank teller. My historical research informed me that he was in the position of assistant cashier for the year 1912. I suspect his use of the newspaper was his best way of visually presenting to me the date—and the sinking of the *Titanic* would have been that year's most prominent news event. It would not be unreasonable for a spirit, one who had risen to the position of president, to oversee the strangers wandering around in the bank vault area. I can reinforce this concept with an EVP that was discovered during the evidence review after the investigation, when Scott had recorded Henry saying, "You should not be here."

When Lorna was informed that the spirit we had made contact with was Henry Schroeder she said she vaguely remembered meeting him when her parents took her into the bank as a small girl in the 1960s. As Henry himself stated, he recognized her.

John Sheets

As previously mentioned, the building next door to the bank was home to the *Todd County Argus* and was constructed from brick in 1909. I then found to my amazement that this property was built by an Arthur Sheets who had published the *Argus* at that time. This was the last name John had told me in the bank office. Could John be a relative of Arthur Sheets?

Lorna then uncovered a remarkable piece of historical evidence at the Todd County Historical Society. John H. Sheets had not only existed as a resident of Long Prairie, but he had actually created and established the *Todd County Argus,* the first newspaper in the county. His obituary in the *Todd County Leader* on July 5, 1928 was placed prominently on the front page and read: "John H. Sheets Called by Death: Died Suddenly Last Friday after a Short Illness with the Flu." [1]

He was born in Randolph County in Indiana in 1848 and moved to Todd County in 1871. He then started the *Todd County Argus* newspaper in January 1876 with his colleague J. E. Cates. John Sheets then purchased the interest of Mr. Cates several months later and operated the paper for twelve years with his brother, Arthur W. Sheets. He then sold his interest to Arthur. John then owned and operated a farm in Browerville where he engaged in the handling of grain. He once again reentered the print trade and in 1916 became the editor of the *Todd County Tribune*. He died on Friday, June 28, 1928.

John Sheets had told me via the ghost box that the year was 1909. According to his obituary this made him sixty-one years of age at that time. This was also the year the building was rebuilt and fireproofed, and although it was solely owned by his brother Arthur at this time, I am sure John would have shown an active interest in the running and success of the newspaper he founded in its new surroundings. It is also interesting to note that John said he made his money from selling. I was unsure of what this may have referred to at the time, but now I know via his obituary that during 1909 he was selling grain, as highlighted in the *Long Prairie Leader* in July 1928.

After leaving the newspaper business in Long Prairie, Mr. Sheets moved to Browerville where he operated a farm and engaged in the handling of grain. He continued this until 1916.

Conclusion

The investigation in the bank provided such an abundance of paranormal activity that it was difficult to sift through all of the individual pieces of evidence. I believe the renovation triggered our encounters, as I have experienced ghostly contact occurring many times in buildings where renovation is taking place.

The interaction with Henry Schroeder fully verified my psychic skills but also showed me that spirits can continue to work and oversee their business and property in the afterlife. He even provided me with the year he had chosen to be there. This would present a sentient form of time travel for a spirit, as Henry could have chosen any time in the first half of the twentieth century, but he chose 1912. This looks like a conscious decision—I want to be in 1912, so I am.

Henry Schroeder believed he was in 1912, and John Sheets told me it was the year 1909. Both men would have known each other very well when they were alive, yet they did not appear to interact with one another. Can two ghosts in the same location, in two different time frames, meet one another? In life these neighbors would have been in and out of each other's buildings freely, as suggested by Henry arriving via the basement wall.

I had no knowledge of Henry Schroeder or John Sheets before I arrived for this investigation. I could not possibly know or remember every individual stretching back to the earliest pioneer days of every town I investigate in the Midwest. Nor do I have the time or inclination to look them up, even if the records are still available. Yet in this investigation these two individuals came through in spirit not only to introduce themselves in person, but to provide corroborated historical dates and information that could be found using historical research. Even if I had prior knowledge of these gentlemen before the investigation, I could not have manipulated the multiple devices used to communicate with them. I even saw Henry Schroeder's appearance via my psychic skills, only to be corroborated much later when I saw his portrait, proving that it is possible to accurately see spirits psychically.

The brief encounter we shared with the distressed woman leaves me frustrated, due to our inability to help her. We tried persistently to engage with her but to no avail. What was more distressing was the EVP that Scott then found after the investigation recorded during the walkthrough. You can clearly hear a woman saying, "He killed me."

It is very unlikely that a murder had taken place in the bank. But when the property was utilized as the town's police department, it would not be beyond the realm of possibility to suggest that a criminal may have come through the building with the residual energy of a murdered woman attached to him. Lorna and I comprehensively investigated the possibility of a murder taking place involving a female victim in town, and we both drew a blank. The historical society, local historians, and the town's archives did not provide any indication that such a crime had taken place. It may of course be that we have simply not found it yet. But you would have to believe that a murder committed in a small Midwestern town would be remembered and documented.

In the earliest pioneer days, when the town was first formed, it would have been easy to have gone missing, with non-existent law enforcement and with no communication available outside of the letter and stagecoach. People simply went missing then as strangers came into towns and died unknown. The new railroads made a nomadic life possible without the modernity of keeping in touch with friends and family. The infamous murderess Belle Gunness proved this between 1900 and 1908 when she murdered what is believed to be forty individuals, including mostly travelers, at her farm in Indiana.

As we were packing up our equipment to end the investigation and leave, Heather continued to run her DVR. By chance, she managed to capture the EVP of a man's voice that said, "I'm over here, against the wall… I only just got here." As in life, it appears that death is all about timing.

THE KEMP BLOCK OPERA HOUSE

LONG PRAIRIE, MINNESOTA

Could an abandoned theater be haunted by more than one phantom of the opera?

During our investigations in Long Prairie we conducted two separate investigations at the Kemp Block Opera House. This building had always intrigued me and I was eager to see what paranormal activity was inside. Opera houses are always full of energy created from past performances and the congregating of townsfolk. Any spirits still wishing to perform or catch up with neighbors and friends in spirit could congregate here in quiet abandonment.

I approached the owners who were running an antiques business and gift shop from the property. They were very accommodating and allowed me a double investigation. The family was represented by Dee and BryAnna who were our guides on both nights. They provided me with extensive information on the property and a copy of the deeds. I undertook further historical research at the Todd County Historical Society.

History

The Kemp block was built by John Kemp in 1898 at a cost of $15,000 and has the embossed words "Opera House" emblazoned high on the building's stonework. Since its construction it has seen many businesses come and go. It was the James Hart and Sons department store from 1907 to 1916 as well as the Fairway Food Store and the Martin Thom Gamble hardware and department store. The second floor housed the opera house, but this was only believed to be in operation for just a few short years. The weekly *Todd County Tribune* newspaper once utilized the second floor and this area had also been a bowling alley, doctor's surgery, and apartments.

Investigation

It was hard to imagine an opera house being located on the top floor of this building when I finally ascended the stairs and looked around. The evolution and history of this floor has rendered this space into a series of small rooms that now make up individual apartments. There was no longer a wide-open expanse provided for the benefit of Edwardian plays and music. Half-finished constructions and discarded shop floor storage littered the last few open spaces that now remained. No visual evidence was left behind to suggest its cultured and artistic past. Towards the back of this floor on the north side was an area away from the corridors and abandoned rooms. This was where the elevator shaft was located and where we would begin the first vigil.

We started by sitting in silence, allowing ourselves to adjust to the darkness that surrounded us. In the middle of the opening ten minutes, we heard the faint sound of a woman's laughter echoing throughout the location. It was then noticeable that the energy in the room started to rise, mirroring what had happened in the bank. It brought with it a dizzying sensation. I tried to psychically see what this area might have once looked like. I first noticed heavy cigar smoke hanging densely just below the high ceiling. A packed period scene was then presented to me with the chatter of pre-show town gossip. The audience was wearing clothing of the era. It was noticeable how much mud was visible on the austere wooden floorboards.

A turn of the last century Minnesotan town during the height of winter would be a muddy and uncomfortable place to traverse.

Horse manure mixed with human effluent would also add to the soup of muck and mud found on the earthen sidewalks and dirt roads. This was not a grand opera house by any means, just an ordinary, communal open space with moveable wooden chairs set in rows and a simple, slightly raised wooden stage located against the west wall. There were no curtains to signal the beginning and end of a performance.

I then psychically saw a woman sitting at the piano and another group of younger ladies singing. Lorna asked what kind of show it was and in response the piano playing woman jumped in and told me in no uncertain terms that "This is a recital, not a show!" If nothing else, it would suggest that the spirits can hear our dialogue, even if at times we can't see one another. I decided to use the ghost box in the hope of physically hearing the talking and music. I asked any of the spirits present what year they thought it was, as the historical society had no information as to when the opera house was in operation. In response to this question I received the year 1915. I asked if they could clarify this by repeating their answer, and once again the reply came back as 1915. I thought this was significant in terms of the quality of my evidence with the same reply repeated.

"Do you like us being here?" I then enquired.

"Yes!" came the response, now in a female voice.

My initial psychic thoughts pertaining to the heavy smoke became more prevalent as several members of the team started to cough. There was a real physicality about the smoke now and I could actually taste it in my mouth. I asked who was giving me the information, and the ghost box responded, once more in a female voice.

"Abbey," she said.

"Do you remember the opera house?" I asked.

"Yes," she replied.

"How many times were you here?"

"Once," came her surprising response.

"Why were you only here once?" I pressed.

"Mortuary!" she responded.

"So you were here when this was a mortuary?" I continued, thinking that this was too fanciful an idea to even consider.

"Yes," she responded.

"So your body was here then?"

"Yes," she confirmed once more.

I considered that when Abbey was alive she knew of the Opera House building but never entered it.

"Bea," was then said in the same female voice.

I assumed that Abbey was also known by the shortened name Bea. The vigil was coming to an end, so I asked Bea to come with me into the next part of the building we would be investigating. I then met with the team that had been conducting a vigil in the basement at the same time. We exchanged notes and had what I call a plenary (a meeting where we discuss our notes from the previous vigil). The information we would pass on to one another would be useful for the next investigation team going into that area. Remarkably, they told me that they had experienced the sights and smells of smoke and had even taken pictures of it. Obviously nobody was smoking during the vigils, and my investigators are trained not to breathe out when taking their photographs. This removes the possibility of creating a false positive by the element of vapor from their breath looking like an eerie mist when the flash reflects from the water droplets back to the camera.

Light anomalies and smoke in the top left corner weaving between the rafters of the basement

This corroborated what I had experienced on the second floor. They also said, without hearing my own experiences, that they had contact with a spirit named Abbey on the ghost box. This is remarkable when you consider they had accessed the same spirit as we had in a different part of the building without hearing what had taken place on my own vigil.

I have to consider that Abbey was jumping backwards and forwards between the two vigils that were taking place at the same time. Geography seems to be an irrelevance in the spirit world, but I wondered if Abbey had brought the smoke with her from the opera house location into the basement when she had arrived.

The Basement

The basement was typical period river rock construction. It was also damp and bitterly cold. A startled salamander cowered under the beam of my flashlight on the wet concrete floor as my team made its way towards the front of the building. As soon as we started, I felt the presence of what I believed to be a dog. I even saw glimpses of its dark shadowy form racing around the basement at knee height. I was then guided to write the name *Queenie* on my notepad. Then I felt the spirit of a woman arrive. I wondered if Abbey had decided to take me up on my offer to rejoin us. I started to ask her questions psychically.

"What would you like to be called?"

"Bea," she responded.

I started to write down her responses. "So you are Abbey, but you would like to be called Bea?" I ventured to ask.

"Yes," she responded.

"How old are you?" I continued.

"Nineteen," she replied.

"Do you have any brothers and sisters?"

"Yes," she replied once more.

"Was 1934 the year of your death?" I enquired.

"Yes," she responded once more.

I then tried to focus on what may have caused her demise, remembering that just because she presented herself as a nineteen-year-old girl didn't necessarily mean that she had died at nineteen. She may have died in old age and chosen to show herself to me in the form she was the happiest in. If she was nineteen when she died in 1934 she would have been born in 1915. Yet Bea had told me earlier that she remembered the opera house in 1915. This would not have been possible if she was a baby. So once again I suspected she may have died a lot later in life yet had come back to me as a nineteen-year-old.

I then focused psychically on how Bea looked. She was a fresh-complexioned young woman with a jovial round face. Her hair was mousey brown with some blondness, and it was parted in the middle and pulled back into a bun. She was slender in build and wore a long, primrose-yellow dress with a high collar and a simple white pinafore. I noted that although the verbal information I had just received was collected psychically, a faint female voice could be physically heard by the rest of the investigation team as she responded to me.

I then wanted to back up all the psychic work I had done via the equipment so that I could verify the evidence from two separate sources. I asked Scott to lead this session, and he turned on the P-SB 7 ghost box and started to ask Bea questions.

"Are you Bea?" he asked.

"Yes, yeah, yes," came her response, loud and clear for the whole team to hear.

"Adrian," she then called out. I wondered if she was asking where I had gone now that Scott was leading the vigil.

"What is your age?" Scott asked further.

"Nineteen," was her swift reply.

"Is it easy for you to communicate with us?"

"Yes," she said.

"Were you born in Long Prairie?" Scott probed further.

"Yes," was her reply.

"What color is your dress?"

"Yellow," she said.

During my interaction with Bea I was made aware that she played a musical instrument, but I did not inform the rest of the team of that information. I then asked Scott to ask her what musical instrument she played.

"Violin," was her response.

I had been told she had played the violin and I had written the information on my notepad. This was an interesting development since the team had no clue as to what the answer might be.

"Do you have a pet?" Scott then asked.

"Dog," she said.

"What is the name of your dog?"

"Queenie," she responded once more.

So Queenie was the name of the dog I had seen at the very beginning of the vigil. Every piece of information I had received from Bea psychically was now being reinforced verbally by the equipment for all to hear. Scott then asked if she would say goodbye to us.

"Goodbye," came her reply.

The Undertakers

I obviously wanted to research who Bea was. Unfortunately, she did not offer me her last name, despite my insistence. I was also intrigued and surprised by her admission that she thought the opera house space was once a mortuary. This seemed incredible and without any historical merit. So Lorna and I went about investigating this bizarre possibility. Then to our complete amazement we discovered through various newspaper articles that an undertaker had actually operated on the second floor from 1932—the *Clarence Olsen Furniture and Undertaking business*.

Clarence Gerhard Olson was born in Battle Creek in 1895. He had already established an undertaker's business in town from 1925 and was formally housed in the building of the People's National Bank. In 1928 he moved again to a space in the Reichert block. Like many undertakers of this period, he also specialized in pianos, upholstered furniture, and picture framing. His move into the opera house was documented in the *Long Prairie Leader* on September 1932.

> Furniture store now open at new location: Clarence Olson has moved stock to New Location and Invites Customers to Visit Him. Clarence Olson is now established at his new location in the building formally occupied by the Fairway Store. His furniture stock was moved there Tuesday and he invites all of his customers and friends to visit him in his new quarters.

> The building has been completely renovated and its appearance makes it one of the finest business establishments in the community. The interior of the building has been trimmed in ivory and green. At the rear of the large furniture display room is an embalming room and a small reception room, the latter arranged for convenience of those that desire private funerals. On the balcony is a large space devoted to a casket display and on the main floor on the northwest corner is a large workroom for repairing furniture, picture framing and similar work.

> The building provides plenty of space for an adequate display of furniture and as soon as Mr. Olson has arranged his stock he intends to have a grand opening.[2]

It is a testament to the methods we employ as a team that we are able to find history that has been lost or forgotten. We can now reintroduce those details back into the public's consciousness solely through the dialogue we have with the dead. I never thought for one moment that the opera house space could have been home to an undertaking business. This was not known before our historical research.

Conclusion

Many strange things happened during the opera house investigation. Some of them I am still trying to process. It was of course a joy to have the same information presented to us by Bea and verified from two separate sources on two separate vigils. I know that every team member that was present in the basement for that interaction felt it was profound. The physical coughing and the taste of smoke throughout the building was also an odd experience, and I thought I could actually hear Bea coughing during our dialogues. This investigation showed that it is possible for spirits to present themselves at any age they wish. It also suggested that spirits have an awareness they are dead and it is possible to see your own dead physical self at the undertakers laid out in rest. Bea said she had never visited the second floor in her lifetime, but knew she was taken there after her passing.

Unfortunately, I have still not found Bea. The lack of her last name makes her almost impossible to find, as census records and obituaries require this information. Even without this detail, Lorna worked her way through every page of the local Long Prairie newspapers for the year 1934, the year Bea said she had died. We also took steps to randomly walk through the local cemeteries to see if her name appeared on any of the thousands of gravestones. It has been my experience that some individuals have taken up to four years to track down, and my hope is that in a further edition of this book I will be able to include the details of her life. The fact that she said she had never been in the building before she was laid out would suggest that she may have only lived in Long Prairie for a short period of time. I would have expected a lifelong citizen of Long Prairie during this period of history to have visited the town's hardware store at least once.

The details she provided me with were accurate beyond anything we had previously known, especially surrounding the detail of the undertaker's business. I have no doubt she existed. As we have previously seen with the spirits I engaged with in the local bank, we know the team's methods to be successful.

To add to the intrigue of this investigation, Lorna informed me that her deceased father had once worked in this building many years ago, and that her family dog was also named Queenie. This seemed like a ridiculous coincidence as Bea also had a dog with her in spirit named Queenie. It made me ponder the concept that Lorna's old family dog may have been residing in this location due to her close family links and association with the building. I wondered if it was possible that Bea was now looking after the same dog in spirit until Lorna could be with it again. As is the case with all paranormal investigations, we were left with more questions than answers.

Loon Lake Cemetery

Jackson County, Minnesota

*A macabre tale of witch beheadings and curses made this
the most mysterious and unique of paranormal locations!*

When I first became aware of the legend of the Loon Lake witch's
curse, I knew I had to investigate the site and its history. So during
four glorious autumnal days, I ventured deep into the damning undergrowth to try and find the truth behind the myth.

Historically, there is little evolution within a cemetery—unlike
other areas of our overly built-up society. Cemeteries remain static
and immune from the layers of demolition and rebuilding that take
place over the centuries in our towns. They appear as they did when
they were first constructed—aside from their sometimes eroded and
distressed nature. The angel statues remain frozen in time and stone
like the poor unfortunates that once glimpsed into the face of the
Medusa. So within their perimeter fences we find the perfect synthesis of history, art, nature, and spiritualism, surviving relatively
untouched in a vacuum, free from the hammer of modernity. This
makes these environments worthy of academic attention.

I conducted my historical research at the Jackson County Historical Society in Lakefield where I accessed period newspapers,
census records, death certificates, and diaries from the era. I also
used family tree websites, Internet resources, and interviews with
local residents to supplement my research.

History

The old and long abandoned Loon Lake Cemetery nestles on an east-facing hill between Robertson County Park and Loon Lake, just twelve miles southwest of Jackson and a stone's throw from the Iowa border. This location was originally called Black Loon Lake by the Native American tribes and became the first settlement in Jackson County not to be founded on the banks of the Des Moines River. The early pioneers were drawn to this area by the rich soil, plentiful timber, and bountiful lakes. Its natural beauty also drew their attention with its wonderful rolling plains, wild plum trees, pelican filled lakes, and the constant silvery glint of jumping buffalo fish. These attractions were also alluring to our ancient ancestors. In 1975 the Minnesota Historical Society conducted a survey that revealed the area to have been inhabited during the Woodland cultural period as early as 200 BC. The site was then placed on the National Register of Historic Places and is one of Jackson County's most archeologically important.

The abandoned Loon Lake Cemetery

The first recorded burial to take place at Loon Lake Cemetery was that of John Dickinson in October 1877, when Dickinson's father gave up an acre of land for the interment of his son. The final burial at Loon Lake Cemetery took place in 1926, making this location a pioneer cemetery. Any cemetery in Minnesota that has not interred more than six bodies in the last fifty years is categorized as a pioneer cemetery.

I am often asked, as a historian and paranormal investigator, what makes a cemetery distinct from a graveyard. Cemeteries are usually specifically designed on the edges of towns and tend to be organized with walkways, trees, and shrubs. At Loon Lake Cemetery the original local settlers carried buckets of water daily from the lake to help keep the trees alive when they were first planted. The Romans started the convention of burying their dead on the outskirts of settlements since they did not want the spirits of the dead to interfere with the living. Graveyards are usually located near or within the perimeter walls of a church or religious building—so they are generally much smaller than cemeteries. It was only during the medieval period in Europe that newly built churches brought the dead back inside the city walls into the graveyard.

Specifically designed cemeteries were reintroduced when graveyards became dangerous health hazards—especially during the Victorian industrial revolution in Europe. The dead outnumbered the places left to bury them, with corpses having to be stacked on top of one another in shallow graves. Many bodies then broke the surface of the ground. It was wrongly believed during this era that cholera was caused and carried by foul smells, so a solution was sought that placed the cemeteries back on the edge of towns and cities. This was successful in stemming the contamination—even if it was for the wrong reason—because unbeknownst to them it was the decaying matter working its way into the groundwater that caused the outbreaks.

Loon Lake Cemetery has long harbored dark stories of witch beheadings and curses from beyond the grave. During my research I had interviewed several local residents who had frequented the site and they told me of their experiences. One spoke of severe temperature drops without any good reason and the feeling of a paranormal presence, including the sighting of several shadow figures wandering throughout the site. Another even claimed to have been mysteriously scratched and then pelted with broken gravestone masonry.

Folklore states that three witches were murdered in the late nineteenth century by the nearby townsfolk of Petersburg. The witches were executed by having their heads cut off with a sword that was then buried next to the body. The first of these alleged witches was Mary Jane Terwillegar, who died at the age of seventeen in 1880. The story dictates that two further witches were unfortunately murdered over the course of the next few years, also by decapitation. These were said to be Clarinda Allen and Mary Jane Dickinson. Legend suggests that Terwillegar was the most powerful of these three witches due to her superior supernatural powers.

Every child in the surrounding area has grown up with this legend. It has been the talk of every playground, the tale of every campfire, and the test of every teenage boy's bravado. It was a rite of passage to traverse the cemetery and experience the witch's curse, especially to any foolhardy individuals who dared to desecrate and disrespect their final resting place. The curse states that if you tread or jump over Mary Jane's grave (three times appears to be the prerequisite amount) you will succumb to a terrible death. Urban legend has also provided us with a nice example of how this curse is delivered with the tale of a young man who stepped over Mary Jane's grave on a hunting trip. That evening when driving he became disorientated when a dense fog descended, so he pulled his car over. He was then overcome with carbon monoxide fumes and died.

The Mary Jane myth has even made it into contemporary music culture. Dave Ellefson, the bass player for the metal band Megadeth, was born and grew up in Jackson. He would have been fully aware of the story surrounding Mary Jane and used her tale as an inspiration for the song "Mary Jane" from the album *So Far, So Good... So What!* The narrative of the song describes the tale of a witch who is buried alive.

The last recorded witches to be tried in a court of law and executed in this country were hanged on September 22, 1692 as part of the Salem witch trials. The Salem witch trials were a series of hearings and prosecutions in colonial Massachusetts between February 1692 and May 1693. The only other recorded incident involving the death of an alleged witch since then was that of a Native American in Ohio called Leatherlips. He was tomahawked to death in 1810 as part of a tribal feud for encouraging cooperation with the white settlers and for allegedly practicing witchcraft. Based on this research, I believe the deaths surrounding the witches of Loon Lake to be nothing more than urban myth and hyperbole.

Historically, I feel that the legend of Mary Jane and the other accused witches may have resulted in a misunderstanding as the inscriptions placed on their tombstones would appear at first glance to elicit a curse:

> *My friends beware as you pass by*
> *As you are now, so once was I,*
> *As I am now, so you must be,*
> *Prepare yourself to follow me.*

On the surface this looks like a dark and threatening statement. But I have discovered through research that this stanza was very popular throughout the nineteenth and early twentieth centuries. It proliferates on many tombstones in Ireland and in the early colonial cemeteries—especially in New England. The earliest version I have found can be seen inscribed on the tomb of Edward the Black Prince (1330-1376) in Canterbury Cathedral, England. Here it has been translated from Norman French into English:

> *Whoso thou be that passeth by;*
> *Where these corps entombed lie:*
> *Understand what I shall say,*
> *As at this time speak I may.*
> *Such as thou art, sometime was I,*
> *Such as I am, such shalt thou be.*

This verse would certainly have gained popularity during the nineteenth century when a morbid fascination with mortality and the culture of funerary was popular; it was inspired by the mourning of Queen Victoria and the popular literature of the time. So I believe this verse would have been chosen from a local undertaker's book of available passages. Not long after the Loon Lake burials, Sears Roebuck & Company introduced cemetery related products for sale in their spring catalog of 1897. A stone inscribed with this verse could actually be bought for $3 plus postage and packing. The only common denominator between the accused women appears to be this shared inscription.

I then discovered a remarkable document at the Jackson County Historical Society. It was a journal written by J. W. Preston of Baxter, Iowa from May 10 to June 22, 1883. Preston visited Loon Lake for a month and camped on the eastern shore in order to hunt birds and wildlife. In his notes he describes meeting a local man. It is written in colloquial English and was probably scribed by the light of a flickering campfire.

> An old man of 70 years, Peters by name, lives in a miserable old cabin in a beautiful grove of walnut trees which he had cut because people would gather the walnuts. He says he is troubled by witches. He has a chain of silver made by beating 15 silver dollars flat. This he draws around effigies of witches which trouble him and shoots then with his revolver, which is a good one, and in my opinion would do good service should any one try to get money of which he has considerable. He is very pursy and thin, sharp, hard of hearing, has a startled appearance. I think most of his talk of witches is to scare vandals away from him. I talked with him a number of times, found him to be a skeptic, very profane, well informed, and indeed very queer in every way.

It is interesting to note that Peters protected himself with the use of a silver chain. This I envisage to be some kind of adornment stereotypically used by gypsies where coins are linked together to form a headband or necklace. I also found it slightly odd when it describes Peters using effigies, as this practice would be considered to have pagan origins. I would have expected an anti-witch proponent of this period to have embraced Christian ideals and not the practices of the religion he was denouncing. I would consider this to be the thinking of a paranoid man, as highlighted by the description of his demeanor.

Further research suggested that this individual was Sanford James Peters, a pioneer who arrived in Jackson County in 1862 and lived on the shore of Loon Lake. He died on May 14, 1884 and is also buried at Loon Lake Cemetery. Before he settled at Loon Lake, Peters attempted to construct a mill in the Spirit Lake Township, but this venture proved to be unsuccessful. It could be conjectured that he felt his luck was cursed. It was then a further revelation to discover through census documentation that Peters was in fact married to Catherine Dickinson (his second wife) who was the daughter of Mary Jane Dickinson, thus making one of the accused witches his mother-in-law.

Mary Jane Dickinson appears to have been a very interesting character. She was mentioned in a newspaper article written about her during an interview with her granddaughter, Lillian Jones. In the article Jones stated that she could understand why her grandmother was labeled a witch. This was due to her unusual abilities.

She said it was possible that people thought her grandmother was a witch "because she had ESP." The story Jones remembers most vividly is of how one day when Stephen Dickinson, Mary Jane's son, was in the woods, a tree fell on him and he was trapped. "She went there with this man—she went right to where the tree was on him… that was my grandmother… the one that died in Lake Park that they call a witch."

Jones described Mary Jane Dickinson as a very Christian woman who died at the age of seventy-seven after a long illness, not at the hands of a fevered, sword-wielding crowd as purported by local residents.

I discovered that a local storeowner in the 1960s would weave the tale of the Loon Lake witches in order to keep out-of-town visitors in his store longer in order to sell more produce. This also allowed him to furnish beer to those who wanted to test their bravado by experiencing the curse for themselves.

So it would appear the legend was born from several different sources: a misunderstood tombstone verse; the chattering of a strange, paranoid, anti-social old man who perpetrated the myth in order to keep his money safe from unwanted visitors; the psychic skills that Mary Jane Dickinson clearly possessed; and the tales woven by a local storeowner in the 1960s. The simplest task would now be to obtain the alleged witches' obituaries and death certificates. This would finally shed light on the real cause of their death.

I first found Mary Jane Terwillegar's obituary listed in the *Spirit Lake Beacon* newspaper of March 18, 1880. Note that her last name is spelled differently in this article.

> DIED - TERWILLIGER - In Cherokee, on Friday, the 5th inst., of diphtheria, Miss M. J. Terwilliger, aged 17 years. Miss Terwilliger had been in town about a week when she was stricken down, and death ended her suffering in four days. Her remains were taken to Spirit Lake for interment.[3]

We can see in this document that Mary Jane Terwillegar died from diphtheria and not by decapitation. Diphtheria is a very contagious respiratory illness spread through the air or direct contact. It is characterized by a sore throat, fever, and skin lesions. Diphtheria swept through the Midwest during the mid to late nineteenth century and killed thousands of settlers.

Clarinda Allen's death certificate documented that she had died from croup. This is laryngeal diphtheria with symptoms of a swollen neck and throat. It is usually accompanied by difficulty in breathing. Mary Jane Dickinson died in old age after a long illness, as stated by her granddaughter Lillian Jones.

The abandoned Loon Lake Cemetery

Investigation

There is no road to Loon Lake Cemetery, just a narrow snaking path mowed into the wild rolling prairie to guide the most committed of investigators. The long, swaying, unkempt grasses on either side moved hypnotically back and forth at head height. Their slender blades stretched towards the bright turquoise sky. The flora painted the whole journey in a blaze of rich autumnal colors straight from the palette of Van Gogh. It provided cover and refuge for any wild animal that may have felt inclined to test the nerve of a passing visitor by running out. Thankfully, only grasshoppers and frogs jumped onto the swampy, clover-strewn path ahead of me.

A disheveled looking chain-link fence wrapped itself around the overgrown consecrated ground, reminding me that nature had not yet fully reclaimed what man has put in place. The whole tombstone tableau was framed by an impressive collection of towering, twisted pine trees, the kind that only seem to be found in cemeteries. They benefit from having their roots buried deep into the compost rich soil. Only a handful of the original gravestones were visible due to vandalism and aging. The harsh Minnesotan weather had also eroded and distressed the few details remaining in the chiseled stone, leaving many faceless and anonymous. A modern red granite marker now lists the names of the interred. These were some of the earliest pioneers and were hard-working farmers from the communities of Loon Lake, Lakefield, Middleton, and Petersburg. As I entered through the gate I felt a peaceful serenity wash over me. It was not the dark oppressive atmosphere I was led to believe.

Places of burial are not locations the living often frequent, if at all, so there would be little reason to come back in spirit to these sites unless specifically asked for. If you had a good send-off in the company of your friends, family, and loved ones, you would not need to reside in such a place in spirit.

Unfortunately, I did not know the location of Mary Jane's grave, making it impossible for me to avoid stepping over her. The headstone had been removed some years ago in an effort to save it from acts of vandalism. Her marker also would have allowed recidivists the opportunity to try to actually exhume her remains. So I walked into the middle of the cemetery buried up to my knees in burdock, itch-weed, thistles, and cocklebur, and I asked for Mary Jane Terwillegar to come to me. I explained out loud that I wanted to write and research about her life and family. I also spoke of wanting to dispel the myth of her death and the false accusations of witchcraft leveled against her.

At that moment I suddenly felt the presence of a spirit coming towards me across the cemetery. I saw a young girl floating through the undergrowth and getting closer—like one might associate with Japanese ghosts that are believed to travel on clouds. She was wearing a long white gown that I initially thought to be a Victorian wedding dress, but as she moved closer I could see it looked more like a death shroud or just a simple summer dress. She was holding a small bouquet of wild flowers in her hands. I assumed this would have been placed into her clasped hands as she was laid to rest. It was comprised of daisies and other prairie blooms.

Her hair was long, straight, and dark. It was parted in the middle and fell down past her shoulders to frame her pretty face. She had thick, full lips and the dark complexion of a hard-working, sun-kissed pioneer. If it wasn't for her quiet, serene appearance and slow approach I would have been more concerned. I am sure that any spooked teenagers seeing her in this manifestation at night would have screamed and leapt the entire footpath back, no doubt then adding to the rhetorical tales and the canon of local legends when they next visited with their friends. I welcomed her presence and asked if her family came from the area.

"Yes," she replied.

She proceeded to tell me that her father was a farmer and builder. She then told me that her parents had a homestead on the lake. I later discovered this statement to be true through historical research. It would initially appear odd to the outsider that the cemetery was in such a remote location. But wagon paths would have been placed differently then, and the earliest buildings and farms that occupied this stretch of prairie have long since disappeared. She then told me that a number of cabins once dotted themselves around the lake, and there was even a church. Her family had apparently saved enough money through hard work to buy a plot of land on which to build. She then claimed to have rarely seen her father as he was always laboring in the fields.

I then psychically caught a glimpse of her parents' dwelling. As she showed me in I noticed the wooden floor. Most cabins had earthen floors, but as time progressed and constructions became more prevalent and professional the floors began to be finished with puncheons. These were slabs of wood cut as near to the same size as possible like long planks. The upper surface was then smoothed off with a plane after the floor had been laid, similar to the wooden sidewalks seen in early pioneer towns. The floorboards were not nailed down, so if any animal managed to get underneath the cabin the timber would rise up and down as the animal moved around.

I then enquired if she had spent much time in the town of Jackson. She responded by saying, "No." I believed that would have been an unnecessarily slow and arduous journey back then by wagon, especially when other towns were nearer. There were also no cabins between Loon Lake and Jackson during this period, which would make the journey hazardous if the weather turned bad. It was possible that Mary Jane had never set foot in Jackson County, or even Minnesota, in her lifetime. Her parents had only moved to Loon Lake from Iowa shortly before her death.

At that moment, out of the corner of my eye, I saw a shadow figure moving around the perimeter of the cemetery on the inside of the fence. This verified the stories I had heard of dark figures wandering through the undergrowth. I was intrigued by this occurrence but did not want to turn my attentions away from Mary Jane. I then asked her about her job. She presented me with the image of scrubbing clothes by hand with a washboard and pail. I also saw her pumping water. I asked how she managed to gain employment as a domestic servant, and she said the family employing her was acquainted with her father.

All the way through this interaction I kept feeling dizzy. I stood there swaying like the tall grasses I had witnessed on the walk to the cemetery. I tried to undertake grounding exercises to help stop this sensation, but this proved difficult on the sloping, uneven ground with the wind blowing. It was then that I also started to feel a tightening across my chest as I began to channel the difficulties she had breathing. I was well aware of how Mary Jane had spent the last few days of her life, based on her obituary. I was beginning to feel her distress empathically.

I continued my psychic interview and asked her how she managed to end up in a cemetery in Loon Lake, when according to my research she had died in Cherokee County, Iowa. She replied by saying, "It was cold," perhaps implying that the inclement weather during that March had made it possible to take her body from one state to another in a period before refrigeration and motorized transport. I also considered that she may have attributed the cold weather to her death and was perhaps simply stating how she thought she had literally ended up here.

I then asked about her hobbies and interests. She told me that she liked playing the game of pick-up nails. This I assumed to be a version of pick-up sticks. Apparently the family used square, hand-forged nails for this game, and they were probably part of her father's building supplies. She also told me that she liked to read. I then wondered what kind of books she may have owned during the late nineteenth century. She responded by saying, "The Bible." This was an interesting response when you consider that after her death she had been wrongly accused of practicing witchcraft.

I believed her family to have been very religious based on the imagery presented on her father's tombstone. It has faint carvings showing the gates of heaven, depicting the passage from earth to eternal life, with a centrally chiseled crown symbolizing the victory and triumph over death. Small, embossed stars appear on each corner and represent the star of Bethlehem and the concept of creation. Mary Jane's tombstone is now housed in the Jackson County Historical Society and depicts a single rose bloom with a stalk, symbolizing the concept of a life cut short. I then asked if she was a Baptist. "Baptist," she responded. Both her parents had their own funeral services at the local schoolhouse that was also used for Baptist services. The Loon Lake Cemetery was shared by both the Baptist congregation and the local Methodist church.

After talking and engaging with Mary Jane for some time I felt comfortable enough to ask her about the myth surrounding her witchcraft accusation. There was no response to this question and everything suddenly went quiet with no further information forthcoming. I got the impression that she knew little of what I was asking. I then asked her outright if she knew what I was referring to and she said, "No." I then decided to try to verify my psychic work through the use of the ghost box. I turned on the device and asked if I should walk back to the red stone marker at the entrance to the cemetery.

"Yeah, okay," she replied audibly for me to record on my DVR.

"Can you come and talk to me there?" I enquired.

"Yes," she responded. So I walked to the front entrance of the cemetery once more.

"What do you think about people coming here to bother you?" I asked. As I found with my psychic session, there was a pronounced silence.

"Do you find it annoying that people accuse you of practicing witchcraft?" I questioned further. Again there was a silence and a complete lack of a response. This was in contrast to the quick and informative replies I had previously received.

"Okay, what would you like to say to me?" I asked.

"Shut up!" was her surprisingly direct response.

"Do you not like me being here then?" I questioned further.

"Get out!"

"Why would you say that?" I ventured.

"Portal!" was her surprising reply.

This response came as a revelation. I had to consider whether it was in fact Mary Jane who had just told me to *shut up* or perhaps another spirit. She had been very friendly and polite up until that point and it seemed to be out of context and character. I then wondered if Mary Jane was actually trying to warn me and was thus asking me to leave out of a sense of wanting to protect me. If there was a portal in the cemetery, it would certainly explain the phenomena of shadow figures wandering randomly through the grounds. I considered that teenagers may have brought Ouija boards into the cemetery over the years and had subsequently created all kinds of problems. This I confirmed to be true when I spoke to a local resident named Chris, who remembered his classmates engaging with this practice in the cemetery in his youth. I asked once more to gain clarification.

"Is there a portal in this cemetery, a doorway that spirits can come through without any filter or discretion?"

"Yes!" came the response.

"Would you like it closed up?"

"Yes!" she replied once more.

I then decided to focus once more on Mary Jane and asked her to verify where her body was laid to rest.

"What way do I need to go to reach your grave?" I asked as I stood on the edge of the undergrowth.

"Just go in," came the reply. So I set off once more into the middle of the cemetery and asked her to give me directions via the ghost box as to where I needed to go.

I have amended the following dialogue slightly to allow her body to rest in peace.

"Am I going in the right direction?" I enquired.

"Yes," she replied, so I continued to carry on, making my way through the undergrowth.

"Cease," she called out, so I stopped.

"Go back," she added. I stepped back several paces.

"Here?" I asked.

"Yes," came the reply.

"Which direction should I head in now?" I asked.

"Right," she responded.

"Am I going in the right direction now?" I asked, as I started walking off to my right.

"Sure, straight," she added. I carried on walking straight.

"That's okay," she continued.

"Am I still going the right way?"

"Yeah."

"Is this close?"

"Nope," she said.

"Clarify that for me," I asked as I carried on walking.

"I'm here," she suddenly responded.

"Is this where you are?" I asked finally.

"Yes," she confirmed.

This is a remarkable dialogue when you consider that Mary Jane's spirit was actually giving me directions to her final resting place. As I stood on the patch of ground I had been directed to, I thought about the concept of a spirit having an awareness of where it was buried, even if they don't reside there in spirit. This would suggest that spirits have a knowledge of what takes place after they have passed. I guess we all want to see who turns up for our funeral and what is said. I continued my questioning.

"Did you die of diphtheria, a lung fever?" I tentatively asked, knowing that I had already seen her obituary and death certificate.

"Yes, yes!" she shouted out twice, to reinforce the fact.

"Where were you born?" I continued.

"Iowa," she responded.

"How many days were between your passing and being buried?"

"Four!" she replied.

"Writer," she then called out.

I took this statement to be an acknowledgement of the explanation I had given her at the beginning of the vigil when I had discussed why I was there and the book I was planning to write. Perhaps she was asking me in that moment to document the misinformation surrounding her life and death. She then said an extraordinary thing.

"The dead will have you live."

This is quite a statement to make, and I have thought about its meaning ever since it was uttered. Was Mary Jane asking me to leave because she wanted to protect me? Or was this a reflection of the spirit guides I have working with me from the other side? I suspect Mary Jane could see how well protected I am by the dead that surround me, work with me, and follow me. I certainly have felt at times during my life and career that I have been blessed to be looked after in my darkest moments, especially when investigating. It would also be true to say that my life has been shaped and influenced by the dead in terms of my writing and psychic work. Just the process of being a historian means you spend more time working with the details of the dead than the living.

"Is there anything else you would like to say?" I asked in my final dialogue with Mary Jane.

"I appreciate it," was her last response.

I believe she was thankful for the research I was undertaking.

Conclusion

I never normally investigate in cemeteries out of consideration for the dead and their relatives. Many of these God-fearing settlers died painful and terrible deaths and were grieved for by those they left behind. In this regard the investigations were undertaken with the utmost respect in order to right a false historical wrong, to allow the dead to have their say and to lay to rest the rumors and misinformation that have prevailed. I always hope that the individuals involved can now rest in peace without the fear of being disturbed or desecrated.

The investigation proved to be a very interesting and profound experience for me. To be directed to a spirit's graveside by her own words was unique. It was also satisfying to find such a depth of historical research to back up my thoughts and findings. Investigations like this go a long way to prove an afterlife exists, especially when you consider that the information passed on to me in spirit was proven to be correct through the task of historical research. I was also pleased with the way the psychic information received was corroborated through my equipment.

The image of Mary Jane wandering through the cemetery at night

There was one final and remarkable twist to this investigation. I was contacted by a Jackson resident who was staying at the nearby campground who had decided to visit the cemetery late on a summer's evening. She then saw a woman floating across the undergrowth in a white dress. She had no knowledge of my own experiences at this location and contacted me to ask if I knew who the spectral lady was. She even managed to take a quick photograph of this phenomenon. Even though the details of the photograph are affected by the poor circumstances and conditions, you can still make out a white figure illuminating the darkness of the cemetery. This was exactly how Mary Jane presented herself to me. It is therefore significant that an independent witness saw the apparition without any previous knowledge of her appearance. This corroborated my psychic interaction.

It is now my hope that the historical facts presented in this text will go some way to stop the egregious playground rhetoric that is the Loon Lake Cemetery witch's curse. The portal was closed using a Christian ceremony and the whole area is now a peaceful and tranquil habitat for the abundance of wildlife that now resides there. These pioneers deserve our respect for the work and toil they executed in breaking the land in this unforgiving part of the country as we respect and honor their memory and final resting place.

THE PIONEER VILLAGE

JACKSON COUNTY, MINNESOTA

Collecting together so many old pioneer buildings in one place was always going to create paranormal activity.

During the summer, I visited one of the oldest fairs in Minnesota—the Jackson County Fair. The area of the fairground I found most intriguing was the old pioneer village. This was a faux village assembled by moving many of the old, nineteenth century, wooden-construction buildings from around the county into one large location. Throughout my paranormal investigating career one question has always been prominent in my thinking: are ghosts attached to the building they haunt or the space where the building is located? Do the ghosts and spirits move with the property if the property is relocated? This village would now provide me with the perfect environment to answer these questions.

I contacted several Jackson residents who were prominent in organizing the fair and they were open to the idea of having an investigation in the village. I researched the location at the Jackson County Historical Society in Lakefield where they had information on the fairground and the individuals involved in its development. I did this by reading through newspaper articles and other documentation. Local amateur historians and various Jackson residents also presented me with a wealth of knowledge and primary source materials, including photographs. Due to the nature of this investigation I brought one of the largest teams I have ever assembled.

History

Ancient people chose to leave their footprints in the fertile soil, magnificent groves, rich prairie, and riverbanks of Jackson County and the Des Moines River valley. A small but tantalizing glimpse of their existence could be seen through the handful of burial places that were scattered throughout the Des Moines Valley. Such evidence was revealed just west of Jackson in 1873 when a semi-circular mound was excavated by the townsfolk. But little of historical interest was found other than a human leg bone. Several years previously, a solid stone ball was plowed out of the ground of Hans Chesterson's farm. This spherical find was worked with primitive tools and measured about two inches in diameter.

Trappers and explorers were the first Europeans to traverse this land, but the earliest pioneers to settle in this area arrived in the summer of 1856. They were three brothers—William, George, and Charles Wood, from Ridgeville, Randolph County, Indiana. William was the driving spirit of the three and had started as an Indian trader and general merchandise dealer in Mankato in 1854. His goal was to find a location to start a home for himself and his mother's large family. This he did when he ventured into the area now known as Jackson.

The brothers first set up a trading post on the west side of the Des Moines River and constructed a substantial one-room cabin. They saw the potential of trading with the local Native Americans and had the belief that other white settlers would soon join them when they saw the geographical advantages for themselves. They first christened this embryonic town Springfield as a natural spring was found close to where they had built their cabin.

From July to December of that year a number of other settlers started to build cabins and to stake their own claims in Springfield. The majority came from Webster City, Iowa and were descended from English and Scottish heritage. By the winter, Springfield boasted thirteen cabins and forty-two citizens. The growth of this small township from one original log cabin into a community was quite remarkable. Unfortunately, the late arrival of this embryonic town's population meant that it was too late in the season to plant crops and tend to the land. Subsequently, food was in very short supply, as all provisions had to be transported from the nearest settlements of Webster City and Mankato.

Two Native American camps also occupied Springfield at this time. One was located on the east side of the river, occupying land section twenty-two at Belmont. This consisted of four families gathered around a trading shanty house owned by a mixed race Sioux Indian called Gaboo (Joseph Coursalle). The second camp was also made up of four families and was located to the west of the river. This was presided over by Umpashota (hamp-pah-shota) or Smoky Moccasin, a medicine man with the authority of a sub-chief. This was an offshoot band of a tribe from Swan Lake in Sleepy Eye.

As the town prepared to be cut off for the season, they began to experience the harsh winter of 1856-57. This was destined to be one of the most severe winters ever recorded. Several bands of roving Indians then visited the settlers as the conditions were also having a negative impact on their own food supplies and resources. They were always received kindly and the settlers shared their limited provisions.

One of these roving bands was led by Inkpaduta (Scarlet Point). This was a lawless renegade Wahpekute group of fourteen Santee Sioux Indians. They were in conflict with other Native American tribes due to their plundering, robberies, and murders. They also refused to recognize the Treaty of Mendota restrictions of 1851 that had transferred the land in the northwest of Iowa to the United States. Tensions were exacerbated further in 1852 when a drunken white whiskey trader named Henry Lott killed Inkpaduta's older brother and tribal chief Sidominadotah with nine of his family. The US Army was informed of this barbaric act but failed to bring Lott to justice. Tensions then increased when the local prosecuting attorney nailed the dead chief's head to a pole over his house.

Inkpaduta led his starving, revenge-seeking band to the Iowa and Minnesota frontier settlements. Between March 8 and 15, 1857 he launched a series of raids on the Spirit Lake area in which a total of thirty-eight people were killed. This came to be known as the Spirit Lake Massacre. His band took four young women hostage, two of whom were killed along the way as they could not keep up, and the third was released shortly afterward.

Inkpaduta and his band came down from the Heron Lake area straight to the general store in Springfield, owned by William and George Wood, killing them both before replenishing their supplies and ammunition. A number of settlers quickly gathered together in the Thomas' cabin and a determined fight ensued, with the citizens succeeding in keeping the Indians at bay. However, the Indians managed to kill seven and wound three. Terrified of a possible second Indian attack, the beleaguered Springfield citizens left for Fort Dodge. Inkpaduta and his band managed to evade capture. During the following summer of 1858, a successful negotiation and ransom saw the release of the fourth hostage taken, a girl named Abbie Gardner.

Just two months after the massacre, the Minnesota State Legislature made the county a political division and named it Jackson County, in honor of the first merchant that resided in St. Paul. The county seat was to be located in Jackson, the new name for the town site of Springfield. All that was required now was to encourage the citizens to return. But on August 25, 1862, just five years after the massacres in Spirit Lake and Springfield, the Belmont community in Jackson County was attacked during the Sioux uprising. The Indians killed thirteen citizens and wounded three before the townspeople gathered together for protection in the town's small church. The Indians then fled, thinking that the group would offer a stiff resistance. The settlers were once again scared off their land and retreated over the Iowa border, leaving the area deserted for a second time.

Soon after the end of the Civil War in 1865, many chose to return to the depopulated county with the added assurance that a newly constructed military stockade offered. It was constructed on Thomas Hill and manned by the military. It was only with military intervention and guaranteed protection provided in 1866 that growth could flourish once more. A further surge in population and economic growth came with the introduction of the railroad in 1878. Jackson then became the division point for the Chicago, Milwaukee, and St. Paul railroad lines in 1888 with an eight-stall roundhouse constructed. This created a center for commerce and immigration, bringing a new growth that lasted into the 1950s.

It was interesting to note during my research on Jackson that a layer of paranormal history also presented itself. Walter Halloran was born in Jackson on September 21, 1921. He was the Catholic priest who at the age of twenty-six had assisted in the exorcism of a thirteen-year-old boy that inspired the 1971 novel *The Exorcist,* written by William Peter Blatty, and the subsequent 1973 film of the same name directed by William Friedkin.

History of the Fair

The Jackson Agricultural Society was formed in 1869, and the first fair followed that fall. It was called the Jackson Fair. The organization had little money to invest in these inaugural events and the location of the fair was subsequently moved around, utilizing empty buildings and vacant lots about the town. However, some stability was achieved with the availability of the old Central Park block, which was used until 1897. Lifetime memberships were then introduced as a way of securing a better financial footing and issued for the hefty sum of fifteen dollars. Over one hundred people agreed to sign up to the scheme, and land, located south of the old depot site, was subsequently purchased with twenty-five acres secured from B. W. Ashley and George W. Moore.

Buildings were soon erected at a cost of $2,500, including a modest grandstand to accompany the newly built racetrack. A horse barn was also constructed. Unfortunately, attendance dropped dramatically due to bad weather and caused the following fairs to be disappointing. Subscribers then failed to deliver on the money they had first promised and owed. It became a task to keep the organization afloat with such financial burdens. The poor weather was soon becoming a predictable annual disappointment. The regularity of the rain allowed the local community to develop the saying: *rainy weather comes with the Jackson Fair, so put up your hay before the fair.* The fair was traditionally held before the upland hills haymaking of the short grass. Local historian Alvin Glaser commented on this phenomenon in the *Tri County News* in 2007.

> Another complicating factor beyond the control of anyone was the weather, namely rain and more rain, it was unfortunate that so much rainy weather seemed to hit during fair days.[4]

People were expected to spend days, if not weeks, traveling to the fair from locations all over the state and beyond. Most of the locals were more than twenty-five miles away in this unbroken, sparsely populated prairie. If the paths into Jackson became heavily rutted due to the mud, the surrounding community would not be able to attend. As highlighted in the same *Tri County* article:

> If ruts became too deep, another track was taken alongside of the rutted one and tough sod carried horses and wagons pretty well as long as the ruts didn't cut through the sod. Horse and wagon travel or oxen didn't bring attendances up very much from a sparsely settled prairie.[5]

Terrain across the whole of Minnesota was difficult to traverse, so population growth in small towns like Jackson was very gradual. Trails were nothing more than clogged cow paths; in poor weather it was not uncommon for box wagons to be hub deep in mud. The wheels were made with broad rims to help stop them from cutting into the muddy cattle tracks. The wheel rims were made of green rawhide that shrank tight as it dried. A slow progression under these circumstances of fifteen to twenty miles a day was common and tedious.

The settlers in the accessible vicinity would have to make a week-long commitment to attend the event and carry food and grain for horses during the duration. They used a canvas that attached to the wagon like an awning. This provided an area for cooking and would offer limited shelter. The arrival of the railroad was eagerly awaited, but this did not provide better travel options, as most could not afford the fares and the expense of paying for food was now added to the cost of lodgings.

No headway was made into the debt the Jackson Agricultural Society amassed until 1908, when a new organization was created with the backing and investment of $20,000. By 1910 the fair was finally starting to take off, and horse races, good music, merry-go-round rides, dances, and lunches were all introduced. Unfortunately, this investment did not change the event's precipitous fortune, as wet weather continued to cause the fair to be postponed in the summer of 1920.

Investigation

The pioneer village has many buildings including a church, general store, hotel, telephone exchange, dentist's office, blacksmith's shop, caboose, railway station, lawyer's office, print-shop, gas station, coffin maker, pioneer house, and barn. This location was described by Kelly Van De Walle in the *Jackson County Pilot* in 2006:

> The Jackson County Fair Village consists of 20 buildings, ranging from a rustic doctor's office to an old service station. A home, church and various business buildings, complete with furnishings, depict what Main Street might have looked like in a former era. Antique machinery and other items of interest are also on display. Many items from Jackson's past have found their way into one building or another.
>
> The Jackson County Fair Village has brought joy and entertainment to countless people since the first building moved to the grounds in the late 1970s.[6]

I brought a large team to the pioneer village since this was a great opportunity to blanket the entire site and to increase the chances of receiving paranormal evidence. I was handed a jailer's sized set of keys by a board member and the whole location was now at our disposal. Having carried out an extensive walkthrough, I decided the most promising sites would be the general store, the pioneer house (also known as the Baloun house), and the dentist's office. Other areas offered an opportunity to set up audio and video equipment in the hope of documenting paranormal activity in our absence.

We brought with us a twenty-foot trailer that we used as a central command area. This allowed us to run cabling throughout the village so that our infrared cameras could follow and document our investigations. I informed the local sheriff as to our intensions for the night, so that a group of strange people wandering around the pioneer village in the early hours of the morning with flashlights would not cause suspicion. I asked Lorna to lead a team in the general store and for Heather to do the same in the pioneer house. Ashley took a team into the dentist's office, and I explored the barn.

The Dentist's Office

This building was originally erected in the 1880s, a half a block to the east of Main Street on Sheridan Street. The first proprietor was the John Paul Lumber Company that used the property as an office. Unfortunately, this building was swept away in the early spring floods shortly after its construction when the Des Moines River broke its banks. Oral history records that some of the lumber actually ended up in Des Moines, Iowa. To avoid a repeat of this incident it was moved to a new site.

This building has been used for many varied purposes during its history. At one time it was a shoe repair shop owned by Joe Cihlers and was also the home of the Blizek family. The building finally ended up in the possession of Louis Nelson, proprietor of Nelson Feed and Produce, and longtime Jackson citizen. He used the building for storage.

Nelson once described an incident that occurred during the pioneer days when the house was raided. One of the occupants of the house was known to make illicit moonshine on the property and a number of respectable townsladies became upset as they found their husbands coming home late on a Saturday night worse for wear. A group of them pressured Jackson County Sheriff Lee to investigate the rumors surrounding the house. When the sheriff knocked on the door and enquired about the homemade brew he was told, "No, Mr. Lee, outdoor is sunshine—no moonshine in here." The sheriff proceeded to search the place and found three crocks of liquor bubbling in a back room. The sheriff and his deputies threw them into the river.

The property was then moved to the county fairground and placed at its current location in June 1979 where it was restored to its current condition. Many of the buildings have been restored, but some are in need of repair. The harsh, exacting Minnesota seasons have taken their toll over the last 140 years, as outlined by the *Jackson County Pilot* in 2006:

> Structurally the village is in need of assistance. Moss grows on rooftops, windows sit in rotten sills, decks need re-building, paint is chipped on most all of the houses, and tree limbs lay scattered after several ice storms took their toll this past winter.[7]

I had felt during the walkthrough that the dentist's office would be very active, and I sensed a real presence of energy when I stood next to the antique dentist's chair and equipment. It is possible the chair had soaked up all the pain and suffering that was caused throughout its employment during an era without proper anesthesia and with only rudimentary skills and tools. The whole room had a creepy vibe due to the display of prosthetic limbs and all manner of other medical equipment that would have not looked out of place in a medieval torture chamber.

With high hopes, Ashley first took her team into this area to investigate, but came back an hour later, disappointed. She stated that no paranormal contact had been made in this location during the vigil. It may be that energy was present in this area, but energy does not necessarily have to signify a sentience or intelligence. I have energy in the batteries that run my equipment, but it does not follow that I can have a conversation with it. I am of the opinion that poltergeist activity is energy similar to what I believe to be in the dentist's office. Doors may slam and cups may fly, but that does not have to suggest a person resides there in spirit.

Later that evening I went into the dentist's office with my own team and an infrared camera. I still felt the energy but had no discernible paranormal contact. I left this area disappointed, but we had so many other buildings to investigate that I did not want to invest any more time in this building. Remember that just because nothing paranormal happens when I am present does not mean that a building is not haunted. It just means it didn't happen when I was there.

The Barn and General Store

One area that caught my eye was the barn. This was an area filled with antiquated farmyard machinery, carts, and carriages. This was not a location that I would have initially considered to be worthy of a vigil. Yet one carriage caught my eye. It was a horse-drawn hearse used from 1880-1921. It belonged to two Jackson funeral directors, V. W. Avery and Sathe & Son. For the sum of three dollars, it was used for funeral services and pulled by a team of white horses. A trimmer black horse team could be obtained for an extra dollar and was loaned and driven by resident Julius Miller. The hearse had a gold and velvet interior and was adorned with two kerosene lanterns mounted to the front. I placed a DVR inside the hearse where the coffin would have been placed in the hope of recording paranormal evidence. I started a vigil, but once again no paranormal evidence was forthcoming.

Lorna's team went to investigate the general store and also received little in the way of paranormal activity. There was a report of some scratching towards the back of the shop but the site appeared to be the home to several raccoons, cats, and many other wild Minnesotan mammals. I was now starting to believe that paranormal activity haunts the space rather than the buildings since we had uncovered little activity in any of the locations we had so far investigated. I was beginning to feel deflated and hoped that Heather's team could provide the evidence I had been looking for.

The Baloun Pioneer House

Upon entering the pioneer house for the first time during my first visit to the fairground, I had noticed a large amount of psychic energy in the building. As I ascended the tight narrow stairway to the upper level that held three small bedrooms, it became almost impossible for me to walk. It was like trying to wade through paranormal syrup. I felt this same sensation several years previously when I investigated the Melrose Historical Society Museum. That building used to be a nunnery, and I could barely stagger along the corridor on the top floor due to the nauseating and gut twisting energy that was present.

The Baloun Pioneer House first built and owned by Vaclav Soukup

I had Greg join me during this exploration of the house and even his skeptical and analytical thinking was jolted by the feeling of these sensations. Heather led a team in this area first and had her hair pulled during her vigil. She also reported that they had heard what sounded like the noise of somebody moaning and then a mumbled conversation between two men. I decided it would be advantageous to organize another vigil in the same area to see what further evidence would present itself.

As I sat down ready to start the vigil, a big crack of lightning illuminated the sky, followed by a roar of thunder. Throughout our investigation the weather intermittently lit the site like the Fourth of July. I positioned myself in an armchair in the parlor so I could see into the kitchen. Ashley sat to my left with just a small occasional table positioned between us. I could see Heather and Greg in the kitchen, and the rest of the team was dotted around the stairs and bedrooms.

I have come to recognize a familiar sensation through my years of investigating that informs me when something is about to happen. The energy felt so high in this room that I knew a paranormal experience would be imminent. It usually starts a few minutes before the activity begins and is a mixture of psychic awareness and subtle environmental changes that seem to be centered on the temperature and electromagnetic fields. Sure enough, a dark figure then walked into the room from the direction of the kitchen and sat boldly in the armchair to my right next to the piano. Ashley exclaimed that she could also see the figure. Greg pointed his thermal imaging camera in the direction of the chair, and a humanoid figure was seen in the colder shades of blue sitting comfortably in the chair right in the middle of our investigation. I wondered at that moment if he was even aware of us.

Heather started up the ghost box in the hope of communicating with the entity. The first question she asked was, "What is your name?" At that very moment I had the name Bernard shouted at me psychically into my right ear. I turned to Ashley and whispered, "I bet you a thousand dollars that he says Bernard." The ghost box then blurted out the name Bernard. I casually turned to Ashley and informed her that she now owed me a thousand dollars. She later complained that she had never agreed to the deal.

Frustratingly, no further communication was made with Bernard, despite seeing him. I considered that he may have been attached in spirit to the chair he was sitting in. If Bernard had spent thirty years sitting religiously in that chair right up until the moment he died, then he may well still be residing in the chair. I knew this historic home was bereft of furniture when it was reerected. I considered that the building had subsequently been filled with period furniture that had come from many different locations. This I confirmed when I discovered an article written by Rosalie Peters in the *Daily Globe* concerning the house:

> To furnish the house, items were secured through donations, flea markets were visited and scavengers went through attics.[8]

This of course would make it almost impossible to historically find who Bernard was. If anybody in the Jackson area is reading this and once donated furniture and wants to claim Bernard, please let me know.

During the attempted engagement with Bernard I thought I heard the name Soukup coming through on the ghost box. I was aware from my research that Vaclav Soukup was the owner of the property and had actually built it. I thought this evidence to be almost too good to be true. So I said, after the briefest of interactions with Bernard, that I wanted to talk to the individual who said Soukup. I asked him where he was born. I had seen on the historical information presented in the house that Soukup was born in Hocklibien, Austria. Then, psychically, I heard the spirit reply to my question by saying Hungary. But at the same moment the ghost box spat out the word "Czech," to contradict me. I was confused by the three different responses and information I now had. Was it Austria as stated in the historical text, Hungary as given to me psychically, or Czechoslovakia as indicated by the ghost box?

Soukup had immigrated to America with his wife and three daughters in 1836. Unfortunately, his wife died during the voyage and was given a burial at sea. Soukup first settled in Chicago and found himself a second wife who then also died a short time after. He remarried for a third and final time to Mary Halvew Zamezril. Like other settlers into Minnesota they were offered land to homestead, and Mary and Soukup received eighty acres in Hunter Township, Jackson County.

Vaclav Soukup with his family

Soukup was a carpenter by trade and bought the wood for his home pre-cut from Chicago. It was transported to Jackson via the railroad. It was only the second frame house to be erected in the whole of Jackson County. The family had lived in a sod hut one mile east of Highway 86 until the home was completed. The land was uncultivated, and early settlers like Soukup had the back-breaking work of turning over the earth with shovels and plows. It was common practice to plow and turn the soil around the cabin first to stop it from being destroyed by bush fires and to deter animals and insects.

There was little money to buy machinery to help till the soil so the market for these products was initially poor.

Suddenly, the storm now surrounding us illuminated the house in a fizzing electric blue and lashed the building in torrents of rain like the sea cut into vertical strips. Thunder roared and shook the building. The moonlight was now obscured in an ominous blanket of darkness that engulfed us as the tar-black clouds rolled in. I informed the team that we may be required to stop shortly and the ghost box replied, "That's too bad." As the sky became darker so did the tone of the responses. In a very threatening, gravelly-voiced demand that sent a chill down my spine, it yelled, "Get out of the house!"

This was so jarringly out of context that I jumped.

"Fuck off! Get out!" it continued.

Psychically I did not feel that a dark, non-human entity had come through. But the growling and rasping noises that the ghost box presented were certainly chilling and made me sit up and take notice. I decided that it might be a good policy to choose one's battles carefully, and as we were naturally coming to the end of the vigil, I made the decision to remove the team from the house as suggested by the expletive laden request. I certainly did not want to upset any spirits.

My decision was also informed by the heavens that had opened up in biblical proportions. Deep puddles had formed and we retreated to the shelter of the command center trailer. We gazed at the monitor screens in front of us that presented a collection of rooms around the site—all currently without investigators in them. I believe that thunderous conditions can juice-up an environment as a catalyst for paranormal activity in the same way an EM pump would. Unfortunately, electrical equipment and water do not mix well, and many of our cables passed through the streams that were now flowing down each street. Although the investigation sites were inside, the cameras were fed from the command trailer into the buildings by long stretches of exposed cabling. For health and safety reasons, I made the decision to call the investigation short. We had already made it into the early hours of the morning, and I did not want members of my team helping me from the other side.

After the investigation I checked the exact location of Hock-libien. The information provided in the house had stated that Souk-up was Austrian; I discovered that no such place existed. So I re-searched the name Soukup and found it to be a common Czech name meaning a merchant or dealer. I then decided to focus my attention on the towns of the Czech Republic. I found a town called Vysoká Libyně that is nineteen miles north of Plzen and forty-three miles west of Prague—it used to be called Hochlibin. It was common for European towns and villages to be renamed due to shifts in political and linguistic boundaries. I believe this was why Soukup told me in spirit that he was Czech and not Austrian.

Czechoslovakia was a country founded after the First World War in 1918. When Soukup was born at the beginning of the nine-teenth century (he emigrated in 1836) this area was called Bohe-mia and was part of the Habsburg Empire. This would place the country under Hungarian Monarchal rule in what was to become part of the Austro-Hungarian Empire. Austria-Hungary was a mul-tinational state and one of the world's great powers at the time. It was geographically the second largest country in Europe after the Russian Empire and the third most populous. In the autumn of 1918, with a German defeat imminent, and with revolutions in Vienna and Budapest that gave political power to the left liberal political parties, the Austro-Hungarian Monarchy collapsed. The leftist and liberal movements supported the separatism of ethnic minorities and wanted full independence, opposing the monarchy as a form of government. They considered themselves internation-alist rather than patriotic.

It was also common during the nineteenth century that names and birthplaces would be misspelled on census forms due to foreign speaking citizens and the sometimes limited level of penmanship and education of the census taker. So I believed that Hochlibin in the Czech Republic was wrongly documented as Hocklibien (a non-ex-istent place).

My research has proven that the dead are capable of extending our historical knowledge by informing us of inaccuracies from the grave. I then looked to confirm my findings by accessing Soukup's obituary in the *Lakefield Standard* of 1919:

Death Summons County Pioneers

Vaclav Soukup of Hunter Passes to Long Rest December 18: Vaclav Soukup was born in Bohemia August 15, 1836, and died at home of his son John R. Soukup Wednesday, December 18, 1918, aged 82 year, 4 months and three days. Deceased was married in Bohemia and a few years later, in 1869, he and his wife immigrated to America and settled in Chicago where they resided several years.[9]

The home mentioned in the text above was the house we were investigating at the pioneer village. This confirmed that Soukup actually died there and led me to believe it was his spirit with whom we had briefly engaged. I also discovered that the census of June 27, 1900 listed Soukup as Bohemian in origin. Soukup would have been aware that the area in which he was born was now called Czechoslovakia, and he was obviously aware of this new naming. So he would have been born in a town under Hungarian rule that then became Czech in the last four weeks of his life.

Conclusion

Despite my professional undertakings, the local Jackson police department did actually pay us a visit during this investigation. The information I had provided had clearly not disseminated very far. The officer was very friendly and interested in what we were doing. He was also frustrated that he could not join the investigation after I extended an invite to him. He declined so he could finish his shift.

The most intriguing aspect of this investigation was the way Soukup informed me of his birthplace and corrected me. It was interesting to note that Soukup's death in December 1918 was only a month after Czechoslovakia was formed. It would have made little sense if he had died just four weeks sooner and claimed to have been

Czech. I believe the interaction with Soukup proves beyond doubt that spirits remain with the house, even if the property has been relocated. Based on my experiences and research, I believe that spirits have a free will to go wherever they desire, and Soukup wanted to reside in the house he had built and died in.

I remembered when I first read about the history of the fair that the organization nearly went bankrupt due to the poor annual weather. I guess it should not have been a surprise that the investigation was then cut short due to the same problem. Frustration was felt by all of the team as we sat in the command center with a whole village to investigate and a bunch of keys, watching the thunderstorm around us. Yet the weather determined that it would be too dangerous to continue that night.

THE RATHBUN DUGOUT

JACKSON COUNTY, MINNESOTA

Investigating the site of the first recorded death in Jackson County would perfectly combine my love of history and the paranormal.

I was intrigued when I first heard about the death of mail carrier Hoxie Rathbun in 1856. Little is known about his life, and I saw the perfect opportunity to add to the canon of Jackson County history. Rathbun was delivering mail in the height of a blizzard when he lost his horse and tragically died in a dugout. His was the first recorded death in Jackson County. I then discovered that the remains of the dugout had survived in the remote location of Kilen Woods. There are very few areas left from the earliest part of Minnesota's history, and I could not remember accessing many spirits from that era in the Midwest.

I started my research by interviewing several employees of the Jackson County Historical Society. I also accessed rare letters and period documents at the helpful and professional Blue Earth Historical Society in Mankato. I undertook two separate investigations at the site with a reduced team due to the remoteness of the location. We were restricted to the equipment we could comfortably carry through the dense forestation.

History

The dugout is located at the edge of Kilen Woods State Park, Jackson County and is a relatively untouched hilly and wooded landscape. Many rare plant species, like calcareous seepage ferns, thrive here due to the uniqueness of the groundwater that wells up on the hillsides and valley slopes. This area also boasts a number of little known historical locations, including the original Fort Belmont site and the now forgotten town of Brownsburg.

Near the dugout was the Ole Holthe cabin. This was believed to be used as a stopping point for the fur traders coming from Lake Shetek on route to Des Moines and the east. The cabin was donated by the Holthe family to the Jackson County Historical Society and brought to its current location from the farm opposite. It has been suggested that it may have been used as the Belmont Post Office at one time, but I had found no documentation to support that oral history. Any cabins dating back to the time just after the dugout was constructed have long since disappeared.

The postal system played a crucial role in the expansion of the Midwest during the middle of the nineteenth century. It facilitated an inexpensive, fast, convenient communication system for the early settlers and increased migration through information and propaganda. It allowed scattered families to stay in touch, providing much needed support and help, and assisted entrepreneurs in finding business opportunities and commercial relationships. This expansion is highlighted when you consider that Blue Earth County did not have a single post office in 1850; yet by 1860 they were operating thirteen.

In the summer of 1856 a military mail route was founded between Mankato and Sioux Falls, Iowa as a way of connecting Fort Ridgely in Minnesota with Fort Randall in the Dakotas. This fledgling postal service assisted the army greatly in expanding control over the vast western territories. The contract for this service was given to *March and Babcock* of Mankato during the autumn of 1856. George March owned the general store in Mankato, and mail would arrive via stagecoach or steamboat to this location. Joseph W. Babcock of Le Sueur County was already operating a postal service in Kasota Township, which he started on February 7, 1854. They both consulted a map and started to plan. The contract included the purchase of half-a-section of land every twenty miles along the route. At this time no post offices were in operation along the trail, and shanties and dugouts were constructed to enable postal workers to rest with some shelter and warmth. Small provisions were also supplied for the carrier's pony.

The dugout at the Kilen Wood's site was excavated on the side of a natural slope leading down to the river. No record remains of how it originally looked, but other dugouts around Minnesota have been documented. They were usually lined with tamarack poles and constructed to enable half the dwelling to be below the ground. Some were covered to act as a basic shelter from the elements. It was not uncommon throughout the nineteenth century for Native Americans to burn the dugouts in the hope of forcing early settlers away.

Hoxie Rathbun was born in 1813 in Delhi, Delaware County, New York. He married Catherine Brobst Bruce in Minersville, Pennsylvania in 1838. In 1852 he then brought his family to Mankato where he was employed by March and Babcock to carry the mail bi-monthly. During the Christmas delivery of 1856 he became disorientated by the poor weather and found himself stranded in a blizzard. He was missing for so long that the contractors feared for his safety. After being pressured by his wife Catherine, the contractors eventually sent two men to look for him. Rathbun was found in his dugout close to death, unable to light a fire or even speak. He had lost his pony in a snowdrift but still managed to keep his mailbag with him. A letter postmarked in Sioux City indicated that he had been on the route for twenty days.

I then found more information in a rare letter written by lifelong Mankato resident Anna K. Grover Fuller (1891-1975), in a 1934 letter entitled *The Unfortunate Letter Carrier*:

Before he set out on his first trip to Sioux City some friendly Indians came and warned him that if he went on this trip he would never return alive. He did not heed the warning and went anyhow with only one letter to deliver. It was Thanksgiving morn and the snow was four feet deep. He was guided by ten feet poles which were set up a certain distance apart to mark the trail. He went past six shanties on the way from Mankato to Sioux City, which had been put up to serve as warming houses. He delivered Mr. Babcock's letter and then started for Mankato. When he was three quarters of a mile away from the last shack he was forced to abandon his horse owing to the fact that a terrible blizzard had come up. He struggled through the snow to the shanty but he could not start a fire because he was so cold. He laid on the floor for 20 days. In the meantime, many trappers and hunters had passed by the shack but they failed to go in. On the twentieth day after Mr. Rathbun had been in the shack he was found alive by a passing hunter. He died soon after and his horse was never recovered.[10]

Rathbun had the unfortunate distinction of becoming the first recorded death in Jackson County. To put this into historical perspective, it would be another sixteen months before Minnesota would become a state and only nine years after the first postage stamps were introduced by the United States government.

Rathbun spent the last days of his life alone over the Christmas period, with his wife and family worrying about his disappearance. He must have experienced a terrible and miserably slow demise, suffering at the hands of the harsh Minnesotan winter. With the remains of the dugout still present, I considered whether a haunting could still occupy the land after 159 years. It was my hope that I could contact Hoxie Rathbun's spirit to find out more about his death.

Investigation

I walked through the undergrowth and picked a path through the trees and forestation towards the crater that indented itself into the sloping ground. The warm, perfect conditions belied the pain and suffering that once took place here, like walking through a calm, sunshine-painted meadow centuries after the carnage of a battle. I first ran two separate EMF meters over the location, but no reading was registered. I perched myself on a fallen branch in the hollow and started the vigil by using the ghost box. The hissing and click-ing of the device came as a jarring contrast to the quiet and peaceful surroundings that nature had provided. I then asked the most clichéd of opening questions.

"Is anybody here?"

"Sure," came the quick reply in a man's voice.

"Do you remember being here?"

"Yeah," he said.

"Is the shanty you used still here?" I asked.

I knew that the Holthe cabin just yards away had been moved to this location and was constructed much later than 1856, but I wanted to verify the fact.

"No, no," he responded twice, reinforcing what I already thought to be historically correct. I then asked for the name of his pony.

"Max," he replied.

I kept asking who I was talking to in the hope of hearing the name Hoxie Rathbun. Alas, this seemed tantalizingly out of reach. The answers to my questions would suggest that Rathbun was with me, but I wanted verbal verification. I persisted in this vigil but failed to receive any further responses to my questions. I made the decision to walk farther down the slope to the edge of the river. If paranormal activity was not fully forthcoming, then it made sense to look for an area where greater contact may be made.

I then sat by the bank of the river and felt the last embrace of the autumnal sun heat my body and face in a warm reassurance.

Brightly glinting yellow leaves dotted themselves along the ma-
ple tree branches like sparse gold dollars holding on stubbornly as
nighttime winter temperatures crept ever closer. The sound of the
gentle babbling brook streaming over the river rocks filled the air
and reminded me of what a truly beautiful state this was. The whole
scene made a pleasant change from the damp, dark basements and
cold, abandoned factories that my work tends to find me in.

I began to work psychically in order to contact Rathbun further
as the normally reliable equipment seemed to be falling short in this
setting. The first image presented to me was the blank whiteness of
snow, a complete whiteout lacking in any detail or recognizable features. This would be the fearful image seared into Rathbun's vision
for the duration of his ordeal. I then channeled the sensation of having a sore throat and feeling thirsty. If Rathbun was incapacitated for
twenty days, unable to access food or proper water, then he would
have obviously suffered from the effects of hunger and thirst.

What I then received in that vigil were mere glimpses compared to my normal experience of psychic work, like the intermittent poor reception on an old television screen or the limited visual
knowledge gained from a half-finished jigsaw puzzle. Images came
and went in my mind as I was presented with the clairvoyance of
distant pictures and muddled thoughts. Despite the warmth of the
afternoon, I felt the sensation of coldness, a shivering and wetness.
I also saw the flickering thoughts and landscapes of what I believed
to be Britain, perhaps where Rathbun's family had originated. I then
had the experience of tasting a bitterness in my mouth and feeling
the propensity to chew. I thought this to be from Rathbun's chewing
tobacco. I also saw Rathbun briefly in my thinking. He was sporting
a large bushy beard, a common adornment during that era and a necessity during the winter months. He also showed himself as a tall,
athletic man.

I asked about his pony once more, as this seemed to elicit a
strong response during the previous vigil. People certainly develop
emotional attachments to their horses. I could now see the animal.
It was chestnut brown with darker coloring towards the hooves and

tail, almost fading into black. I pressed once again to try and verify the animal's name, and once more (psychically this time) I could hear the name Max. I then felt a strong feeling of concern flood over me. Rathbun was actually worried about the loss of the animal and what may have become of it. I realized through him that he did not own the pony as it had belonged to the contractors. His last few days and darkest moments were filled with the dread of losing the animal and the debt he would have to repay. Despite the duration of the vigil, no further paranormal experiences were forthcoming.

There was one final document that I subsequently discovered after this investigation. It was a letter written by Margaret Rathbun Funk on February 24, 1922. She was the daughter of Hoxie, and it gave me a tantalizing insight into how her father looked:

> Father had blue eyes and light hair and he was 6 feet tall and always healthy. Our father's name was Gideon Hoxie Rathbun. He was always particular for us to spell our name Rathbun.[11]

This information confirmed that Rathbun was a tall and athletic man, exactly how I had seen him in spirit.

Conclusion

There are many inherent problems attached to outside investigations in the woods: noise pollution, poison ivy, wild animals, the elements, and the inability to use any equipment that requires an electrical supply. The bright, daylight-bathed environment also made it impossible to see the energy of orbs that may have been present, as it is more difficult to see a faint light emitted against a well-lit environment compared to the contrast of darkness.

It was frustrating that I had only received short bursts of contact with what I thought to be Rathbun's spirit. He came through strongly but disappointingly intermittent through both the equipment and my psychic work. It was interesting to note that a spirit could still be present in this location from 1856, even if the contact lamentably faded after the initial dialogue. I have considered the possibility that his energy may have been used up by the first initial interaction, like the final dim moments of a fading battery.

One cannot imagine the pain, suffering, and fear experienced by Rathbun in his last moments. I find it remarkable how the weather in this part of the country can be so schizophrenic. It can change from a clear, calm, serene day to the harsh, life-threatening deadly veil of sub-zero blizzards in the blink of an eye. It was only through the braveness of Hoxie Rathbun and other fearless early pioneer settlers that this state and country were forged in the worst of conditions. Running through their family DNA was the propensity to leave their homes and countries behind in order to embrace the unknown of a new continent, landscape, and culture. With the diligence of historical research and the skills and equipment of the paranormal investigator, we can make sure they are not forgotten.

WINDOM AREA CENTRAL SCHOOL

WINDOM, MINNESOTA

*The pupils of Windom Area Central School have remained
present long after the final bell.*

The Windom Area Central School looms prominently and impressively against the urban townscape and exudes the look of a haunting building. Heather resides in Cottonwood County and many of
Lorna's relatives were born and raised in Windom. It was through
them that I contacted Cathy who was the former Business Arts and
Recreation Center coordinator. We then gained access to investigate
this monolithic icon to twentieth century education and I set about
organizing an experienced team to enter the property.

Cathy volunteered to be our guide and provided me with useful
historical information. I also accessed online archives to expand my
research and spent many hours in the friendly and helpful Cottonwood County Historical Society where I found period newspapers,
articles, obituaries, and high school yearbooks.

The History

Windom is named after William Windom (1827-1891) who served
as a US Senator and Secretary of the Treasury. The land was platted
on June 20, 1871 by A. L. Beach who was an engineer for the Sioux

City and St. Paul Railroad. Just twelve lots were originally designated and all sold within a day for one hundred dollars. Windom
was then incorporated as a village in 1875 and reincorporated on
September 9, 1884.

The first school in Windom was organized in the upper room
of the Loop & Wood lumber office in the early fall of 1871. Miss
Lawson was the teacher. By the end of the year the school rented the
ground floor of a building owned by Harvey Klock, with the Masonic Lodge occupying the second floor. The first purpose-built school
was constructed on railroad land in 1873 at a cost of $2,995.00 and
was located on the corner of 10th and 6th Avenues. It was a classic,
wooden-framed, two-story, white pioneer structure with two side extensions and a central body. A round attic window set below a bell
tower completed the building. Mr. William Prentiss was the principal.

In 1894 a new, resplendent neo-gothic brick building was built.
It was constructed at a cost of $38,392.65 and boasted many impres-
sive architectural features. It had thick, rough-cut limestone ground
floor exterior walls that complemented the deep-reddish-brown
brickwork. White, triangular neo-classical pediments were positioned at the end of each roofline and a dominating central bell tower was finished with a steep, four-sided pyramid roof. Queen Anne
influences could also be observed in the rounded, arched, elongated
doors and windows. Ironically the school opened to a full capacity
and a series of extensions had to be quickly planned and implemented to accommodate the burgeoning number of children.

In 1931 an ambitious postmodernist school was designed and
built that covered an impressive 76,000 square feet on the same site.
This development was seen to be financially foolhardy during the
height of the depression, but it made an impressive statement that
reflected the importance the town placed on education. The new
building included a commercial area, a music department, and all
the academic areas for the senior high school. It also had a new auditorium with seating for 883 students. Various additions were then
built throughout the middle of the twentieth century, including a
gym extension in 1953 and a north wing in 1961.

Then in 1999, after 126 years of educational service in various forms, the school closed its doors. Just weeks before it was due to be demolished in 2001, a group of local residents rallied together to create the Business Arts and Recreation Center (BARC). They purchased the school for a single dollar with the intention of making the building available for community use. Through fundraising, generous donations, and hard work, they developed the site and implemented a program that would help to bring economic growth to Windom. This would be achieved through the creation of office spaces and the refurbishment of the early childhood and special educational needs classrooms in the south wing. Local community activities were also encouraged to utilize the space.

The Investigation

This building has all the character and architectural features associated with a school built in 1931. Its postmodernist concrete and brick construction shows symmetry and stoicism in equal amounts. It also has all the robust imagery of a fort and appears too big and expansive for the school district it once served. I ventured into the building and felt a brisk unwelcoming atmosphere provided by the frosty autumnal night and a broken heating system. A long, reflective, cold and clinical, high-ceilinged corridor led to a set of sturdy double-doors with a worn patina from children's fingers on the wooden surfaces. I pushed them open and the faint omnipresent smell of floor cleaner met me on the other side.

The team utilized the old school library as a controlled area, and we organized our equipment in preparation for the walkthrough and baseline tests. All manner of empty storerooms and disused cupboards were then witnessed as we made our way through the building. Some may even have been used for the illicit activities of a sneaky kiss or a surreptitious cigarette. Our presence was certainly noted by any residing spirits by our echoing footsteps that audibly bounced around the abandoned classrooms in a way that can only happen in a municipal building. We then found ourselves in the basement where a collection of narrow tunnels twisted themselves beneath the building. They were smelly, musty, narrow, and littered with grime and debris—they would remain unexplored.

Room 206

On the second floor we discovered that room 206 was still used for the teaching of religious education. As I passed the open door I heard a child's laughter. I psychically asked who was there and received the name "Michael." I made a note of his name and the room number. The team then agreed that this location would be the best place to start our first vigil based on this brief interaction.

We arranged a semi-circle of seating and left an empty chair for Michael to join us. The temperature fell dramatically as we started the vigil, and the power on three of our devices just drained and died. Greg's handheld infrared video camera went from fully charged to inoperable. Lorna's static full-spectrum camera was facing the classroom doorway. It also failed, as did my ghost box. It was a chilly evening but not to the level of coldness that would have accounted for so many power and battery drains. I wondered if a spirit was energy starved and was feeding off the batteries.

I placed a K2 EMF meter in the corridor in the hope of registering the presence of any curious and cautious spirits that did not have the courage to join us. The team then started to notice the corridor becoming very active, and we stared at the shadowy movement that weaved its way through the gloomy darkness. We noted that our view of the dimly illuminated green light of the K2 meter kept being broken by the forms that passed in front of it. We could also hear the distant sound of children playing, like the eerie residual audio recordings of yesteryear. I then replaced the batteries in my ghost box and turned it on in the hope that Michael would step forward to communicate.

"London!" was suddenly shouted in a fake English accent. This was not the first time a spirit had mimicked me, and I confirmed that he did well to recognize the fact. I don't have a standard, or 'received,' English accent due to my East London upbringing. My cockney influenced vernacular leaves many Americans wondering if I am Australian. Interestingly, I have rarely been questioned by the spirits about my accent. Perhaps ghosts from a distant era recognize my origins successfully and have a better ear for language due to the proliferation of European immigrants flooding into the country during the later twentieth century.

"Lorna!" Michael then exclaimed.

Lorna acknowledged the disembodied voice and said, "Hello."

"Happy birthday!" he said.

It was Greg's birthday and I wondered how the spirit could have known this. It certainly suggested an element of stalking or eavesdropping. Was it possible that the entity had been listening to our banter and chit-chat from the very first moment we had entered the building? I then tried to engage with Michael further by asking him to count with me. I asked him to jump in with the next number in the sequence as I started to count upwards. A sense of anticipation built slowly as I verbalized each integer.

"One, two, three, four, five, six, seven…" Then I paused.

"Eight!" was then shouted out from the ghost box.

This was a very simple response, but it provided me with a wealth of information. It confirmed that the spirit could hear me and was able to respond in an intelligent manner. I was aware that numbers are the most common words heard on the radio, used in reference to roads, the time, sporting numbers, chart positions, and in the names of the radio stations themselves. With that in mind I proceeded to run through the alphabet to reinforce my evidence.

"A, B, C, D, E, F…" Once more I left a pause.

"G," came the reply! I was delighted at this result and asked who was playing with me.

"Michael!" he confirmed.

This corroborated the name of the spirit I had previously heard on the walkthrough.

It is a common and frustrating experience that interactions like this suddenly end without any noticeable reason. This was the case with Michael. Despite the successful contact we were witnessing, the equipment just stopped producing results, and everything went quiet. Even psychically I felt that he had left the room. I then spent ten minutes trying to reestablish a connection with Michael, but to no avail. As previously explained, perhaps Michael was low on energy. During this part of the vigil I did notice that paranormal activity appeared to be more active in the corridor outside as shadows darted about. So with the expectation of receiving greater contact, we moved to the third floor corridor where the science labs were located.

Third Floor Corridor

As we ascended to the third floor, Cathy recognized that the lights were illuminating the abandoned lockers that stretched parallel along the corridor walls. Cathy had turned these lights off when we left this area after the walkthrough, and we were the only people in the building that night. The phenomenon of lights being turned on and off was also experienced between vigils in the restroom. I recalled turning the light on and then off again during my first visit, yet later that evening I found the light was no longer operable.

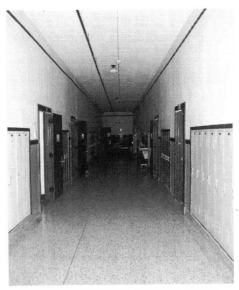

Windom Area Central School third floor corridor

At the end of the evening, when we were leaving the property, I noticed the light was back on. I had to consider that the spirits were up to mischief. It was certainly odd that the light initially worked, then failed to work, and then came on by itself.

I first placed three K2 meters along the corridor floor at twenty-yard intervals. So if an entity arrived it would activate the meters as it traveled, giving an indication of its movement and speed. This provided an ever-dimming row of green lights that eventually disappeared into the blackness—like an airport runway at night. I also placed a DVR next to each K2 meter. Halfway down the corridor I positioned an oscilloscope in the hope of registering any small noise that might activate the sound waves displayed by the meter in real time from some distance away. I also placed a series of calibrated flashlights along the length of the floor, with the farthest positioned towards the second stairwell at the other end of the corridor. I believed that no entity could make it through this space without being detected.

Within moments of starting the vigil, we heard a walking noise in the auditorium directly behind us, on the other side of the stairwell wall. The footsteps were not uniform and we heard three or four steps on each occasion with a short break between each before they started up again. They were accompanied by a dragging sound that was reminiscent of a chair being pulled across the floor. Everybody on the team clearly heard these sounds.

Then a voice spoke to me psychically. It requested in a very forceful manner that I should go to the farthest end of the corridor. I gazed to the far end into the blackest, haziest gloom and pondered whether I wanted to sit that far away from the team. Then the farthest flashlight came on at the end of the corridor and lit the entire area like a beacon. I now had to walk to where the spirit had requested me to go in order to turn the flashlight off. I felt like I was being manipulated.

I slowly paced down the length of the corridor with my shoes tip-tapping in the quiet void. I verbalized my movements to inform the DVR recordings that the footsteps belonged to me. The rest of the team were now at the other end of the corridor and seemed a long way away. I sat on the floor with my back to the wall and watched and listened in my isolation. Then the same flashlight, no more than ten yards away now, was picked up and dropped back down to the floor.

The metallic sound resonated and reverberated all around. The flashlight came on and the beam spun around like a crazy lighthouse as it spilt random light into the darkest corners. It rocked slowly and progressively to stillness and turned itself off once more, allowing the blanket of black to reassert itself. It is one thing to see a flashlight turned on; it is another to see it rolling around the floor after being picked up and dropped. This could be described as poltergeist activity, as this was definitely a noisy ghost.

I became tense and wondered what might happen next after such a show of physicality. Then to my left a whirlwind of shadows flitted up the stairs like a group of naughty children left to run wild in a deserted school. Their braveness was complete when I saw them psychically stand in front of me making faces, which amused them greatly. They were unaware I could see them as one of the older boys opened up his arms and said in a mocking fashion, "So what am I?"

"You are a ghost," I calmly replied, but they already knew that as they ran off laughing and surprised at my ability to witness their behavior.

The Music Room

The music room felt considerably colder than the rest of the building, probably due to its larger size. Random instruments were liberally distributed around this space, and several large tympani drums stood isolated on the stage. I thought these impressive percussion instruments might encourage further poltergeist activity, since what child can resist banging on a drum?

It reminded me of a famous historical ghost story called the *Drummer of Tedworth* about a home plagued by ghostly nocturnal

drumming noises. This was documented in 1668 by Joseph Glanvill in his book *Saducismus Triumphatus*. Glanvill told the tale of
a local landowner named John Mompesson who owned a house in
Tedworth (now Tidworth in Wiltshire, England). He brought a law-
suit against a local drummer who was accused of extorting money
from him. After the legal ruling went against the drummer, his drum
was confiscated. Mompesson then found his home plagued by the
drumming noises. It was assumed that the drummer had brought
about this macabre action by way of witchcraft. This story is often
considered to be one of the earliest accounts of poltergeist activity,
supernatural noises caused by a mischievous spirit.

I placed a K2 meter and a DVR on one of the drums, plus
several trigger objects. A monotonous, low, droning sound became
more noticeable as we settled into the quiet of the music room vigil.
It was emanating from an exhaust fan located in the nearby gymna-
sium. I wondered if it would affect the quality of our audio evidence.
We positioned chairs around the expanse of the tiled linoleum floor
and waited to see who would arrive.

I had the impression that this was an area where spirits were
congregating in large numbers. I turned on the ghost box and asked
if they would like to introduce themselves.

"Matthew," the device uttered.

"Hi, Matthew," I responded.

"Did you play an instrument here?" I continued.

"Trumpet," was his reply.

Heather then exclaimed that she was psychically witnessing
what looked like some sort of graduation or end of show party taking place in the room. She specifically witnessed a spirit dressed in
a full football uniform, complete with a helmet and pads, enjoying
the celebratory atmosphere. I asked Heather if she could provide me
with any more detail to help with my research. She then informed
me that she could see the number 52 on his jersey. Matthew did not
respond further despite our prompting.

After the investigation I pondered the significance of why
Heather psychically saw a football player in this environment. It

was only some weeks later when I was driving through the town on my way to the Windom library investigation that I noticed a larger than life statue of a football player located on a plinth situated in the grounds of the courthouse. I stopped the car and walked up to the bronze sculpture to look for the name of the individual immortalized. It was Larry Buhler.

Lawrence 'Larry' Buhler was born on May 28, 1917. I discovered that he actually attended Windom High School and graduated in 1935 before playing football for the University of Minnesota Golden Gophers. He helped the Gophers win their third consecutive National Championship and was the team's leading rusher and scorer from 1936-38. He then played fullback and halfback in the National Football League for the Green Bay Packers from 1939-41. The Packers won the championship in 1939, and Buhler was selected for the Pro Bowl in 1940.

Buhler's football career was then tragically cut short by a car accident. He then returned to Windom to manage a local liquor store and to work on the family's hatchery and mink farm. After his death in 1990, at the age of seventy-three, the town honored him with an eight-foot-tall, $26,000 bronze statue that was completed in 1993. It was created by a sculptor from Granite Falls named Arthur H. Norby (who also created the Minnesota Korean War Memorial in St. Paul). It depicts Buhler standing in his University of Minnesota uniform holding a football in his left hand and a helmet in the other.

I considered that Larry Buhler might have been the spirit that Heather had sensed celebrating in the music room. I then remembered that she had told me his number was 52. Yet the number presented on the uniform of the statue was 72. I was initially disappointed, but I continued to research further and came across a photograph from 1939. It was of the Green Bay Packers team that won the NFL Championship for that year. Proudly at the back was Larry Buhler in the number 52 jersey. It would now be very coincidental if it was not the spirit of Larry Buhler attending the ghostly party. We never engaged in a dialogue with him, and many students over the years would have worn the number 52 football jersey. But it would be nice to think that one of the school's most famous pupils was still visiting the building in spirit.

The Girls' Locker Room

The boys' and girls' locker rooms were located in the basement of the school and only a utility room separated the two areas. The boys' locker room was noticeably damp, with a musty underlying smell of stale sweat that mixed with the olfactory lingering base notes of well-worn sneakers and old wet towels. The team witnessed several shadow figures moving in the half-light between the aging dusty lockers and the long, heavy wooden benches. A constant dripping sound came from the shower room.

I then ventured a few paces into the girls' locker room and felt a slight brushing upon my face. Thinking I had walked through a cobweb, I dropped my flashlight and DVR as I failed to juggle the equipment successfully in an attempt to feel my face. The flashlight blinked randomly as the percussive sound of its fall penetrated the eerie silence as it skipped and scuttled across the concrete floor.

Ashley walked into the room behind me and her face was also touched. Heather followed, unaware of our experiences and exclaimed that someone had just pulled her hair. We then inspected the entrance area thoroughly. There was no physical indication as to what may have caused these phenomena. Lorna then swept the entire area with an EMF meter and registered a considerable EMF reading of over 2.0 milligauss halfway up the door. This would suggest an area of energy located at around waist height. The EMF energy then fluctuated like it was transient and Lorna struggled to follow it with the meter.

We arranged ourselves on the available benches and started our next vigil. I decided to try a different approach and asked Heather to listen to the ghost box through her ear buds. Heather would be able to hear the responses more accurately using this method and would be able to call out the words and responses the spirit was relaying.

Heather would also be unaware of the questions I would be asking and the timing of them.

I then noticed that the EMF activity was present and predominant once more around the entrance where we had been touched. It was fluctuating, but I recorded a reading of 1.5 milligauss that jumped to 2.9 on my Melmeter. I believed that contact would be imminent. That contact came in short bursts of dialogue.

"Bob," said Heather, telling the team what the spirit had just said to her.

"So your name is Bob?" I asked.

"Yes," the spirit responded as Heather relayed without hearing my question.

"What year did you work here?"

"1961," Heather said, repeating what she was being told through the ear buds.

"Were you a teacher or a student?" I continued.

"Maintenance," came his reply. I acknowledged that we were next to the maintenance area.

"Pipe," he then said.

"Do you need to repair a pipe?" I enquired.

"Touch the pipe, burnt, help me!" came his response.

"Did you get burnt by a pipe?" I asked. He did not respond.

After an hour of fruitlessly trying to coax more information from Bob, we ended the vigil.

In the following weeks I visited the Cottonwood County Historical Society. We were very fortunate that in the brief moments we had shared with Bob he had provided the team with a date he worked at the school. I went straight to the 1961 high school yearbook and flicked through the musty smelling, black and white pages. I then saw a photograph of the maintenance team and sitting in the middle of the photograph was Bob Underwood.

Now that I had uncovered his last name I went to the obituaries. Robert 'Bob' Eugene Underwood was born on March 6, 1921, in Ludington, Michigan. Robert joined the US Army at the start of the Second World War and served for four years in transportation.

He came to Jeffers, Minnesota after the war and married before settling in Delft, gaining employment at the local gas station and at several local funeral homes. He moved to Windom and became a custodian of both the elementary and high schools for a total of thirty-five years. Even after his retirement in 1983 he still helped the school when needed. He died at his home on July 27, 1999.

Bob was a hardworking, dedicated, and good-natured employee whom I believe still frequents the school out of a sense of duty and a love for the job. I am sure he must have wondered what a strange group of people was doing next to his office in the early hours of the morning, especially someone with an English accent. It is possible that during Bob's career he may have burned himself on the pipework, as this may be considered to be an occupational hazard for a custodian working with the boiler in the maintenance room.

Conclusion

At the end of this investigation we were in the process of packing our equipment away when a series of strange electrical events occurred surrounding the team's cars. Heather found two of her car windows had wound themselves down automatically and could not be put up again. Then Ashley found she could not even initially get into her car without a struggle! I then checked my car and discovered that my passenger side window was also inoperable. These faults eventually corrected themselves, some after we had left the location. The influence spirits have over electro-magnetic fields is measurable, so spirits certainly have the tools to hamper the electrical systems in our cars. Perhaps they were trying to deliver a final message, or looking to create more childlike mayhem.

The history found in the three school buildings used in Windom's past represents a linear timeline of American architectural styles, beginning with the earliest whitewashed wooden pioneer structure, to the neo-gothic and classical influences of the late Victorian period, and finally to the post-modern inspired geometric square building that we see today.

A linear timeline is also something we personally undertake in educational buildings like this one. Starting at the beginning of our lives, we spend our formative years in school and our experiences in them literally shape our paths and the way we think and behave. We arrive with a blank slate and leave with a slate covered in experiences and knowledge which we gained both emotionally and cerebrally, from the friends we meet, the bullying we encounter, the loves and crushes we experience, to the qualifications gained that affect our life choices. These are all played out during a time when our bodies are undergoing puberty; we arrive as children and leave as adults. For some it is the best time of their lives, for others the worst.

Under these circumstances, it was no surprise that this building presented a treasure trove of spirits and activity, from the interactions we experienced with the ghostly children, to the witnessing of a moving flashlight. Those who chose to interact with me from the spirit world were once part of the building's fabric, whether they were children, teachers, former famous pupils, or maintenance staff. The Business Arts and Recreation Centre has invested in preserving this building and proudly proclaims that this is now a treasured place to develop and sustain a positive environment for the arts, education, recreation, and business in southwest Minnesota. I believe it was dollars well spent.

THE STATE THEATER

WINDOM, MINNESOTA

*Where the ghost of a young girl asks for money
to keep the theater open.*

Small town theaters were once the hub of the community. This was where your great-grandfather first kissed your great-grandmother in the back row. Your grandparents then played raucously in the aisles during Saturday morning pictures, pretending to be Flash Gordon, Tarzan, or Zorro. Popcorn littered the aisles and every child came back the following Saturday to see the outcome of the previous week's cliffhanger. Subsequently these buildings were imprinted with the memories and energy of humanity, and despite their refurbishments they stay intrinsically unchanged in terms of their layout.

The Windom State Theater was built in 1914 and is one of the oldest theaters in Minnesota still in operation. It is now run by a non-profit organization that is very supportive of my work. With their help I arranged two separate visits to the property, allowing my team to conduct a follow-up investigation. My contact was Nick. He had worked at the theater for many years and was enthusiastic about promoting its history. Nick was in possession of the original architectural blueprints and shared his knowledge of the building's history. He also spoke of several incidents involving paranormal activity.

It was not uncommon for staff to hear noises from the stage area when the building was empty, as well as experience the sensation of being watched and followed. I complemented my history notes by accessing period newspapers and documents from the Cottonwood County Historical Society.

The History

In 1908 Windom residents Phil Redding and Thomas Bonnallie started a theater called the Wonderland. They purchased second-hand equipment, including an exhibition model Edison Projector, and procured around 120 kitchen chairs. They then erected a white canvas screen and went about entertaining the Windom public with early cinematography. Thomas left shortly after the business started, and Phil continued to run the venture on his own, utilizing the Redding building for his productions. This location later became the Windom Oil Company building. Phil then moved to a better site at the Besser building (where the Hakes Creamery used to be) and introduced opera seating and a new Powers camera-graph carbon arc projector. In 1912 Redding partnered with his brother-in-law John Stroud. Stroud was the son of an English Episcopal clergyman and came to Windom in 1886. The two businessmen went about constructing a purpose-built theater on the west side of the town square in 1914 to show films and to attract live vaudeville travelling acts. The new Wonderland Theater enjoyed a pipe organ to accompany the silent movies of the era, a ventilation system, and new projection machinery. The *Windom Recorder* documented the opening night in an article published on September 11, 1914:

> Those in attendance at the opening of the Wonderland Theater were well pleased with the entertainment afforded by the management. We bespeak a big success for Messrs. Stroud and Redding from the fact that these gentlemen are in the money when it comes to this line of business, having had the possession of the theatre ever since it has started in Windom. Programs

were gotten out for the entire week's program. It will
be time well spent to attend this popular playhouse.[12]

Many significant cinematic events were also taking place in
1914. The first film solely created and completed in Los Angeles
appeared. It was titled *In the Sultan's Power* and was directed by
Francis Boggs. Thomas Edison also formed the Motion Picture Pat-
ents Company during this year with the goal of controlling the production and distribution of films.

John Stroud passed away in 1926, and his son Charles replaced
him in the partnership. The theater continued to keep pace throughout
the early twentieth century with technological advances, with sound
being added to the auditorium in February 1929. Henry Hower and
his son Gay already owned two successful theaters in Worthington
when they bought the business from Redding and Stroud in 1937. The
Howers went about introducing a large refurbishing program that included a name change. The remodeled State Theater had a new neon
lighted marquee and an interior that embraced the Art Deco age with
chrome fixtures and hand-painted wall panels that displayed geometric shapes common for the period, such as lightning bolts, zigzags,
and curves. In 1992 this renovation placed the theater onto a historic
preservation resource database. The Barbara Baer Capitman Archives
Art Deco Database in Miami, Florida collates examples of Art Deco
architecture from around the United States.

In 1955 the theater appeared on the front page of the *Cottonwood County Citizen* to announce the winner of an unusual compe-
tition. The old theater seats were being replaced by Jim and George
Le Tourneau who had operated and owned the theater from 1946.
They had decided to count the number of individual pieces of gum
that were stuck to the underside of each chair as it was removed and
asked the citizens of Windom to guess the final number. This was
to highlight the mess that depositing gum can make on fixtures and
fittings. The judges counted a staggering 8,067 wads of gum, and the
winner was declared to be Mr. John Rupp who received the prize of
a year's free theater pass for two.

Jim and George Le Tourneau then sold the business to Mick and Barbara Christians who ran the theater from 1974-1995. The first film they played was *The Exorcist* on October 1, 1974. Four people picketed the theater that night and handed out religious material advocating that patrons should stay away from the film. The former owners joked that in twenty-eight years of business they had never ever been picketed. Over the years other owners came and went until a non-profit organization was started in 2011 to keep this splendid Art Deco building in operation as part of the Windom landscape.

After many hours of dedicated volunteer work, the theater reopened its doors once more in the summer of 2012. Then, in 2013, a symbolic moment came when the original Art Deco neon lit marquee was finally reinstalled back in its rightful place, allowing the evening sidewalk to once more be heartwarmingly illuminated in the resplendent glow that is the glamor and glitz of the movie experience.

The Investigation

I have investigated many theaters throughout the Midwest. In my experience they are normally large buildings that are not suited to paranormal investigations. They were designed specifically so sound can be accessed from all parts of the auditorium. This means that one vigil can easily contaminate another team's evidence in another part of the building. Despite the large floor footprint there are very few rooms to investigate. There is normally an auditorium, a projection booth, and a basement, with perhaps some sort of crawl space that goes under the stage floor and possibly a small underground dressing room.

Auditorium

It was noticeable as soon as I entered the auditorium that the carpet had been torn up. I could clearly see where the carpet had once been glued onto the naked, exposed floor. Nick confirmed they had recently pulled out the old carpet and were in the process of replacing it. This may well have stirred up all kinds of paranormal activity. Carpets are not often thought about in terms of providing paranormal activity, but if furniture and walls can store and soak up residual energy, then surely carpets must share the same qualities. You are not always in contact with an armchair, but you are always in contact with the floor.

The auditorium of the State Theater

I believed paranormal contact would most likely be in the auditorium due to the carpet's removal. So we started the first vigil in the aisle between the seating that led down to the screen. We sat during the silent part of the vigil hoping that the noises Nick had described would be audible. Unfortunately, silence prevailed. It is not uncommon for the first vigil of the night to be lacking in contact. Previous to the first vigil, the team worked diligently setting up the equipment and cameras. This required running cable throughout the property. There was a lot of commotion and noise created as each member moved from room to room in preparation for the investigation. It then took time for the spirits to venture back and to gain confidence. By the second vigil they had calmed down and had a better understanding of who we were and why we were there.

I then turned to the ghost box to try and facilitate a dialogue, since the vigil had yet to provide any evidence of paranormal activity.

"Is there anybody here who wishes to communicate with us?" I enquired with my opening question.

"George," came the response.

"Hi George. Is there anything you would like to ask me?" I continued.

"Who are these people?" was his reply. This was an interesting response because it suggested he may have been talking to a second spirit and not directly to me. I explained that I was interested in documenting the history of the theater.

"Leave," he replied.

This was not meant as a derogatory response, and there was no malice in his tone. I just got the impression that he had no time for me or the team, perhaps because he was busy in the spirit realm and did not like the interruption. No more evidence was forthcoming and I finished the vigil.

In the weeks that followed the investigation I frequented the Cottonwood County Historical Society and spent many hours searching through their archives and documents. I discovered a list of previous managers and owners of the cinema. One gentleman caught my eye. George R. Le Tourneau was born on June 6, 1925, in Mountain Lake and had graduated from Windom High School in 1942. He had spent eight years as the Windom Police Chief and owned a service station and a record store with his brother James. He had also gained employment as the manager of the local liquor store. Remarkably, George also owned and operated the State Theater with his brother beginning in 1946. George died at the young age of forty-one after a six-day illness in Mankato on March 23, 1967. James continued to operate the theater on his own until 1974.

I believed that the George who had briefly engaged with me in the auditorium was George Le Tourneau, who had dedicated twenty-one years of his life to running the theater. I also considered that the second spirit he engaged with was that of his brother James, with whom he jointly owned the theater.

The Stage

We agreed that the old stage behind the giant white screen would be a good location for the second vigil. As soon as we started I felt the electrical residual energy of the area seeping through the floor and into my feet. I then psychically heard the sound of footsteps running around the stage, like the pitter-patter of a child running back and forth. This young spirit apparently liked the sound of her feet stomping on this echoing stage.

I asked psychically for her name and she responded by saying "Lucy." I engaged with her in the opening silence of the vigil by receiving a series of clairvoyant pictures. I ascertained that she was the daughter of a 1920s actress who was part of a travelling vaudeville troop that was passing through town. She was running around playing while her mother was below in the dressing room applying her makeup in preparation for a show. I believe she said her mother's name was Rita. I informed the team of my initial thoughts at the end of the designated silence and suggested that the ghost box might confirm my psychic work.

From the 1880s to the 1920s, vaudeville was the most popular form of entertainment in America. Performances would consist of a dozen or more unrelated acts, performed by singers, dancers, comedians, contortionists, gymnasts, jugglers, and magicians. The first act to play in the new theater was advertised in the *Windom Recorder* on October 2, 1914:

> Opening Play: The Lawrence Deming Theatre Company will be at the new theater three nights next week. This will be the real opening of the new theater and promises to be a rare treat, as this Company is recommended as one of the best now on the road, carrying twelve people, six big vaudeville acts.[13]

An advertisement on the same page described the troop as delivering the show, *The Man on the Case*. This was a comedy play written by the English-born playwright Grave Livingston Furniss in

1907. It was to be shown in four acts with six other big vaudeville features each night with an admission charge of either twenty-five or fifty cents, depending on your seat. I suspect the vaudeville team drummed up business during the day by engaging in street entertainment, as the article instructs us to watch for the *Megaphone Quartette* each day on the street. The Lawrence Deming Theatre Company was also documented in the *Sioux City Journal* the previous week and delighted audiences with performances described as the "snow-storm-girl-driven-from-home-sawmill" act, and a piece entitled "Illustrated Songs Drama".

Below the stage were two dressing rooms for the male and female actors. There was a plethora of graffiti in this area from many of the protagonists who had walked the boards above. I scoured this area looking for Lucy or Rita but did not find either. I did discover graffiti dating from 1916 for *Father Flanagan's Boys Show* and a message scrawled on a door that read, "Women, don't peek through keyholes." Today a large furnace dominates this area. I continued with the vigil on the stage.

"Do you like being here?" I asked.

"Please help me!" a little girl's voice responded.

"Help!" she said again.

"Why do you need help?" I enquired.

"Adrian, you should know," she replied. This was an interesting response that indicated she knew who I was and had an awareness of what I knew based on my experiences with the theater.

"Hello," I said. "What is your name?"

"Hi," she replied, followed by "Lucy." This was a confirmation that I had received the right psychic information.

"Patience," she then said, and continued to lead the conversation.

"So is your name Patience?" I asked quizzically.

"No!" she said, allowing me to believe that the word patience was referring to the act of waiting diligently.

"Broke!" she said again, once more taking control of the discussion and the information I was receiving.

"Do you not have any money?" I questioned.

"Yes," she responded and then said, "Help me" once more.

"Do you want some money?" I enquired. "Is that the reason you said 'help me'?"

"You are right," she said.

"Money for who?" I continued. At that moment several strategically placed flashlights came on and illuminated the vigil. I took this as a sign of encouragement.

"Tell me what you need and I can help you," I said.

"Give me something!" she retorted.

"What?" I asked, but I did not receive a response.

"Is the money for you? I asked.

"Yes," she replied. "Thousands."

"What do you want the money for?" I enquired.

"You are ignorant!" she bluntly replied and left as quickly as she had arrived.

This was a very interesting dialogue and I believed I knew what Lucy was asking for. The non-profit organization that ran the theater was under the threat of having to close its doors. Like many other small-town historic theaters, it was struggling to finance the hefty cost of a digital projector as film distributers moved from celluloid film to digital technology. The raising of funds was proving to be a difficult task with the sums of money involved. I believe Lucy was highlighting her concern for the theater's future, as she would no longer have a stage to play on if the theater was demolished or turned into a grocery store. Perhaps there was also the belief that her mother would be out of a job. This sounds fanciful to suggest, and I was glad Nick and the rest of the team were there to witness the encounter.

I began working diligently to help raise an awareness of the theater's plight. I explained the situation on various radio shows and played the audio recording of the little ghost girl asking for money to keep her theater open. It was astonishing that an audio recording of Lucy asking for money then became a catalyst for money being donated. In some small way she contributed in spirit to the theater staying open. With the proactivity of the board and the support of the local press and townsfolk, the money was raised and a digital projector was purchased and installed.

I arranged a follow-up investigation for the purpose of asking Lucy what she thought of this success and the efforts of the theater board. I was eager to start the first vigil in the same place as before, behind the big screen on the stage. I felt a presence appear standing over my shoulder and there was the same buzz and electricity I had felt before. This time I psychically heard the chatter of a preshow audience. I could clairvoyantly see grayish-blue wooden stage boards in the wings, and there were prominent vases filled with flowers on the stage with an easel facing out towards the auditorium with a board on it that presumably had writing on it. I could then make out individual men dressed in military uniforms coming onto the stage one-by-one as their names were called. They looked like soldiers from the First World War.

It was only after this second investigation that I discovered a newspaper article in the Cottonwood County Historical Society. It described a farewell gathering held at the theater for the county's soldiers about to enter the First World War. It spoke of a lunch and a ceremony at the theater before they went across to the courthouse to be photographed. They departed directly from there via the train depot. Some would never return.

I started the vigil by turning on the ghost box with high hopes of contacting Lucy once more.

"Would you like to say hi?" I asked and broke the silence.

"Hi," was said in a girl's voice.

"Do you remember us?" I enquired.

"Money," she said.

"Are you happy the money arrived?" I continued.

"Yes, yes!" she responded twice to reinforce the answer, followed by "Thank you!"

"You are welcome," I responded.

"So you are happy it stayed open?" I asked.

"Yes!" she replied.

"Will you say goodbye?" I asked.

"Goodbye," she replied.

I had received the information I was looking for in spirit and finished the vigil. Throughout my years of paranormal investigating I had never experienced a more remarkable and touching encounter.

Conclusion

It is often the case that the preoccupations of the living are not the preoccupations of the dead. This investigation showed that the dead and living can interact for the common good. It also shows that the spirits have a unique and in-depth knowledge of current affairs. They apparently have the same fears and worries as the living and the same uncertainties about their own futures.

Without a last name it was impossible historically to find out who Lucy was, and due to the nature of her mother's work she could have come from any area of the Midwest. I believe Lucy chose to stay at the Windom State Theater because it represented one of the buildings she visited in her youth. I have often experienced spirits visiting locations that they once frequented in the physical realm due to their love of the location or through curiosity.

The theater is a quiet environment for most of the week as films are only shown on the weekend. During the week spirits can play and roam freely without fear of being seen or castigated. The life of a vaudeville performer sounds like a fun and carefree existence. Running away and being an actor, especially during a period of history considered to be one of the most exciting and enlivening, was an idealistic dream. This time was not called the "Roaring 20s" for nothing. There was the glamor of the films, the makeup, the adoration, and the thrill of a new town every week with the added adventure of rail travel at its peak. Even as I write this I am envious of Lucy's spirit and the childlike naïveté she showed, running around the stage, pretending to be anybody she wanted to be. It appears that death is not something to fear but a fun and exciting journey of nostalgia that we should all be ready to embrace.

Windom Public Library

Windom, Minnesota

It's hard not to feel the presence of sleeping spirits as you walk along the shelves and drag your fingers across the spines of the books.

The arrangements for the library investigation started when I walked into the building and asked the surprised librarian if I could paranormally explore the property. This process was then facilitated further when she actually recognized me from the back of one of my books that was in the library's collection. I was subsequently asked to submit a proposal to the local town council and they generously agreed for my team to access this fabulous building for two separate investigations.

The head librarian was very accommodating and provided me with local historical knowledge. I accessed period historical documents, newspaper articles, and obituaries at the Cottonwood County Historical Society. This was supplemented with online historical research.

History

The library building in Windom is perched on the corner of the main square on 4th Avenue and 9th Street. It is a neo-classical renaissance revival building displaying a typically sturdy, square construction in resplendent gunmetal grey blocks of sandstone. Fluted columns support the pediment where chiseled gold indented words present, "First National Bank." The style of the whole building mirrors the architectural ideals of the Roman classical period a millennium before and delivers to the passerby a lesson in symmetry and harmony. It displays all the visual information that one associates with strength and fortitude, an impression any bank would wish to instill in its customers.

The building was constructed by the J. B. Nelsen Company of North Mankato, Minnesota. J. B. Nelson was an architect who left his influence on many buildings throughout the Midwest, including the South Dakota Agricultural College in Brooking, the courthouses in Windom and Fairmont, the original Carnegie Public Library building in Mankato, and the Gustavus Adolphus College in St. Peter.

The Windom Public Library built in 1912

The Bank of Windom began doing business on this corner in 1881. It then consolidated with the People's State Bank and became the First National Bank. In 1911 a fire in the building next door destroyed the bank, leaving only the vault untouched. The rebuilding process started at the beginning of 1912, and the town witnessed the use of horses to raise the columns into their current position. Out of the ashes of the old wooden construction a resplendent building appeared. In 1977 the bank relocated to 10th Street where a purpose-built facility allowed improved security and for the modernity of banking technology. Hallmark First Floral then occupied the relinquished bank building until 1985, when it then became home to its current occupier, the Windom Public Library.

Before 1985 the library did not have a permanent location and regularly moved around town. Early records show that a library was organized in Windom as early as 1883. The *Cottonwood County Courier* documented the swell in public support for its inception:

> Several of our citizens have suggested calling a meeting to consider the practicability of a public library in Windom. Surely, in these days when standard literature can be purchased at such low prices, it would seem that Windom might support a quite extensive library. Let someone secure a place and suggest a time for a meeting, at which committees may be appointed, officers elected, etc., and, if proper interest is taken, we are satisfied as to the result. It is certainly a needed acquisition to our village.[14]

The library was then documented as residing in the Johnson brothers' office in 1893, before an area was found to house a cache of books in the basement of the courthouse in 1900. The Windom Library Association took over the "library room" from 1928 and went about moving the books to Windom High School in 1932. It then moved once more when it occupied what is now the city hall in 1963.

Investigation

As I entered the building I was reminded of the opening scenes of the 1984 film *Ghostbusters*, where the protagonists were confronted with paranormal activity in a library. I made doubly sure to look for ectoplasm and any old, dead ladies. We began our investigation by undertaking a walkthrough and a series of baseline tests. Lorna, Heather, and Kim started in the children's library and within seconds a book flew off the top shelf from one of the central bookcases and landed directly in front of them. This building had never been investigated before, and I wondered if a spirit now wanted our attention in order to gain a communication. My team had rarely experienced such a prominent use of physical energy demonstrated from the spirit world. The book in question was a children's hardback outlining the difference between geckos and salamanders. I believe the action was significant rather than the content.

The Children's Library

Due to the strength of the poltergeist activity we decided to set up the first vigil in the children's library. I placed motion detectors and trigger objects on the shelves and recorded them using a series of infrared cameras. The opening fifteen minutes went by without incident until a fishing bobber trigger object fell in the same way the book had done. The bobber also triggered several motion detectors on its descent, illuminating the room in a confusion of colored blinking lights. To add to this cacophony, a flashlight then came on by itself. I thought now would be the best time to ask who was wanting our attention and I reached for the ghost box.

"Who turned on the flashlight?" I asked.

"Doug," came the response.

"You turned the flashlight on?" I continued.

"Yes," he replied.

"Doug Davidson!" he then added, presenting what I believed to be his full name.

The children's section of the Windom Public Library

From that moment all went quiet. I tried every piece of equipment at our disposal to gain further contact but without success. I had only shared the briefest of moments with the spirit, but he had given me a name to research and I was eager to find out more about Doug and why he was in the library. Then in the darkness Greg saw a cold humanoid shape working its way between the shelves on his FLIR thermal imaging camera. It appeared that the spirit was now moving around the location after our brief interaction. This verified that paranormal activity was present around the bookshelves.

The Vault

The steps leading down to the basement were as I expected—cold, concrete, and unwelcoming. At the bottom to my right was the large, four-inch-thick, reinforced, peeling green door of the bank vault. Its cogged mechanism of linkages and locks reminded me of this building's past. This relatively small walk-in vault was now used as a storage space for the library's paperwork and miscellaneous items. The combination of the bank vault and books reminded me of the famous 1959 *Twilight Zone* episode "Time Enough at Last" starring Burgess Meredith, where the protagonist is the sole survivor of a nuclear bomb, saved because he took his lunch in the vault of the bank where he worked. A lover of books, he sees the town library and realizes he has all the time he wants to read, but fate steps in and changes his plans.

Directly opposite the vault door was an opening into an area of the basement under the children's library. This was a dusty environment as the floor was not concrete but a mixture of dirt, sand, and masonry dust, an asthmatic's nightmare and the source of many false, unwanted orb photographs. I did my best to move around this space without kicking up the contamination. This was not a crawl space, but I could not stand fully upright and went about the baseline tests with a stooped posture.

Architecturally, the basement showed the scars of renovation and rebuilding over a prolonged period of time. Brick and stonework of all historical ages seemed to make up the walls in random stretches. Windows and doors had been bricked-in suggesting that the sidewalk once stopped short of reaching the building, providing light and steps that may have led down into the basement.

The Main Basement

Low overhead pipework further hindered the locomotion of walking upright as the main basement opened up to reveal a number of wooden pallets and cardboard boxes. They littered the floor randomly in this otherwise sparse environment. In the center of the room there was a book graveyard where a large number of discontinued texts were strewn and left alone with their own thoughts. These were put to good use as seating during the vigil. It was a large area that showed the scars of remodeling and change. The aging furnace produced random mechanical noises to which the pipes responded by gurgling to keep us company during the silence of our vigil. As always in such places I found the obligatory dead bird and an abundance of cobwebs.

We sat in the circle of our vigil and started to see some very odd shapes forming in the darkness as an entity began to move around.

It seemed to weave between each of the investigators and gave the impression that we were the ones being investigated. Ashley thought that the spirit was now standing next to her and Heather. Both women felt watched, and a coldness emanated from the space between them. Greg directed his thermal imaging camera into the area in question and witnessed the cold image of a standing humanoid depicted in varying shades of blue.

I then felt something brush against my legs and had the psychic impression of a dog joining us to run around in spirit. Other team members also felt this sensation. It is not uncommon to come across dogs and cats in spirit, but in a library basement was a little odd. I spoke into the dark, echoing space and asked if the spirit who brought the dog with it was a bank employee. The flashlight came on in what I believed was a response to my question. The ghost box had worked very well in the children's library so I used the device again.

"Jeff," it shouted out as I turned the device on.

"Hi, Jeff," I responded.

"Do you prefer Jeffrey or Jeff?" I continued.

"Jeff," he replied.

"How many are watching us?" I enquired.

"Four!" he said.

"So there are four of you watching us?"

"Yes, four."

Psychically, I believed that Jeff was sleeping in this area of the basement when he was alive, and I asked him to confirm this.

"Were you once sleeping in the bank?"

"Yes," he confirmed.

"Do you like us being here?" I continued.

"Nope!"

"Was that your job?" I asked, looking to gain as many historical details as possible.

"Yes," he replied. I was puzzled as to why a bank would employ anyone to sleep.

We then heard a very distinct whistling sound coming through on the ghost box.

"Why are you whistling?" I asked.

"For the dog," he said.

He was trying to gain the spirit dog's attention in order to have it return.

"Would you like us to leave?" I pressed.

"Yeah!"

"So we should not be down here?" I enquired.

"Just do it," came his reply.

Out of respect for his wishes we ended the vigil.

The Cell

In the back right-hand corner of the main basement was an area that had been segregated into a small cell-like room. This annex could not have been used for the captivity of an individual as it was poorly constructed of sheetrock. An old, rusting, single bedframe was positioned in the center of this area and dominated the space. I believed this bed to be as old as the building. It looked like the bottom part of a bunk where the top half had been removed, leaving the four corner bed supports to protrude upwards beyond what was functionally necessary. The mattress support was a decaying skeleton of woven metal and springs that indicated a squeaky night's sleep for any restless sleepers.

When I first entered this little room I had the most nauseating psychic sensation run through my body. I felt sick to the pit of my stomach. This was the only part of the entire building where I felt such a strong psychic revulsion. The room was only large enough to occupy the bed and three other investigators, including myself. I placed many trigger objects on and around the bed in the hope that the energy I had experienced would move them, as we had experienced in the children's library upstairs.

What became instantly recognizable was the presence of the same spirit dog we had encountered in the main basement. It is not uncommon for a dog to come through in spirit if I am asked to contact its deceased owner. A pet would often arrive first in spirit to signal the owner's imminent presence. This reflects typical canine behavior as when a dog bounds up to the gate or door to greet you shortly before the owner appears.

I then started to be given glimpses of information psychically, and I could see how the layout of this area looked during its time as a bank. I believed, based on what I was observing, that this room was constructed for a bank employee. The employee would have been hired to stay in the basement overnight to ensure that the town's finances were safe from the threat of any potential robbers. The bed was in place to allow them to reside in limited comfort. This would have been the same role John Wayne played in the 1934 film *Blue Steel,* when he also slept at the bank in a bid to prevent the Polka Dot Bandit from busting the safe. I believe the spirit dog belonged to Jeff, who was given the task of protecting the safe. I continued the vigil, but despite using every tool, device, and the experience of wisdom, no further contact was made. Only the quiet and darkness that seems to precede a sunrise remained.

Douglas Davidson

After the investigation I was eager to research the name of Doug Davidson at the Cottonwood County Historical Society. I meticulously explored the town's obituaries, but it appeared that no one named Doug Davidson had ever died in the local area. I did not let this deter my efforts though, and I refocused my attention on the files based on the library's history. As I looked through the file of documents I discovered the name Douglas Davidson. He was the president of the First National Bank and was responsible for its relocation.

Douglas was a native of Long Island, New York, and had graduated from Montana State University in Bozeman. He was thirty-nine when he stepped into the presidency of the Windom First National Bank in July 1977. Before coming to Windom he worked for the First National Bank of Bozeman, Montana, from 1961-72. He then became the vice president of the First National Bank in Havre, Montana. It was Doug who had supervised the completion of the new bank building on 10th Street and oversaw the preparations to relocate it from the present library building.

It would make perfect sense if Doug's spirit wanted to see how the old bank building now looked, especially as he was responsible for moving it from this location. In spirit would you not want to see who was doing your job and how your work environment now looked? I then interviewed several long-serving members of the current bank staff in the hope of finding out more about Doug's life. Unfortunately, they could not provide me with any more details, but they did remember him working there. They told me Doug had left the area in the early 1980s. I then published an article in the *Cottonwood County Citizen* newspaper asking if the residents of Windom had any information on Douglas. I had no responses.

Despite my extensive research, I cannot at this time verify if Doug is currently dead or alive. At the time of our investigation he would have been seventy-seven years old. If he is still alive the possibility remains that a former work colleague may have been calling out his name in spirit in the hope of making contact with their former friend and colleague. If he is dead then I know where he is residing in the afterlife, dutifully overseeing the smooth running of what was his bank.

Conclusion

To witness such a force of paranormal activity in the children's library was very impressive. It is not every investigation where you witness a book flying through the air. The brief interaction with the spirits I encountered was also remarkable and provided me with researchable historical information. I suspect that after this book is published more details pertaining to Douglas Davidson will surface. I will then be able to include that research in a second edition.

If a spirit craved a quiet existence, then haunting a library would certainly satisfy that need. Libraries do not entertain the busy bustle of department stores or the noisy traffic associated with restaurants and schools. There is a reverential energy surrounding books and learning, the weight of knowledge and history. I think that while in a library you can feel in some mysterious way that you are absorbing through your skin the wisdom contained in those books without even opening them. They are untouched by the modernity of our homes and society. There are no televisions here, no music, no computer games, no instruments, no phones, and no washing machines to disturb the dead. I hope and pray that there are libraries in heaven.

THE BRADSHAW HOUSE HOTEL

BALDWIN, WISCONSIN

*Where five separate ghosts haunt the oldest
building in town.*

For many years I have hosted events and investigations at the beautiful St. James Hotel in Red Wing, Minnesota. It was during one of these occasions that Scott H., the booking manager, told me about the historic Bradshaw Hotel in Baldwin, Wisconsin. He suggested that it would make a great location for a paranormal investigation, and I agreed.

Located opposite Bailey Park, the Bradshaw House has been known by many other names since its construction in 1871 including: the Foster House, the Baldwin House, the Park Hotel, the Martin Hotel, the Streeter Hotel, and Main Street Residence. It even served as a community nursing home during the middle and latter part of the twentieth century. Scott H. purchased the six-thousand-square-foot building in 1999 and divided the property into small apartments. The Bradshaw House now stands vacant and presents a myriad of silent corridors and deserted rooms for any resident ghosts to call home.

I accessed information about the Bradshaw family through historical documents and researched the property through the St. Croix County Historical Society. Scott H. was also very knowledgeable about the building's past.

History

Baldwin is located thirty miles east of Minneapolis and forty miles west of Eau Claire in St. Croix County. It was founded in 1871 by Dana Reed Bailey and was first known as Clarksville. It was later renamed Baldwin after the manager of the Western Wisconsin Railroad, Mr. D. A. Baldwin, who was responsible for the railroad coming through town.

The Bradshaw House Hotel

Stacy D. Bradshaw was born on October 24, 1819 and came from Vermont via Hammond, Wisconsin. He opened the doors of the newly built Bradshaw House on December 12, 1871. The hotel was originally painted red, as this was the only color available in town during this era. The interior was whitewashed. The building soon became a refuge for all those arriving via the railroad seeking temporary lodgings. This is documented in the book *Pioneers Peek Out from the Past* by Sandy Burleigh:

> S. D. Bradshaw opened his 2 ½ story, 42 room hotel around Thanksgiving, 1872. His grand opening coincided with Baldwin's first anniversary. He and his family took in travelers at their old Main Street boarding house up until the day their new Front Street Hotel opened. People traveling by train from Menomonie to Hudson frequently chose to stop off at Baldwin's Bradshaw House for a night of dining and rest.[15]

The Bradshaw family then left the hotel in 1874 and opened a smaller boarding house and restaurant in town. The book *Pioneers Peek Out from the Past* suggests that the family may have grown tired of violent undesirables residing in the hotel:

> They found out, firsthand, what "big business" could do to a family. I believe the "last straw" had been when three rowdy St. Paul men, guests at the hotel, fired a few pistol shots. They had been playing cards and decided that one of the hotel's regular boarders next door was making a bit too much noise to suit their fancy. So they threw him down the stairs. The gun shot followed, the constable was summoned, and soon, the three men were on the next train back to St. Paul. Enough was enough! No, the St. Paul men did not get their money back![16]

Mr. S. D. Bradshaw fully embraced community life and was given the title of street commissioner. This position allowed him to help build the town's bridges and road infrastructure. He was also made a chimney inspector in 1875. The Bradshaw family eventually moved to Hersey, Wisconsin where Mr. Bradshaw died on April 26, 1884. He is buried in Hammond Cemetery.

Investigation

On one of those balmy August nights, under the illumination of a full moon and with heat lightning creeping ever closer from the west, we ventured into the oldest building in Baldwin. From the outside, its modern sidings and windows belied the fact that it was constructed in 1871. Only once inside did I receive a visual understanding of its true age via the original, polished wooden floors and stairways. It was a large property with many long corridors that swept throughout the building on each floor, providing access to numerous empty rooms and apartments. This location had been unoccupied for many years and the slow strain of dilapidation was showing in the broken windows, peeling paint, and abandoned possessions that randomly littered the rooms.

Scott H. believed the property was haunted due to the spooky tales he had heard from former residents. He spoke of one tenant in room twelve who woke to see an elderly lady sitting in her chair. The ghost said her name was Florence and promptly disappeared. The property had been used as a retirement home and many of its residents would have died in the building. Scott H. said he had discovered many old documents in the basement that were from the nursing home era. To his surprise he found paperwork that showed a lady named Florence once resided in the home.

Scott H. had also made the grisly discovery of a man who had died in his room overnight. He found the body in bed with his face straining towards the open window, perhaps in a desperate bid to access fresh air. The cold winter's night had frozen the corpse solid and the poor man's face had a covering of frost forming over it. Scott H. contacted the coroner.

There were also many recorded deaths in the early years of the hotel. It was not uncommon for hoteliers across the Midwest to fall ill and die as a result of the diseases and illnesses that travelers brought with them by train. The subsequent owners of the Bradshaw House Hotel were not as lucky as the Bradshaw family, as documented in the book *Pioneers Peek Out from the Past:*

> The Bradshaws were fortunate in having avoided sickness, as many hotel keepers became victims of disease carried in by boarders. Pat Dillion's family managed the Bradshaw House around 1879, and Mrs. Dillion and two of their children died of disease brought in by hotel guests.[17]

Room 12

I started the investigation in room 12 as this was the area in which a former resident had been visited by the spirit of Florence. The vigil began in a stifling hot atmosphere, but within minutes a spirit joined us. I psychically saw a fourteen-year-old girl with frizzy dark hair suddenly appear. She had a pallid complexion with freckles, blue eyes, and a bony, thin childlike figure. She wore a simple, floral print dress decorated with a pattern of small, brown, autumnal flowers on a black background. It was cut high to just below the neck and was finished with a simple, white lace trim. She stood directly in front of me with a blank expression that made it difficult to judge her emotion. I asked for her name and I thought she said "Adel," but her response was not as clear as I would have hoped. At that moment there was a loud bang heard from the floor below. The whole team acknowledged the sound and we wondered what had been knocked over or slammed. I continued with my psychic dialogue.

"What are you doing here?" I asked.

"Looking after the hotel," she replied.

She appeared inquisitive, so I told her why we were there and introduced the team. I thought she had the aura of being the hotel's guardian. I wondered if her father had owned the business. Perhaps she was tasked with making sure everybody was comfortable and that nothing untoward was happening in the rooms.

Greg was seated a way down the corridor with Scott H., looking towards room 12 through the screen of a thermal imaging camera. He told me that they could see a cold humanoid shape standing directly opposite me as I had believed. Greg then told me to put my arm directly out in front of me. I did so and instantly felt a bitter coldness like one might experience from placing your hand in a fridge. Greg then exclaimed that my hand had turned blue and disappeared inside the entity. Humans are seen in hot shades of orange, yellows, and red on such devices. I had literally put my hand through the body of a ghost.

The doorway into room twelve where I placed my hand
through a ghost

I wanted to corroborate the psychic information I had just received from the girl, so I turned on the ghost box in the hope of having an audible dialogue. Instantly a girl's voice said "Scott," followed by the word "Somerset." Somerset is a town just twenty-five miles from Baldwin. Perhaps this was a location that was important or familiar to the girl. The ghost box then shouted out "dead" as if to clarify her own understanding of why she was there. A male voice then jumped into the conversation and said "Scott." Scott H. was proving to be a good catalyst for the paranormal activity in this building, as the spirits clearly recognized him and had an understanding of who he was. I started to engage with this new male spirit.

"Is your name Scott?" I asked to clarify if he was referring to himself or the owner.

"No," was the emphatic response.

"Did you work here?" I continued.

"Yes," he said.

"In the nineteenth century?" I pressed.

"No."

"In the twentieth century?" I continued.

"No," he said once more.

"In the twenty-first century?" I ventured, not believing that I would receive a positive response.

"Yes!" came the surprising reply.

"So were you some sort of housekeeper or maintenance man?" I asked.

"Yes," he said once more. At that moment Scott H. told me that there was a maintenance man he employed from 2001 who had died in 2005. Scott H. asked me to find his name.

"So what is your name?" I enquired.

"Jeff," came his reply.

"So your name is Jeff?" I asked for confirmation.

"Jeff, Jeff, Jeff!" He repeated three times in a row.

I looked to Scott H. and asked if the maintenance man he employed was named Jeff. With a look of disbelief and total astonishment he said, "Yes, the maintenance man was named Jeff and he died in 2005." I believed Jeff to be one of the youngest in spirit I had experienced in a historical property. I found it ironic that in one of the oldest buildings in the Midwest I had made contact with a spirit from 2005. Did Jeff not realize I was writing a history book?

"Do you hang out here a lot?" I asked.

"No," he replied.

"So why are you here now then?" I questioned.

"I like it… it's important," he said.

"So do you keep an eye on the property in spirit?" I continued.

"Yes!" he replied.

This short engagement had proved that he knew he was in spirit and what had happened to him.

"Can you show yourself to me then?" I asked.

"I can't," he replied.

I did not press this line of questioning further. He obviously did not have the capability to manifest himself for whatever reason so I continued with my questions.

"Are there any other spirits here?"

"Yes, I hear voices," he said.

"So you cannot see them?" I replied.

"No," came his response.

"How many spirits do you hear?" I continued.

"Five," he said.

"Can you give the name of one of those spirits?"

"Sure, Stacy," he said.

"Is that the first name of Mr. Bradshaw?" I asked.

"Yeah."

"Is Mr. Bradshaw with us now?"

"No," he said.

I asked the same question again for clarification and once more he said, "No." I then asked Scott if Jeff had any recognizable features. Scott said that he used to have a moustache.

"Have you got a moustache? Yes or no."

"Of course, yeah," was Jeff's response.

Scott H. then informed me that Jeff once fell through the stair bannisters and they had to be repaired.

"Do you remember falling through the stair rails and then fixing them?"

"Sure," he said.

"Do you want to give Scott a message?" I asked.

"Nothing, I am fine," he replied.

"Would you like to say goodbye?" I continued.

"Goodbye!" he said.

"Where is the best place to have contact with you in this building?" I then enquired. I then heard him say, "Where is the best place to make contact?" as if he was asking another spirit for his opinion on the matter. I did not receive a reply to this question.

"Will you come and talk to us later?" I asked finally.

"Yep," he said.

Scott H. thought that it sounded like Jeff and that his responses sounded like ones he would have given when he was alive. I ended the vigil.

Basement

Heather took a team into the basement as I investigated room 12. When Heather turned on the ghost box at the start of the vigil she was greeted with the words "Get out!" shouted in a male voice without any question or stimulus from her team. Heather then reported to me in the plenary between vigils that they had also heard the bang our team had heard at the beginning of our own vigil and made a note of a time that corroborated with my own notes.

Heather had the psychic sensation that a woman was hiding in the basement. She was picking up the feelings of panic and distress that she believed came from a residual haunting. When Heather's team came back from the basement and told us of their experiences, Scott H. informed us that one of his tenants in the past had hidden in the basement in a bid to escape domestic violence.

The interesting aspect concerning this residual haunting was that the couple involved were still alive. It has always been assumed that those individuals presented in a residual haunting would have to be dead. Yet if an emotional or tragic incident imprints itself in the fabric of our dimension only to be replayed at specific times to the observer, it would make sense that from the exact moment that event has physically finished it is then available to see, even if those involved are still living. How would an inanimate concept, like the replaying of a traumatic event, know if the individuals involved were dead or not? In theory it could start replaying that incident, like a video tape, the following hour, day, week, or year.

The Attic

Modern technology now allows me to access detailed historical records online via my cell phone during breaks between vigils. After the first vigil I decided to research the 1874 census records for Baldwin in the hope of discovering more about the Bradshaw family. I noticed straight away that their children were listed as Ada, Wealthy, and Robert. Could it be that the spirit I thought was saying "Adel" was in fact Ada. I hoped that armed with this new information I might be able to communicate further with the young girl to confirm the briefest of research.

We ascended the antiquated stairs to the attic. This area would have been unbearably hot earlier in the investigation, but now during the early hours of the morning it was tolerable. It was a large, simple area with no furniture or clutter. The edges of the attic were low and offered the possibility of banging your head. Wooden planking adorned the ceiling that rose high into the apex of the room, reflecting the inside shape of the roof line. I asked Heather to lead the team so I could concentrate on my psychic skills without the interruption of managing a vigil or organizing equipment.

The girl I believed to be named Adel arrived psychically as we started. Heather asked her how old she was, and I was once more given the answer of fourteen. I asked Caroline if she had received a psychic response and she agreed with my acknowledgement of fourteen. Heather asked what year it was and I was presented with 1887.

"Did you go to school in town?" Heather continued.

Adel's reply was "Yes."

"Can you see us?" Heather then asked.

And the spirit girl once again said, "Yes."

In the darkness Kim then asked if anyone could hear squeaking. I turned on my flashlight and the biggest bat I have ever seen swooped in at head height through the beam and presented what looked like the Batman logo. It circled the room flapping and randomly zig-zagging in all directions, making it hard to judge which way to run for a speedy exit. Everyone hit the floor and I glanced around to witness Heather flailing around with her arms and legs kicking and her sweatshirt pulled over her head out of fear of being attacked. Eight seasoned investigators fled screaming from the attic with their arms bulging full of random equipment. The potentially rabid bat thought it would be good sport to follow us down the stairs as we ran before it flew off into a side room.

We made it back to the kitchen area on the ground floor where we decided to continue the vigil. I had started to engage in an interesting psychic dialogue with Adel, so I thought we should jump straight into a ghost box session to see if any further communication was possible.

"Adrian," was the first word out of the ghost box.

"Is anyone down here with us?" Heather asked.

"Yes," was heard in a male voice.

"What is your name?" Heather continued.

"Edward," he replied.

"So your name is Edward?" I asked.

"Yes, sir," was his response.

"Do you go by Ed?" I continued.

"Yes, sir."

"Did you live here?" I asked.

"No," he said.

"How many are with you?" Heather asked.

"Five," he replied. This was the same number that Jeff had given me in room 12 earlier in the evening.

"Can you name them?" I ventured to ask.

"Girl," he said.

"Who is the girl?" I continued.

"She is dead," was his reply.

"I would like to talk to the girl," I asked. "What is your name? Is it Adel?"

"Yes!" came her retort, now in a girl's voice.

"Is your full name Adeline? Yes or no."

"Yes."

"What did you do for a job?" I continued.

"Teacher," she said.

"What year did you die?" I would not normally ask questions of spirits surrounding their deaths for fear of upsetting their sensibilities. But it was clear from my conversations with Adel throughout the building and through her choice of wanting to appear as a fourteen-year-old girl, that she was fully aware of her spirit status.

"Did you have children?" Heather asked.

"Yes," she replied.

"How many children?" Heather continued.

"Three," she said.

"Can you confirm that?"

"Three," was her same response.

We received no further evidence during this vigil, so we collected the equipment and finished.

After the investigation, I had the opportunity to research further the ghost of Adel. I discovered in the book *Pioneers Peek Out from the Past* that Stacy Bradshaw's daughter appeared to be known as Addie with the census record listing her as Ada. I was confident that I had heard her say Adel and it was not uncommon for names to be listed incorrectly in old census records. A small glimpse of her life and personality can be seen in the following extract taken from *Pioneers Peek Out from the Past:*

> Bradshaw's daughter, Addie, was a real go-getter in the village. A teacher, and secretary of various organizations. She and Wealthy ran a millinery shop.[18]

This new evidence now informed me that she was a teacher, exactly as she had described herself. Upon further investigation I discovered that she was a teacher at the Millers' School in Baldwin from 1869 to May 1872. I now believe beyond all doubt that the young spirit residing in the hotel that night was Addie, the daughter of Mr. Bradshaw. Several weeks later I was searching for the burial spot of Stacy Bradshaw that I had discovered to be in Hammond Cemetery, St. Croix County; next to the marker for the plot he shares with his wife was the grave of Adel. His daughter's full name was Adelaide T. Bradshaw, and she died in 1900. I was right to persist with what I thought she had told me, that her name was Adel.

Conclusion

This building represents a microcosm of society, as every aspect of humanity has been experienced within its walls. The energy that comes from the process of living is imbedded in its very fiber and every floorboard. People were conceived here, born here, lived here, worked here, slept here, and died here. This sentiment was reflected in the residual fear Heather's team felt in the basement.

Paranormal evidence received from two separate sources suggested that five spirits were residing in the building. They were Stacy and Adelaide Bradshaw, Jeff, Edward, and one other who remained unknown—perhaps the spirit of Florence who failed to make her presence known during the course of the investigation. I was further informed by Jeff that he could hear the other spirits but could not see them. This represents five different dimensions all bleeding together in one location, as they all came from different historical eras. In our own dimension we rarely see ghosts, but I have regularly heard them.

Adelaide appeared as a fourteen-year-old girl but answered questions about her adulthood in terms of her career and children. This suggests that spirits can present themselves in any form they wish, but can still retain their memories and experiences from later in their life. I also had the unique opportunity of putting my arm through Adelaide. I didn't know whether this action represented poor etiquette or not, as there are no conventions for such an experience, but Adelaide did not complain and I did engage with her in two separate locations after this event.

The Bradshaw Hotel showed the perfect synthesis of paranormal investigating, evidence, and historical research. I believe that future vigils will provide me with further details regarding Edward and the unknown fifth spirit. During that investigation I will be sure to include a tennis racket in my equipment case for the possibility of investigating in the attic once more.

THE WIETING OPERA HOUSE

TOLEDO, IOWA

Has the ghost of the Wieting Opera House now died?

The Wieting Opera House is one of the oldest and grandest theaters still operational in the Midwest, and its glorious interior provides patrons with a rare glimpse into Edwardian entertainment. Having been placed on the National Register of Historic Places in 1979, the theater can now boast an impressive roster of over one hundred volunteers dedicated to the smooth running of the building.

The Wieting Opera House

Many can tell stories of their own paranormal experiences over the years. Several spoke of hearing prominent footsteps striding across an empty stage. Another discussed the sensation of feeling a cold presence walking beside them. One lady even told the tale of seeing a random lightbulb fall from the height of the catwalk onto the stage below. We were also told of spirits hiding and moving objects in the projection booth. Spools of film would regularly disappear in the 1980s after the projectionist had changed the reel. I was eager to find the truth behind these prolific activities. So, on a balmy, rain-soaked August night I pushed the heavy, brass-trimmed opera doors open and ventured inside.

Sarah is the founder of the Iowa-based team S.E.E. (Seek, Experience, and Educate) Paranormal, and I extend my thanks to her and the team for organizing this investigation. Sarah is also a resident of Tama County and was able to conduct extensive historical research on my behalf. I supplemented her notes with online documents and information taken from the theater's own website and literature. I also interviewed several members of the board.

History

Dr. Philip and Hellen 'Ella' Wieting moved to Toledo, Iowa in the spring of 1867 from Worcester, New York. Philip initially practiced dentistry in Toledo and ran several other business interests, including founding the Toledo City Bank in 1878. At the turn of the nineteenth century the Wieting family moved back to New York State and settled in Syracuse where Philip found further financial success with a manufacturing business. Philip died on February 12, 1906, and in his memory Ella gifted theaters to the towns of Worcester, Syracuse, and Toledo.

The Toledo building contract was awarded to Mr. C. W. Ennis, and construction began during the spring of 1912 at a cost of $20,000. Ella stipulated that the workmen should be employed from the local community. The finished theater boasted an ample stage, orchestra pit, main floor, a balcony, two boxes, dressing rooms, and a ticket office. The theater curtains were parted for the first time at eight o' clock on the evening of September 12, 1912. A full house saw the Sheehan English Opera Company's presentation of Verdi's *Il Trovatore*, starring the tenor Joseph F. Sheehan and a hundred-strong supporting cast.

Located conveniently on the Chicago to Cedar Rapids mainline railway and the Marshalltown to Omaha route, the theater was able to attract some of the biggest names in the Midwest show-business industry as well as travelling vaudeville acts, minstrel performances, lyceum courses, class plays, graduations, political conventions, and medicine shows. The large seating capacity of 650 provided a strong financial return.

Historical documents also indicate that Art Ludwig was paid for operating the cinematography equipment as early as 1913. Art's wife was also employed to play the piano as an accompaniment to the silent films of the era. Popular releases of the day included *The New York Hat* with Mary Pickford and Lionel Barrymore and *Dr. Jekyll and Mr. Hyde* with King Baggot. This was a period of early cinematic history that pre-dated the first films of Buster Keaton and Charlie Chaplin.

Ella then proceeded to gift a further $1,000, in 1923 to help pay for a new basement and foundation work. When Ella died on May 23, 1933 in Worcester, New York, she bequeathed another $10,000. Unfortunately, only $7,900 was ever received since, while many bequests were made, few could be adequately covered by her estate. In 1932 Mr. and Mrs. F. J. Sichra leased the theater, which remained under their management for the next twenty-six years. Mr. Sichra died in 1948, but his wife Lucille continued to manage the theater on her own.

By the late fifties, audiences were starting to dwindle and the golden age of cinema was over. The new disposable income of the youth was spent on records, clothes, and magazines. The cinema felt like the entertainment choice of their parents. Unfortunately, their parents now wished to stay at home and watch the rapidly expanding success of the television, where they could see performers showing off the very skills they had honed in vaudeville. With a heavy heart, Lucille closed the building and business in November 1958.

It was during the spring of 1960 that six like-minded residents gathered to discuss the plight of the Wieting Opera House. They felt the loss of the movie theater and missed the role it once played within the community. They also felt the pressing realization that its trust fund would soon be lost unless it could be reopened. Forty citizens attended an impromptu meeting. They created the Toledo Community Theatre Guild and penned a constitution that attracted others to the organization. On May 18, 1960 the lobby doors were once again unlocked and a musty, dilapidated, cobweb-strewn auditorium presented itself. The equipment was purchased from Lucille, and many local men, women, and children volunteered their time to help clean and refurbish the building.

The dream was fulfilled when the theater opened for a second time on September 16, 1960 to a full house, rekindling fond memories for many patrons who remembered the first opening forty-eight years earlier. The initial sale of over a hundred family season tickets enforced the belief that the community of Toledo wanted this fabulous building back on their community landscape.

The theater was renovated once again in 2012 at a cost of $1.4 million and now has a seating capacity for three hundred guests. Owning and operating this historic building is expensive and funding remains a concern for the board. It is my hope that the ghosts and spirits of this magnificent building from beyond the grave will help raise its profile.

Investigation

It now appears to be the convention that wherever I arrange a paranormal investigation, adverse weather will follow. Thus a warm pleasant evening in August turned into a night of monsoon filled skies. We had the kind of lightning that suggests God has stepped on a Lego brick. Flood warnings were in place throughout the night and deep into the morning.

I believe that wet, damp, humid conditions are better suited to finding paranormal activity. The charged, electro-magnetic, lightning-filled skies would benefit rather than hinder our investigation. I am aware that the best seasons for paranormal activity are the spring and fall. Investigations in parched, arid, hot summers, and cold, dry, snow-chilled winters are often disappointing.

The building first treated the theatergoer to the sight of a large, white pediment supported by four Ionic columns, with an architrave that announced "The Wieting" in black Roman letters. These features transformed this plain brown rectangular building into a Greek revivalist gem. I ventured through the lobby with its highly polished brasswork and gleaming glass. Rows of rich, plush, red-patterned cinema seating then greeted me, with shiny, light wood armrests and curved, wave-inspired backrests. The walls were colored with subtle and subdued tones of sage green and were painted with intricate laurel motifs that reflected the assiduity of the theater's history and enduring nature. At every opportunity red and green complementary colors enhanced the décor with vibrancy.

The authentic, vintage 1912 stage curtain, with its original painted pastoral scene, was recently valued at $100,000 and is framed resplendently with thick scarlet drapes. The landscape theme was also presented on either side of the stage in hand-painted murals. Every facet of this building displayed the perfect synergy of old and new, as the modernity of functionality integrated with a backdrop of antiquity. It was my hope that our modern equipment and techniques would now access the voices and ghosts of the past.

The Basement Dressing Room

The dressing room below the stage had a stereotypical row of illuminated, framed theater mirrors running along the wall. It opened out into a damp utilitarian basement and crawl space once used for storing coal and stage props. This was going to be the inauspicious setting for one of the most impressive recordings I have ever received.

We placed our chairs in a crescent with our backs to the mirrors facing the open space and the stairs that led up to the stage. A static infrared camera recorded the vigil and several DVRs were positioned around the room. Within minutes I could see a ghostly person walking along the far end through the darkened haze. He hovered around at the end of the stairs and occasionally went between the rooms. The whole team saw his dark and smoky outline.

The basement dressing room

I began to reach for any psychic information I could find. He was a man and I believed him to be local. I could psychically see him once more loitering at the bottom of the stairs, and I verbalized this to the team. I turned on the ghost box and asked for his name.

"Peter," he replied.

I turned off the ghost box briefly and repeated what the spirit had said to clarify his response. In those mere seconds of silence that followed a Grade A EVP was recorded when the man's voice clearly stated in a raspy whisper, "Peter, Peter!" Without realizing at that moment what the DVR had just captured, I turned the ghost box back on and asked, "Do you prefer being called Pete or Peter?" The ghost box responded once more by saying, "Peter."

The recording of this brief interaction started with me verbally describing the spirit's location to the team. Directly after that statement, the ghost box then received the name "Peter," followed by an EVP of "Peter, Peter," followed once more by the equipment saying, "Peter" when prompted. I had an audio recording where my psychic skills, the ghost box, and a spirit talking in real time had come together in one golden five-second clip, with each aspect corroborating the other.

The perfect conclusion to this contact would be in the historical discovery of this gentleman. Sarah and I went about the laborious process of researching the town's history in the hope of finding him. But without his last name or any further detail I was resigned to disappointment. Then in the book *The History of Tama County*, on the top of page 897, we discovered a statement that described the opening of a newly formed county lodge:

> Anchor Lodge, No. 32, of the Iowa Legion of Honor, was organized July 30, 1879 by Grand Deputy, H. S. Bassett. The following were the charter members.[19]

Halfway down the proceeding list of names was the resident Peter Peters! I had never considered that Peter was mentioned so many times because of his first and last names. I went back and listened to the recording armed with this information. Upon further review, the EVP definitely sounded like a spirit trying to communicate both names—Peter Peters. It would be remarkable if we had found the needle in this historical haystack.

We scoured the census records for 1880 and discovered further details surrounding the life of Peter Peters. He was born in 1847 in Schleswig-Holstein in the northernmost state of what is now Germany. He worked as a salesman and was married to Catherine, who was born and raised in the same location. He was a founding member of the Tama County Anchor Lodge in 1879 at the age of thirty-two. He died in 1914 and is buried in Polk County. The opera house was opened in 1912, just two years previously, and the strong possibility exists that Peter would have visited and known about the theater.

It was then a further revelation to find that Heather's team had received the name Peter repeatedly during its first vigil in the projection booth, without any knowledge as to what we had received in the basement at that time. This now suggests that Peter was flitting between each vigil. Heather's team had also received the name Catherine from a female spirit whom we now know to be Peter's wife. It would suggest that they are together in the afterlife.

The Balcony

I started the second vigil at the back of the balcony next to the projection booth. This was an area of the building that we knew to be active from the experiences of others and from Heather's previous vigil. Her team had also discussed the phenomenon of seeing faint glowing orbs weaving about on the stage below. After thirty minutes of dull, uninteresting tedium I started to experience the same event, as dim lights slowly drifted around the stage like fireflies in the breeze. I turned on the ghost box in an attempt to gather evidence.

The top left corner of the balcony is where I made contact with
Emmanuel Dvorak

"Is anybody there who wants to speak with me?" I asked. "What is your name?"

"Manny," a male voice replied.

"It's great to meet you. Is your name Manfred?" I continued.

"No," he said.

I asked the team what Manny might be short for and Emmanuel was suggested.

"Is your name Emmanuel?" I asked.

"Yes," he replied.

"What do you do?"

"Soldier."

"Where are you based?"

"Dodge."

"What do you miss most about being alive?" I continued.

"My mother," he replied.

"What's your mother's name?" I asked in a bid to retrieve as much researchable data as possible.

"Mary," he said.

I wondered why he was missing his mother if we assumed both were in spirit. It was my experience in working with the dead that deceased friends and relatives should be able to congregate together. Was Manny still of the belief he was posted away from home, perhaps engaging in a foreign conflict or another part of the country? I received no further contact from the soldier.

Once more I had failed to secure a last name, despite my persistent requests. I realized that finding Manny would now be difficult. I started my historical quest by accessing the veteran's lists that are available online for most major conflicts. There were no shortcuts and many hours and days were dedicated to this task. I started by looking for any Iowan soldier with the first name of Emmanuel who had participated in the American Civil War (1861-65). This proved to be fruitless, so I moved on to the American involvement in the First World War (1917-18).

After many countless days I found an individual named Emmanuel Dvorak who participated in the First World War. And the more I looked, the more I became convinced that I had found our spirit soldier. He was born on December 15, 1896, in Tama County and was the son of Mary and Joseph Dvorak. Manny had claimed his mother was named Mary and excitement grew as I continued to look. He entered the service on September 5, 1917, at Camp Dodge and was then transferred to Camp Devens, where he entered Company 47 of the 163rd Battalion Brigade. I recalled that Manny had said he was at Dodge. Once again I had received confirmation that this was the Manny I was looking for. He was then mustered out on December 24, 1918. He died on March 1, 1974 and was buried in Clutier, Tama County. When I return to this part of Iowa I will visit his grave to photographically record his headstone and to see if he psychically visits me again.

Emmanuel Dvorak c1917

I wondered why Manny had come through so prominently at the back of the auditorium. It was not uncommon for First World War soldiers to be given a party and send off at the local town theater. Perhaps Manny had worked at the theater or had fond memories of seeing films there with his love in the back row. He may have only been passing through on his way to check his old Toledo home and stomping grounds when he became curious as to who we were.

As a caveat to this paranormal incident, Heather's team came back from its second vigil in the basement with further evidence. Throughout their investigation the name of Elise was called out from the ghost box several times. Once I had found the identity of Manny I was able to discover his wife was named Anna, and their daughter was Elise. This was the final proof that Emmanuel Dvorak was present in spirit in the auditorium.

The Stage

Many of the paranormal occurrences are attributed to the ghost of Hellen 'Ella' Wieting, who built and donated the opera house to the people of Toledo. This assumption is made by those who have seen and heard activity, as there is the natural belief that Ella would be linked to the building in the afterlife, and very few historical figures from the town are so well known. It is believed that Ella sits resplendently in the fourth row of the auditorium in a period dress and hat which I'm sure would displease all those spirits seated in the fifth row. The final vigil on the stage, looking out into the auditorium, would hopefully reveal whether she frequents the theater or not.

The entire team positioned itself around the well-trodden stage and peered into the darkness of the expansive auditorium, looking through the gloom to pick out the fourth row. The energy was surprisingly lacking, and my hope of feeling the excitement of a residual atmosphere left behind by a century of adrenaline and acting seeping into the boards, was sadly missing. The orbs we had witnessed from the balcony were now nowhere to be found.

I asked over and over if Ella was present, if she wanted to come through, if she could give us a message. Every piece of equipment was tried, every technique exhausted, every persuasive way of asking, asked. The minutes ticked into hours without a single light or creak breaking the paranormal dormancy. I tried the ghost box once more, having already sat through several other long, protracted periods of static hissing and monotonous, rhythmic popping sessions.

But this time my persistence was rewarded with a staggering revelation from beyond the grave.

"Is Ella there?" I enquired.

"No!" came the reply in a voice that sounded like Manny from the previous vigil.

"Can you go and get her?" I continued.

"She's not here," was the response.

"Why is she not here?" I asked.

"Because she's dead!" was the astonishing answer.

"So was she once here as a ghost then?" I asked.

"Yes," he continued.

"So she was once a ghost here, and then her spirit died so she can longer be here?"

"Yes!"

"So is it possible to die twice, once in life, and once again in spirit?" I pressed.

"Yes," he verified.

There were no further responses to my questions. I believe Manny provided the information during this conversation, but he did not verify his identity.

The content of this short discussion was very thought provoking and intriguing. I had always considered that if ghosts and spirits required energy to make their physical presence known, then that energy must slowly diminish, or dissipate over time, unless the energy can perhaps be regiven or resourced from an electrical storm or EM pump, for example. Through the ghost box, the spirit had suggested that Ella had once haunted the Wieting Opera House, and that historical sightings by staff and patrons alike may have been correct in their assumptions. But could it be that Ella had now passed for a second time in spirit, so is no longer able to haunt the theater?

Ella died on May 23, 1933. This means at the very most she was only able to haunt the theater for a possible eighty-three years. Would this number then be seen as a reasonable amount of time in spirit if your energy was slowly used up by throwing lightbulbs, walking around the stage, and appearing in the fourth row? Does this now explain why some spirits are seen solely as shadow figures, as they no longer possess the energy to fully manifest? Is this why paranormal activity in buildings can subdue over a period of time? Is this why we rarely make contact with a ghost from more than 150 years ago despite mankind roaming the planet for hundreds of thousands of years?

If a spirit has measurable energy that can dissipate or be charged-up, then it could be theoretically possible to ground a ghost to dispose of it. How this would be possible is beyond what I know at this time, and from an ethical perspective would it be morally acceptable to kill a spirit when a spirit is already considered to be dead?

I then considered most prominently the thought of what happens when you die for a second time. Where do you go? Do we then reside fulltime in a place we can call 'Heaven,' without the opportunity to then dip back into the physical dimension as once we could? Perhaps paranormal investigators should not be investigating the dead, but the dead that have died.

Conclusion

The investigation in the Wieting Opera House provided some of the best evidence and historical corroborations I have ever experienced. The short audio recording of Peter in the basement was the perfect synthesis of verbal psychic information with two ghost box responses and an EVP, all on the same five second clip. To then find the gentleman in question through extensive historical research was sublime. The interaction with Manny at the back of the auditorium also provided enough evidence to suggest Emmanuel Dvorak was there in spirit. To then receive details in connection to Ella and her inability to haunt the building was astonishing in its content and frankness, and when placed under scrutiny makes perfect sense.

In the summer of 1960 the Wieting Theater was featured in the *Wall Street Journal* as a movie house that was making a successful financial comeback. Its renaissance and continued success has been through the considerable efforts made by the citizens of Toledo, all working together for no profit throughout several generations from as early as January 1913. Records show that individual donations helped to pay for operating expenses. I am sure Ella Wieting would be very proud of the time and effort the town has placed into the opera house. It is a matter for conjecture whether she can now see it or not.

Sanborn Railroad Crossing

Sanborn, Minnesota

Does a headless ghost haunt the site of his murder?

It was during a private investigation at a property in Sanborn that I was made aware of the mysterious circumstances surrounding the possible murder of a former resident. The tale had now fallen into local legend, and the exact details of the incident had long passed into the mists of time, making many believe that the story was now purely a myth. As a paranormal investigator and historian I had the tools to unravel the facts from the fiction.

I spent many hours researching at the very helpful Redwood Public Library in Redwood County. The facility allowed me to access a raft of period local newspapers via microfiche and numerous census records, books, and documents. Local Sanborn resident Barbara, who was knowledgeable and enthusiastic, helped me greatly in my research. It is of course dangerous to investigate at a fully functioning railway crossing, so diligence and care were taken.

History

The area now known as Sanborn was first populated several years after the Sioux Uprising of 1862. During the war, no white settlers were known to be living in this part of Redwood County, and the nearest populations were found east to New Ulm or to the west at

Lake Shetek. By the 1870s several scattered Native American families could still be found living in log cabins, but slowly more hardy
pioneers started to find their way here. Some of the early hardships
they had to endure were documented in the book *Sanborn Centennial History 1881-1981*:

> There were other problems the settlers also had to
> face. Some of the old-timers would tell about how
> bad the wolves were in the area. They also told of the
> terrible blizzard in 1881 that piled snow forty feet
> high in places. The trains stopped at Christmas and
> did not run again until the middle of April. The snow
> was packed so tight it could be cut like ice and pulled
> out by teams of oxen.[20]

The railway was intrinsic to the development of Sanborn by
bringing families, commerce, goods, and building supplies to this
fledgling town. The Winona-Tracy branch of the old Winona and St.
Peter line now extended throughout the southern part of Redwood
County. The east-west line was completed just west of New Ulm in
June 1872, and by October the first construction train passed through
Sanborn. During the harsh winter of 1873, this embryonic service
was suspended until the spring. In April it was able to operate again
and the first regularly scheduled train passed through the territory.
Sanborn was then platted in 1881 and was incorporated on November 17, 1891. It was named in honor of Sherburn Sanborn who was
an officer of the Chicago and Northwestern Railway Company. The
town then became a thriving railroad center during the early 1900s,
with fifteen railway families residing in Sanborn. At one time there
were as many as one freight train and four passenger trains running
through the town daily, each way.

Murder or Misadventure?

I became intrigued by the stories surrounding the alleged murder
at the railroad crossing because nobody seemed to know when the

incident took place, or if it had even taken place at all. An article written in the *Sanborn Sentinel* newspaper on May 13, 1994 asked the same question: "When Did it Happen? A Ghastly, Mysterious Death." The report described the macabre death of Louis Miller at the town's railroad crossing but had no further information as to the date and details of the event. The article asked for help in finding more information related to the incident, as no living Sanborn resident could remember when this gruesome death took place.

Any individual who died in the earliest history of a Midwestern town would be interred in the local cemetery due to limited transportation and no refrigeration. So, based on this concept, local resident Barbara explored the local cemetery at my behest, looking for the name Louis Miller taken from the 1994 newspaper article. After an extensive search, a small, flat grave marker was discovered; it read Lewis F. Miller, born October 30, 1875, died March 13, 1910. Despite the first name spelling discrepancy, I was now in possession of his death date. This would allow me to accurately access archived newspapers to learn of the details surrounding his demise.

I then found that the local *Sanborn Sentinel* was no longer in circulation, and nobody could tell me where it was archived. The Redwood County Historical Society did not hold copies, and the Minnesota Historical Society Library in St. Paul had a mysterious gap in their archives for the year 1910, with no explanation as to why. This was now looking conspiratorial. Despite this setback I believed that other local newspapers from the surrounding area would have also covered this event. My hunch proved correct, and I finally found the headlines I had been searching for at the Redwood Falls Public Library. I then pieced a timeline of events together from several articles collected from the *Redwood Gazette*, the *Redwood Reveille*, and the *Lamberton Star* for the period of March to April 1910.

Freight train No. 75 had pulled into the town of Sanborn at around six a.m. on Sunday morning. Members of the train crew then found a decapitated body lying on the tracks. This was the body of Lewis Miller, the son of Mr. and Mrs. Henry Miller. Lewis Miller had four sisters and five brothers. He was born in St. Peter but grew up in Sanborn after his parents moved the family. He then left home at an early age and went to the Pacific coast to farm in Sacramento. He had recently come back to visit his family and had gained temporary employment at the *Northern Pacific Railway* out of Minneapolis.

He was found lying at the crossing by the stockyards with his head completely missing. At first it was thought he had been killed by a passing train since his body was found about ten feet west of the sidewalk close beside the south track of the rails with his neck resting upon the rail. His head was then found ten feet east of the sidewalk, between the rails. The body was removed to a nearby fur- niture store to await the coroner. It was initially suggested in the first newspaper reports that Mr. Miller had been in a terrible accident or had committed suicide.

One theory suggested that he may have come across a station- ary train that was blocking his path. He then perhaps crawled under the cars to get to the other side when the train suddenly started up, causing him to be pulled under the wheels. I see this theory as im- plausible though, as trains are not known for their quiet acceleration from a standing start. It was also put forward that he may have com- mitted suicide, but his family said this was unlikely as he seemed to be in good spirits with a happy disposition. There appeared no rea- son for him to take his own life. To add to this mystery, the rail com- pany then proceeded to inspect all of the trains that passed through Sanborn that weekend and found no evidence of an accident.

The *Redwood Reveille* then continues the story in an article one week after the incident called "Was it Murder? Death of Lewis Miller at Sanborn Still a Mystery":

> A post mortem examination of the remains was held
> Sunday evening and outside of a few minor bruises
> on the right arm no other bruises were found which
> put a different aspect to the mystery. The condition
> of the clothing, the position of the body when found,
> the blood marks on the ground where the body [sic]
> found and all things in general show that the man

might have been murdered with robbery as a motive as no money was found in the clothes and relatives report that he had over $100 with him.[21]

Many questions were unanswered, like how did a train manage to hit him hard enough to detach his head but leave his body and clothing unscathed? I thought that any bruising on his right arm would suggest he used his favored arm to protect himself from an attack. The theory of foul play is reinforced when you consider that only five cents was found in his pocket when his family claimed that he had over one hundred dollars with him. This was a considerable sum of money during this era.

Miller also had in his possession an additional fourteen dollars that he won at a poker game that evening. He was returning from the game when the tragedy struck. The four individuals he played cards with were the last people to see him alive at a little after eleven p.m. It was also noted that the inside pocket of his coat was torn, suggesting that a struggle had taken place for his money. All of the other men who played cards with Mr. Miller that night were examined at the inquest, and there was no evidence to implicate any of them. They did say that the group consumed five bottles of beer that evening, but this would represent a moderate allowance that would not have left Mr. Miller helplessly intoxicated.

The fourteen dollars' worth of winnings seems too small an amount to justify a robbery and murder by one of his card-playing companions, but one of the party may have followed him after the game if Mr. Miller had disclosed that he had one hundred dollars with him. It could also be suggested that a vagrant transient traveler may have met him at the railroad crossing and taken an opportunistic moment to attack Mr. Miller, who put up a strong fight due to the money he had in his possession. This theory could be made stronger if a pattern of similar attacks could be shown in the surrounding areas during this era.

Research revealed an incident that had taken place in a town called Tracy in Lyon County, just twenty-six miles from Sanborn.

The *Tracy Herald* of 1896 states that a little after twelve o'clock on the previous night, a man was found dead lying across the railroad track with the wheel of a boxcar across his stomach. Whether the car running over him was the cause of his death remains a matter of speculation with those who first found him. His position under the train when found could not be accounted for. He was lying flat on his back with his feet outside of the track with a car on top of him. The man had been seen eating lunch at eleven o'clock in the morning having just arrived on a freight train, showing that he was killed between eleven a.m. and twelve o'clock midnight. The yardmen were of the opinion that he was actually hit on the head and placed there. He had a large bruise on the back of his head that seemed to corroborate this opinion. The strange position he was found in also makes this theory sound probable.

The Sanborn railroad crossing where Lewis Miller was murdered

I suspected that a common crime of this period was to rob, and possibly murder, local residents and then leave their bodies on railroad tracks to make it look like an accident or suicide. The assailant could then abscond from the crime scene and remain transient through the railroad network without being traced.

This historical research raised many questions. Was Lewis Miller's death a suicide, accident, or murder? Did he know his assailant? The jury at the inquest gave the verdict of death in a manner unknown. I guess all that now remained was to ask Mr. Miller's spirit those very questions.

Investigation

This was a very ordinary looking landscape located between a lumber yard and a grain storage facility. It looked like every other featureless railroad crossing in a small Midwestern town. It was difficult to imagine the horror that once took place there. Passing traffic intermittently interrupted the vigil with noise pollution, and a freight train slowly rumbled close to the team with a shuddering unstoppable mass.

Outside investigations are not preferable since there are many factors that can negatively influence the vigils. Any subtle changes in temperature that can be measured in a closed indoor environment with a thermal imaging camera are untraceable. Wind, traffic, barking dogs, and other random everyday noises pollute the sensitive recording equipment. Visual energy presented as orbs are almost impossible to see against an outdoor landscape compared to a darkened room. The elements are also unpredictable and harsh. Trying to access a spirit through psychic means will be affected by attention-sapping high humidity, excessive heat, cold, rain, and mosquitos. I was also bracing myself for an enquiring visit from the local police department as I turned on the ghost box.

"Who is here?" I started by asking.

"Ed," was the response. I did not know who Ed was, but I wanted to make contact with Lewis.

"I wish to speak with Lewis Miller," I said, then explained who I was and why I was there.

"Can you talk to me, Lewis?" I continued.

"Hello!" came the reply.

"Did you lose your head at the railroad crossing?" I asked by jumping straight in with pressing and pertinent questions.

"Yes," he said in a male voice.

"Were you born here?" I enquired further in a bid to retrieve as much verifiable evidence as possible.

"Here," he claimed. I pondered whether he thought I meant America, Minnesota, or Sanborn.

"Were you born in St. Peter?" I then asked, based on the research I had undertaken.

"Yes, yes!"

"How old were you when your parents came to Sanborn?"

"Ten, ten!" he said.

"So you were ten years old when you moved to Sanborn with your family?" I asked once more to make sure the facts were correct.

"Right, yes," he replied, followed by the word "move."

"Can you tell me your name?" I continued.

"Yes," he responded. This was not the definitive answer I was hoping for. I then asked a further four times for his name without receiving a single reply.

"Do you remember playing poker?" I asked, looking to change my questioning in order to keep the answers flowing.

"Yes," he said.

"What was the name of the person who attacked you?"

"Why?" he responded.

I then spent a further minute explaining why I was there and what I was hoping to achieve. I also told him that he now had a chance to right a wrong if he could give me the precise details surrounding the mystery of his demise. "Were you murdered?"

"Yes!" he said.

"Was that a yes?" I asked once again due to the importance of the question.

"Yes!" he responded for a second time.

"Who murdered you?" I continued.

"Bob!"

"Can you confirm that name again?" I pressed.

"Bob," he said once more.

"What was Bob's last name?" I asked, but I did not receive a response.

"Did Bob play cards with you?"

"Yes," he replied.

"So did you have an argument over money?"

"No," he said.

"Did you fall out over a woman?"

"No."

"So why were you murdered?"

"Theft," was his reply.

"So you had something stolen?"

"Yes, hunter," he said. I wondered if the word 'hunter' referred to a hunter-case pocket watch. This is a timepiece with a spring-hinged circular metal lid or cover that closes over the watch dial and glass protecting it from dust, scratches, and other damage.

"Did you lose a watch?" I asked based on my hunch.

"Yes!" he responded.

"So you had your watch stolen?"

"I think so," he said.

"Are you Lewis Miller?" I asked once more due to the strength and quickness of the current responses.

"Yes!" he replied, providing me with the definitive proof of who I was interacting with in spirit.

"I need you to verify for me that you were murdered," I said.

"Yes!" he said loudly and clearly for all to hear.

"Once again, can you confirm for me that you were murdered?"

"Yes," he said again.

"And was the name of the person that killed you 'Bob'?"

"That's right, yes," he responded.

"Are your parents with you in spirit?" I asked.

"Yes," came his reply.

"Was your head removed with a knife?"

"Weight," was his odd response. I considered that he may have been referring to the weight of a passing train.

"So you were followed after your card game, a man named Bob attacked you and stole your watch, and you were knocked unconscious and left with your body positioned on the railroad tracks in such a way that the next train that passed through removed your head?"

There was no reply, just silence. I sometimes wonder if individuals with a limited attention span would reflect this trait when they are dead.

"Lewis?" I stated, to try and verify that he was still with me.

"What?" he asked.

"How were you killed?"

"Beaten!" he replied.

"But there were no marks left on your body other than your right arm."

"No," he verified.

"So, you were followed after the card game, you had a fight, you bruised your arm trying to protect yourself, and were left on the rail tracks?" I pressed once more.

"Yes," came his reply.

"So were you dead before the train came along?"

"No," he said.

"So it was the train that killed you? Were you placed under the wheels of a stationary train that removed your head when it started rolling?"

"Correct," he said.

"What was the name of the person who killed you?" I asked once again, looking for verification of his previous answer.

"Robert," he responded.

I felt I had now obtained the answers to the questions I wanted surrounding this macabre event.

"Have you a last message you want to give?" I asked.

"Friend," he said.

"Would you say goodbye to me before I leave?"

"Goodbye," he said, and I ended the vigil.

The interaction with Lewis Miller at the railroad crossing was one of the longest and most successful ghost box sessions I can recall. Based on his answers, it appears that he was followed after the poker game by one of the players, a man named Robert or 'Bob.' Lewis was then attacked, bruising his arm in self-defense as he tried to defend himself. His watch and money were then stolen. He was then positioned in an unconscious state on the rails beneath a stationary train. Obviously, Lewis would have been able to identify his attacker if he would have survived the incident. In 2011 an FBI document reported that 79 percent of all murders in the United States are committed by the victim's friends, loved ones, or acquaintances. This appears to be true in the case of Lewis Miller, 106 years earlier. Unfortunately, the names of the poker players from that night were never recorded.

Conclusion

This story had seemed very surreal and bizarre from the first moment I started to undertake research, and many more facts began to appear as I probed deeper into the mystery. One piece of information that left me scratching my head involved the discovery of who owned the *Sanborn Sentinel* at the time of Lewis Miller's death. The *Sanborn Sentinel* was first published on May 5, 1893. In 1908 the paper was sold to Grover Posz, the son of George Posz who, I discovered, was the brother-in-law of Lewis Miller. The Posz family then sold the paper after a short period of ownership in 1912. Just one month later the entire building, including the newspaper print shop and post office, mysteriously burned to the ground, destroying all of the back issues of the newspaper. This was why there were no researchable archives available for the year that Lewis Miller had died. This seemed like a strange series of events considering the relationship between George Posz and Miller and the short length of time the family owned the paper, followed by a convenient fire that destroyed all the reporting evidence of the case. Accusations are not being proposed, but one cannot deny the strangeness of some events.

Then an even more surreal twist came when, by pure luck, I found a newspaper article that told the unusual tale of a second gentleman named Lewis Miller. Just weeks after Lewis Miller's death at the railroad crossing, the *Redwood Gazette* published on April 6, 1910 spoke of a gentleman from Morton also named Lewis Miller, who hanged himself in mysterious circumstances in a barn in Portal, North Dakota. The deceased was also in good circumstances and there was no reason for him to take his own life. Just two hours previously he had written a letter to his brother asking for a quick response to the nature of a business enquiry and the health of his relatives. He was from the same county as Lewis Miller, the Sanborn railroad victim, he shared the same name, both died within weeks of one another under mysterious circumstances, and both were made to look like suicides. I cannot account for this, and the whole scenario defies belief and rational thinking. It makes one wonder if the wrong Lewis Miller was originally murdered.

What I then discovered was remarkable. During further research I uncovered a second railroad tragedy in Sanborn, just three months after the Lewis Miller incident, as reported in the *Redwood Gazette:*

> A bad wreck occurred on the North-Western just south of Sanborn Thursday morning, when a north-bound freight train, drawn by the Engineer Ed Loomer crashed through a bridge which was being repaired. Mr. Loomer is seriously injured and has been taken to Rochester for treatment. He is well known in this city, but his home is at Mason City, Iowa, where he has lived since his marriage to Miss Elma Town, of Tracy, several years ago. His fireman, a Mr. Miller, was also seriously injured. – Since the above was put

in type the engineer died and the fireman is in critical condition in the hospital at Rochester.[22]

I believe the fireman mentioned in the text to be one of Lewis Miller's brothers. It was documented in the article surrounding Lewis Miller's death that he had a brother working in the roundhouse at the time, a building used for servicing locomotives. What I did notice from this text was the name of the engineer that was seriously injured, Ed Loomer. Ed was the first name that came through during the vigil with the ghost box, a spirit I inadvertently ignored due to the arrival of Lewis Miller. As always seems to be the convention when researching history and the paranormal, the truth is always stranger than the myth or legend.

FOREPAUGH'S RESTAURANT

ST. PAUL, MINNESOTA

Rumors of a macabre suicide at the Forepaugh mansion are now part of Minnesotan folk lore.

Forepaugh's mansion is an established and much loved restaurant and celebrated venue for weddings and business dinners, located east of Irvine Park in the wealthy historic downtown district of St. Paul. No paranormal investigations have been permitted on the property until now, so the team's presence represented a unique opportunity to be the first to access the resident spirits.

The Forepaugh mansion is an opulent, Victorian, three-story building with a wonderful landscaped garden. Classical urns, magnolia trees, and a winding gravel road draw the visitor to a resplendent, multi-pillared, wooden, colonial construction, with an under-lit covered carriageway. Above this feature, a high, sloping roof meets a balcony terrace surrounded by wonderful wrought iron railing work. Every elegant architectural style and order is beautifully melded together in this glorious ensemble, consisting of ivory cream trim, red brick, and dove grey siding.

Many paranormal incidents have been recorded by staff and guests alike on this property, with a spooky female phantom wearing a nineteenth century dress frequently seen gliding along the hallways and through the walls. Place settings, cutlery, and chairs are often found rearranged in the dining room, and cold spots and the disturbance of kitchen equipment have also been experienced.

The owners and staff of Forepaugh's Restaurant were very accommodating and provided me with stories and historical documentation. I researched the property and its previous owners further by utilizing the Library of Congress online newspaper archives.

History

Joseph Lybrandt Forepaugh was born on January 6, 1834. He arrived in St. Paul on a riverboat in 1858 after completing an apprenticeship with an imported dry goods wholesale company in Philadelphia. Forepaugh wasted no time in starting a successful business in Minnesota and became the senior partner in the J. L. Forepaugh and Company, a dry goods store that provided much needed supplies to the Union troops during the Civil War. This business grew to be one of the biggest in the upper Midwest with a huge yearly turnover of half-a-million dollars. During this time Forepaugh also started the Forepaugh and Tarbox company, a manufacturer and wholesaler of boots and shoes.

In 1870 Forepaugh bought five lots of land in the exclusive downtown St. Paul area, where he built a ten-thousand-dollar mansion that he filled with the highest quality, finely crafted furniture and decor. This grandiose house was designed so each window could look out over the neatly manicured grounds. It was also one of the first buildings in St. Paul to have running water. Forepaugh's continued business success allowed him to retire early in 1886. He sold the mansion to General John Henry Hammond and auctioned off his fine imported furnishings and paintings. This allowed Forepaugh to travel extensively for three years throughout Europe with his wife Mary.

Forepaugh's early retirement and lengthy foreign excursions were undertaken to try and improve his health. Unbeknownst to most outside of his own personal circle of friends and family he was suffering from a debilitating depression, exacerbated by

chronic stomach pains and a fear of financial ruin. When Forepaugh returned from abroad in 1889, he built a second expansive
home on Summit Avenue that offered a view of his previous property and the city. Unfortunately, just three years later his health
and perceived circumstances overcame him and he took his own
life on July 8, 1892. This was documented in the *St. Paul Globe*
newspaper:

> Bullet in His Brain. John F. Forepaugh, A Prominent
> Citizen, Takes his Life. His Health for Many Months
> has Caused Him Much Trouble, and he Mentally
> Worried Himself over Very Foolish Fears. He Dis-
> appeared Friday and was Found Dead Yesterday:
> Joseph F. Forepaugh, a retired merchant and highly
> respected citizen, committed suicide in a small grove
> on Selby Avenue Friday night. Mr. Forepaugh left
> his residence on Summit Avenue Friday morning at
> 9 o'clock. He was at his business in the block that
> bears his name on East Fourth Street until after 10
> o'clock. About 10:30 one of daughters saw him on a
> cable car going west, between Nina and Farrington
> Avenue. As her father usually left his car at Nina Av-
> enue to reach home she was somewhat surprised but
> thought nothing of the circumstances until later in the
> day. The absence of Mr. Forepaugh at luncheon did
> not cause any anxiety at his home and the employees
> at the office supposed he was at home. Early in the
> evening the family became alarmed and a search was
> commenced. No trace of him could be found, the last
> person to give any account of him being his daugh-
> ter, who saw him in the car that morning.
>
> How the Body was Found: Early yesterday morning,
> Mr. Shepherd being informed that Mr. Forepaugh
> was last seen on a Selby Avenue car, started to make
> a thorough search in that direction. He had carefully

examined the territory on both sides of the avenue for blocks and was about to give up the search when he noticed a small lake or pond about 100 yards from Selby Avenue, near Syndicate Avenue. On reaching the water he found several boys there bathing. Explaining he was in search for a lost man, and giving the description of Mr. Forepaugh, one of the lads said he saw the man answering that description near there Friday afternoon. The boy was certain he could not be mistaken in the description. Mr. Shepherd, assisted by the boys, formed a line and started a systematic search of the grove at that point. About one hundred feet from the pond the body was discovered by one of the lads. The body lay on the right side just in front of a large tree. A bullet hole in the head between ear and eye and a revolver grasped firmly in the right hand explained the cause of his death.[23]

His family then reported that he had been feeling unwell for several years due to dyspeptic symptoms that left him in poor spirits and a general debility caused by a decline of his vital organs; his prolonged periods of melancholia were also revealed. It was then confirmed that Forepaugh was also harboring the false belief that financial misfortune would be just around the corner. This thought may have been triggered by the number of times he had frequented court regarding financial disputes in the years leading up to his death. In December 1879 he won a financial case that granted him $467 plus costs. Then three years later, in November 1882, he was the defendant in a case that looked to foreclose on a chattel mortgage. In August 1890 an action was commenced against Forepaugh to enforce a mechanic's lien for $185, and he was back again for another lien case worth $300 in May 1891. These cases may have been prominent in his depressive thinking, but reality reveals that Forepaugh was a very wealthy individual, and his fears of financial ruination were unfounded.

General John Henry Hammond bought the mansion from Fore-paugh in 1866. He was born in Maryland on June 30, 1832 and came from Scottish-Irish descent. Hammond gained great success in the military, being initially commissioned as a second lieutenant in the 5th California Infantry in 1861. He was then promoted to major in September 1862 and served as an acting adjutant general and chief of staff to General William Sherman who was so impressed with Hammond's leadership skills and discipline that he made him a brigadier general. Hammond was then placed in command of the 1st Brigade, 7th Division and Cavalry Corps, of the military division of Mississippi, where he saw heavy action during the Vicksburg Campaign.

After the war Hammond married and settled in Louisville, Kentucky, where he started a family of six children: Mary, Ogden, Sophia, Vernon, John Henry, and Margaret. His second child, Ogden, was travelling on the *Lusitania* on May 7, 1915 with his wife Mary when the ship was torpedoed and sunk by a German U-boat with the loss of 1,198 passengers and crew. Ogden survived but John's wife died.

John Hammond's family then settled in Chicago, Illinois, in 1873, where he served as president of the Manitoba & Southwestern Railroad and of a local bank. Hammond became a builder and pioneer of railroads and in Wisconsin became known as *the father of Superior* for his role in transforming the Wisconsin swamp into a thriving city. Hammond plotted early land allotments, built the first important office buildings, and brought major railways to Superior, making full use of the harbor at the western end of Lake Superior. The Panic of 1873 forced the bank to close and President Hayes took the opportunity to appoint Hammond as Inspector of Indian Agencies in 1876, and he relocated with his family back to Minnesota.

Hammond fell ill and died in St. Paul on April 30, 1890. He left behind an estate worth over half-a-million dollars, a hefty sum during the late nineteenth century. His death was recorded in the *St. Paul Globe* the following day:

Death of Gen. Hammond. At his Home Yesterday—
Sketch of His Eventful Career. Gen. J. H. Hammond
died yesterday at his residence on South Exchange
Street, at the age of fifty-seven years. It was scarcely
known about the city that he was ill, and his death
will be a shocking surprise in the community in
which he has resided so long.[24]

Moving into the twentieth century, the Irvine Park area started to
decline, and the Forepaugh mansion began to show signs of deteriora-
tion. Many owners came and went until the property became a boarding house up until 1973, operated by the St. Paul Housing and Redevelopment Authority. In 1983 the current owners bought the building
and began the long process of renovating and restoring the mansion
back to its original beauty. They also unwittingly inherited the many
resident ghosts and spirits that roamed the hallways and rooms.

Rumors

I wanted to get to the bottom of the rumors that surrounded the
ghosts that haunted Forepaugh's Restaurant, to uncover what was
actually there. No team had investigated the mansion before, so no
validation could be made for the stories and tales that proliferated in
many paranormal books and websites. This became apparent when
I read about the infamous ghost named Molly, believed to haunt the
building.

It has been written that Joseph Forepaugh took a shine to a
young maid in his service. It was allegedly noted that staff would
witness Molly and Forepaugh disappearing into rooms in order to
embrace an illicit affair. It has been told that Forepaugh's wife discovered the two during one such encounter and demanded that her
husband stop the liaisons. It is rumored that Molly then found herself pregnant with Forepaugh's child in 1866 and in a moment of
desperation tied a rope to a third-floor chandelier and placed the
other end around her neck. She then threw herself out the window
and ended her life.

Yet this story does not appear to be based in reality when you consider that the house was not built until 1870; you cannot hang yourself from a property that is yet to be built for another four years. Other claims have been made that Molly actually killed herself just before or after Forepaugh took his own life in 1892. But the family had already sold the house six years previously, so once again this tragic event could not have happened on the property during the Forepaugh's occupancy.

The Library of Congress operates an extensive online digitized resource that includes the *St. Paul Globe* newspaper and many other period Minnesotan newspapers. It has a unique feature that allows the researcher to look for individual words, or word groups, within each page of every document. After considerable research, I believe with reasonable certainty that the story of Molly is nothing more than a factless urban myth, without any historical merit. No relevant matches were found for many individual words, including hanging, suicide, third floor, window, Molly, or Forepaugh. I then extended the same search to all of the available historic Midwestern newspaper archives with the same negative result.

I believe that a maid hanging herself outside of the house in such a dramatic fashion, in full view of the town, from a property owned by one of the wealthiest entrepreneurs and socialites in St. Paul, would have been documented had it taken place. Newspapers from this period did not shy away from the harsh facts and realities of such incidents, regardless of any social standing, as seen in the descriptive and detailed report of Joseph Forepaugh's own suicide. It must also be recognized that I have already uncovered the reasons why Forepaugh took his own life and that his obituary was laden with glowing and positive references to his character and noted devotion to his wife.

> We trace the career of a man with pride and pleasure,
> and by the distinctive features that make him a good
> citizen we accord him a place among his fellows.[25]

Yet during my research I did find a remarkable story in the *St. Paul Globe* from 1893 that bears a remarkable resemblance to the Molly rumor and may provide us with the genesis of her fictional story.

> Was it Intentional? Mary Anderson Appears to have Attempted Suicide: Mary Anderson, a middle aged woman, employed as a domestic in the family of Rabbi Samuel Marks, at 827 Ninth Avenue South, seems to have attempted suicide. At 7:30 yesterday morning the family of the rabbi were astonished at the next door neighbors loudly rapping at their back door, and on inquiring the cause, discovered Mary Anderson lying on the ground. Her bedroom window, which was on the third floor, was open, and the girl had evidently jumped or thrown [sic] herself out. She was picked up in a very poor condition. The doctors called in said they feared her shoulder was broken and her hip dislocated.[26]

Mary was a domestic servant who threw herself out of a third floor window just eighteen months before Joseph Forepaugh killed himself in the same town; the name Molly was also a derivative of Mary during this era. If most townsfolk were unaware of Forepaugh's failing health and history of depression it would be easy for them to make up their own stories to account for his shocking demise. Mary Anderson did not die in her suicide attempt and I believe the two would not have met, as their social circles would have been very different. It is also worth questioning whether Forepaugh could have even fathered a child in his late fifties, with depression, failing organs, and severe stomach pains. The term *Molly the maid* is also a stereotypical alliterated term for a Victorian servant, as popularized by the Joseph Dale song from 1803, *Molly Put the Kettle On* (Molly later evolved into Polly'. Any thoughts of a fictionalized maid from this period would most commonly be given the moniker of Molly.

I was now intrigued to start the first paranormal investigation on this property as this would hopefully allow me to interview Joseph Forepaugh about his life and also meet the ghosts that haunt the restaurant. Would contact with the dead corroborate my research?

Investigation

The weather took a turn for the worse when we first arrived at the property and many of the major roads in and out of the cities were experiencing closure and white-out conditions. It left the town eerily quiet and deserted as we went about bringing the equipment through the dune-like drifts into the building. Flakes of snow suspended themselves motionless in the frozen, pink-tinted night sky as the beauty of the property suddenly glinted like a magical snow globe.

The Forepaugh's Restaurant

During the walkthrough and process of setting up the equipment, I began to see shadows moving around the first floor hallway corridor. This was experienced and verified by the team. I also recognized the phenomenon of seeing a white mist appear and disappear in the same location. I organized three teams to investigate throughout the property in the hope of gathering the most evidence possible. I started my first vigil in the second floor dining room area where Mary Forepaugh's original dining room table was located. I placed several fishing bobber trigger objects on the table and around the room and waited with anticipation.

Second Floor

The room was rich with heavy, dark wooden furniture, sumptuous, cozy, burnt red and burgundy walls, with complementing fine textiles. Its warmth made me forget the cold harshness of the conditions outside. Beaded paneled woodwork, heavy, ostentatious, brass crystal chandeliers, floor lamps, and historic black and white plate photographs in ornate, gilded frames completed the look. Matching rugs left gaps where I glimpsed well-worn floorboards that presented and documented the movement of human traffic over the last 176 years.

A hazy, dim darkness descended as I waited in heightened patience. I had a perfect view of the dining room through to the hallway and then the second dining room beyond. I started by introducing the team and myself and I then ran through the numerous ways in which the spirits could interact with me during the course of the vigil. I verbalized that I had placed various fishing bobbers around the room and asked if any listening spirits would pick one up. Almost instantaneously, a bobber I had positioned on Mary's table launched itself across the room with some alacrity. It hit the wooden floor five feet away from its starting position, bouncing around the floor with a silence-shattering sound before rocking to a halt. We sat in bated silence for a minute, not even daring to breathe, listening and waiting intently for what might happen next. The room charged and filled with energy. It raised the hairs on my arms, and I braced myself for a full-bodied apparition to manifest out of the gloom. After a minute of actionless tension I grabbed my K2 meter and ran over to the bobber in the hope of registering an anomalous energy—no reading was recorded.

I broke the silence by asking if the spirit was still in the room, and if it could knock over a second bobber to reinforce its presence. This time a bobber I had placed on the newel post of the hallway stairs could now be heard bucking and bouncing down the steps in a progressive journey that ended distantly on the floor below. I then noticed a stale odor that wafted past me. It was an olfactory sensation that suggested a spirit from a period of history where regular bathing and hygienic regimes were not possible or desired. It was not an offensive smell, but it was recognizable as another human being and not a living one. I reached for the ghost box and turned it on with a fumbling anticipation.

"Good day!" shouted a female voice without prompting.

"Hello," I said in response. "What is your name?"

"Amy," she replied.

I greeted her and explained who we were and why we were there.

"How many spirits are in this property?" I asked.

"Eight!" she said.

"Can you give me the name of one of those spirits?" I enquired.

"Hammond," was her reply.

"Who else?" I pressed further.

"Dad, Dad, Father!" she added.

"Did you live here?"

"Yes!" she replied.

During this interaction we could hear footsteps working their way around the second floor and the distant sound of polka music, almost like a residual audio haunting of music from yesteryear. Despite further questioning, the answers dried up and this brief connection was lost. I had witnessed a very impressive show of poltergeist activity and the confirmation that a Hammond resided in the building with seven other spirits. This made me optimistic for the proceeding vigils.

Team leader Heather had started her investigation on the first floor and was shocked to see my bobber appear from the floor above via the stairs. Her team had also experienced the same stale smell, which made me believe that an individual in spirit was wandering from vigil to vigil throughout the house. This may explain why my dialogue had finished so suddenly. Heather had received the name "Joseph" and the statement "Hi Daddy" through the ghost box. I hoped this was the spirit of Joseph Forepaugh. I was also aware from my historical research that both Forepaugh and Hammond had raised many children in the home. Heather then asked if John was present, referring to General John Hammond who resided and died on the property. "Yes!" came the reply.

To confirm my theories, Scott then informed me that on the third floor he had also experienced the smell of body odor. Remember that we had three teams all working in isolation from one another in three separate parts of the building, all now with the same corroborative notes and experiences. Scott asked if Joseph and Mary were in the room with him and received the reply "Yes." He then asked Joseph to tell him about his death and heard the reply "Woods." This response may have been in reference to the wooded area where his body was found. Scott then asked why he had taken his own life and heard the clear response of "Debt."

It was an encouraging start and it led me to believe that Joseph and Mary Forepaugh were present in spirit, as was John Hammond. I did not recognize the name Amy from my historical notes but I hoped to find more information about her as the evening progressed. I was eager to talk with Joseph, so I organized another vigil on the third floor where Scott had made considerable contact already.

Third Floor

The third floor dining room had neatly arranged gleaming silver cutlery, wine glasses, and perfectly folded napkins, all presented on pristine, white tablecloths for the ideal dining experience. This was the area in which Molly was believed to have committed suicide. As we started the vigil I began to cough. This is usually a sign that a spirit wants to talk through me psychically. I started to see a clairvoyant picture of what the area used to look like: it had trunks and stored luggage with suitcases and hatboxes. They were all adorned with various tags and tickets that suggested extensive train and boat travel. Based on Scott's evidence, I started with the ghost box in the hope of gaining a dialogue with either Joseph or Mary Forepaugh.

"How old are you?" I asked in my opening statement.

"Nine," was the response, said in the same female voice that sounded like Amy from the second floor. It now made more sense that she was telling us her father was also present if she was a child.

"Nearly ten!" she added.

"Can you go and get Joseph?" I asked. "I would like to chat with him."

"Of course," she replied.

I waited for a brief moment and asked, "Do you prefer being called Joe or Joseph?"

"Joe!" he replied.

"So are you here with us Joe?" I pressed for clarification.

"Yes!" he responded. I thanked him for coming to have a dialogue with me and thanked Amy for bringing him.

"Did you have a maid named Molly?" I enquired, looking to add some facts to the story surrounding the rumor of Molly.

"No!" he replied. It has been my experience that since they are dead, spirits are not defensive in their responses; any incidents that occurred when they were alive, no matter how shocking, are now an irrelevance.

"Did you have a lady named Molly in your service?" I continued for verification.

"No... no!" he said twice to add emphasis and clarification.

"Did anybody hang themselves in this property?" I asked hoping that the strong responses would continue.

"No!" he said.

"Did anybody die here through suicide—a hanging, or throwing themselves out of a window, or by any other means?"

"No!"

"Do the rumors surrounding the suicides annoy you?" I continued.

"Yes!" he responded.

"Would you like me to write that you are unhappy with the rumors that surround your philandering and the suicide of Molly, especially if you did not do anything wrong?" I asked further.

"Yes!"

"Did you commit suicide due to the pain caused by your stomach complaint?"

"Yes!" he said once again.

"Did financial worries play a part?" I continued.

"Yes!" he reinforced once more. Joseph was only giving one word responses but he was answering a lot of key questions.

"Was there a woman involved?"

"No!" he replied.

I once again noticed that shadow figures appeared to be moving around in the other rooms on the floor, so I set up a laser grid system that projected a network of small dots into the spaces. This would allow me to see if an entity passed in front of any of the hundreds of shotgun-like beams by breaking them with its movement.

"So your suicide was through a feeling of being down?" I continued.

"Yes!" he said in his now usual one-word response.

I then started to feel an intense stomach pain as if I were empathically feeling his troubling ailment.

"Why did you use a gun?" I asked.

"Debt," he replied. This was not what I meant, but it was useful as a response to add to the previous evidence in regard to the reason why he took his own life.

"How many spirits are residing in this house?" I asked again, having previously quizzed the spirit of Amy on the same subject.

"Eight," he replied, reinforcing our earlier response from the previous vigil.

"Would you be happy to talk to me again if I came back?" I continued.

"It's a great thing," he said.

I believe he was referring to the experience he was having of communicating so freely with the living.

"Where would be the best place to make contact with you if we came back?"

"The third floor!" he responded.

"What room on the third floor?" I continued.

"Johnson," was his reply.

The Johnson room was the room behind the back of the dining room, currently used as office space for the restaurant manager and owner. I wondered if the high level of EMF associated with the computers and telecommunications in this back location would play a factor in why Joseph felt it would be easier to make contact there. I could not complain though, having spent thirty minutes interviewing him from our current location. I gave him my thanks and hoped that we may chat again soon. He said "Goodbye," and I turned off the ghost box.

Conclusion

The investigation at Forepaugh's Restaurant left me in no doubt that eight spirits resided in the building. This was clarified many times in many areas with different teams with different equipment. Based on my time there I believed four of them to be Joseph and Mary Forepaugh, John Henry Hammond, and a young girl named Amy. I have subsequently searched for an individual named Amy in both the Forepaugh and Hammond family trees but without success. Without her last name it would be almost impossible to find her identity, especially when you take into account the thousands of individuals who resided on the property and consider its age and one-time usage as a boarding house. As Amy presented herself as a young girl it would be reasonable to suggest that the ghost of the woman walking through the building was most likely Mary Forepaugh, especially if she was seen in a fashionably expensive nineteenth century dress that no maid would have been able to afford.

It was interesting to hear Joseph Forepaugh dispel the rumors surrounding the haunting and suicide of Molly. Many might say that he would say that, but historical research would back up his statements, and we now have definitive proof as to why he sold up and eventually committed suicide himself. It is also worth mentioning that if Molly was prominently haunting this property, she had an ample opportunity to come through to the team, considering the eight vigils we conducted that night spread over three floors with extensive equipment and the team's psychic abilities. Yet not a single EVP or mere mention of her name existed in our evidence. I also completed a second, follow-up investigation several months later and still had no contact with any individual named Molly. This may be disappointing for those who love the macabre story of a domestic servant love triangle with a tragic ending, but the reality remains that eight ghosts haunt the Forepaugh Restaurant, and Joseph Forepaugh and John Hammond were individuals who have remarkable histories, whose achievements helped shape not just Midwestern history, but the history of the United States.

What has also gone unrecognized in this chapter, despite what some religious teachings would lead us to believe, is that those who have committed suicide are not damned in spirit to an eternal life in hell. They are present in spirit and appear happy and ready to be engaged with. This has been my experience from years of psychic work with clients who wished to have closure by contacting those close to them who had taken their own lives.

The team felt honored and privileged to be the first to investigate this wonderful property, and my hope is that Joseph might receive some peace from the false accusations he has endured in spirit, as he himself requested for me to write. He must have felt a great frustration at not being able to voice his own side of the story. This may even account for the ghostly disturbances on the property, as he looked to gain the attention of the living. This investigation goes to prove the old adage wrong when people say, *he took it to the grave with him*—because we now know that it *can* be retrieved.

THE LUND-HOEL HOUSE

CANBY, MINNESOTA

Does a matriarchal ghost still oversee the running
of the Lund-Hoel House?

My investigation in Canby started at the Christie House in Long Prairie. I had arranged an evening of fund raising for the property, and tickets were sold for a ghostly candlelight tour. Jan is the president of the Lund-Hoel House and attended the tour. She heard me talk enthusiastically about my work and was interested in arranging similar events in Canby by investigating the house and the local theater.

I assembled a large team of experienced investigators and traveled into the west of Minnesota with our mobile command center. The organizing of these investigations came together in the quickest time, a rare occurrence in my experience.

Jan presented me with a documented history of the Lund-Hoel House, which I supplemented with online research. I also interviewed several local residents and staff. Canby was a very welcoming town, and the word soon spread of our arrival.

History

A post office was organized in Canby as early as 1874, which was platted just two years later. Like most small Midwestern towns, its existence was due to the expansion of the railroad. The settlement was named after Edward Canby who was a general in the United States Army.

John Grant Lund was born on June 23, 1868 and was brought to Canby by his parents when he was eight years old. They arrived from Rushford, Minnesota in 1876 to open a general store. John married Flora Miller at the age of twenty in 1888 and started a real estate business in the same year. The *Canby News* highlighted his impressive business acumen in an article from August 18, 1893:

> He has sold a very great many farms during the time he has engaged in business and has probably done more to bring in actual settlers than any other firm or agency in Minnesota or the Dakotas.[27]

The Lund Land Agency was located in a double stone building on St. Olaf Avenue. It proved to be a very successful venture and sold over 60,000 acres of land in 1889. Agencies were then established in Watertown, Iroquois, Goodwin, and Henry in South Dakota, Jamestown in North Dakota, and Northwood in Iowa.

In 1891 he built a house on a lot that covered more than half a block in only forty-nine days. Further additions were then added until 1900, including a surrounding stone wall, servant's quarters, balconies, porches, and a turret. This extravagant home also boasted a gas plant in order to illuminate the rooms. As the new building work developed, a lack of continuity evolved. This is best shown by the eccentric sight of seeing a door positioned directly above another door in the second floor hallway.

Lund expanded his business interests further when he was appointed president of the local bank. He was then made the town's mayor from 1898 to 1900, winning with a landslide victory. In 1903 the Lunds sold their home to John's sister Mary and her husband Reverend Olaf Hoel for $10,000. Canby historians believe the money was raised by Mary's family. John and Flora then moved to Minneapolis where John was elected to the Minnesota House of Representatives where he served in the 1905-1906 term. Flora died in Minneapolis in 1907 with John passing the following year.

The home stayed in the Lund family until 1958, although no family members resided in the house after 1932. John's niece Nella then moved to Minneapolis and took most of the original furniture and family mementos with her. She subsequently leased the home to at least two separate families and eventually split the house into several apartments. Nella and her husband eventually sold the property to a couple who wanted to turn it into a care facility for the elderly. The sale closed on April 1, 1958.

The Lund-Hoel House has been maintained and administered since 1976 by the nonprofit Museum Encompassing Canby Community Area board. It is on the National Register of Historic Homes and is dependent upon the generosity of members, volunteers, and donations.

Investigation

On my first visit to Canby I was taken on a tour of the Lund-Hoel House so I could formulate my plans for the investigation. Jan told me that she had regularly heard voices coming from different parts of the house when no one was there. I had also spoken with the neighbors that lived in the house across from the library window. They had seen the drapes moving late at night, as if somebody was trying to peer through them. Once again the house was unoccupied during these occurrences.

The Lund-Hoel House

I was taken through what would have been the old library and into the ground floor bathroom. The room had an intricate, tessellated design of burnt terracotta and black decorative tiles inlaid on the floor. A square, upright, white porcelain sink and a claw-footed enameled bathtub filled the rest of the room. I then felt a familiar overwhelming sensation. There was a feeling in the air that weighed heavily on me with the resistance and thickness of energy. It was the electricity of knowing that another person was standing next to me—a dead person.

I opened myself psychically to the possibility of having contact with the deceased, and I asked for their name. In an instant a spirit said in a firm, clear female voice, "Jo." She proceeded to repeat the word "Jo" over and over. "It's Jo. My name is Jo… Jo," she continued. She wanted to make sure I knew who she was. I psychically believed this was a shortening of the word Joanne or Josephine; this would make perfect sense even without psychic help. I then walked out of the bathroom through the opposite door and found myself in the dining room.

Jan was open to the idea of ghosts and spirits residing in the house, and I told her fully of my experience. As I explained the details I became distracted by seeing Jo's head (in spirit) poking in and out of the bathroom to look at me. I didn't wish to appear rude, but it is very difficult to have a conversation and look that person in the eye, when over their right shoulder a ghostly head is darting back and forth. I arranged to come back with my team in the hope of finding out more about Jo and why she was there.

During the weeks leading up to the investigation, I began the process of researching Jo. I discovered that John Lund's mother was named Johanna Huseby Lund. Johanna was born in Norway at Gue Solor on March 9, 1835. She married Ove Nicholai Lund who was born in Saysborg, Norway, on April 21, 1825. I then accessed the census records and found she was living in Canby during the time her son was residing in the house. Her obituary informed me that she had died in Canby on June 24, 1898 at the age of sixty-three. I then confirmed that she had died in the house while staying with her family.

The Bathroom

The Lund-Hoel House bathroom had already provided me with paranormal activity, and I was eager to confirm Jo's identity. I began by sitting in the darkness with the dull glint of equipment dotted around the room. A static infrared camera recorded every captivating second. The tiled floor meant that each sound and whisper was amplified to jar the eerie stillness. I asked if Jo was present and if she would like to come through and speak to me. Straight away I heard the familiar words of her name spoken to me psychically, as I had previously experienced.

"Jo," she said once again.

I greeted her and explained who I was and why I was there. I asked her psychically if her full name was Johanna.

"Yes," she replied.

I asked her where she thought she was.

"The kitchen," came her response.

I had suspected that this area was not always a bathroom, and I believed this location to be the kitchen in the original plans and construction. There are many theories that link the presence of flowing water to the manifestation of ghosts, but on this occasion it would be more in keeping with the traditions of the period to find the woman of the household in the kitchen, the hub of the entire building.

Johanna Huseby Lund c1890

I then asked how long it took her to travel to Canby from where she was living. I did not receive a definitive number, but I felt the tiring empathy of a protracted journey involving several forms of transport, perhaps a carriage and a train. She almost cursed under her breath at the thought of traveling.

I enquired what she thought of all the people coming through the house, with almost daily visits. She responded by acknowledging that she liked the people admiring the house and the comments they made about the furniture. Still, I had an underlying feeling that she didn't quite have an understanding of why they were there and why they kept coming through the kitchen with such regularity.

During my contact with Jo I felt tight across my chest and experienced an uncomfortable shortness of breath that led to coughing. I wondered if the residual energy of her last few months in this house were creeping through. I asked her what made her ill. She responded by telling me it was the "night air." Night air was believed to be poisonous during the late eighteenth and early nineteenth centuries. It was believed that stepping out into the night and breathing the air would cause you to become sick and possibly die. Such was the persistent belief in this theory that all the windows and doors in households across the country were securely closed during this era as soon as the sun went down.

This myth was perpetrated by the misconception that smelling decaying organic matter caused disease. This idea was eventually replaced by germ theory. The smell from overcrowded graveyards in many large cities, unable to cope with population growth brought by the industrial revolution and new transportation links, was thought to cause cholera. This was called the miasma theory. Smells from swamps and graveyards seemed to be more prevalent at night.

The American educator Catherine Beecher and her sister, Harriet Beecher Stowe (author of *Uncle Tom's Cabin*), promoted this belief in their 1869 housekeeping guide *The American Woman's Home*:

Thus it appears, that the atmosphere of the day is much more healthful than that of the night, especially out of doors.

Experiments seem to prove that other matter thrown out of the body, through the lungs and skin, is as truly excrement and in a state of decay as that ejected from the bowels, and as poisonous to the animal system.[28]

Peter Baldwin, in his 2003 essay *How Night Air Became Good*, recounted a story from John Adam's (1735-1826) autobiography that described Adams travelling with Benjamin Franklin in 1776. The two men had to share a room together in a crowded inn. Adams claimed he was afraid of the air at night and closed the window. Franklin then demanded that he reopen the window and proceeded to lecture him on why he was such a jackass.

The superstition of the air turning poisonous when the sun went down was probably encouraged further by the necessity in the bitterly cold Midwest winters to hermetically seal homes. This convention was also in place for the south due to the hordes of insects that at night would be looking to feast on human blood.

More recently, science has suggested that a link between smells and paranormal activity actually exists. A study by Clarkson University in New York has shown that haunting experiences in a room or building can be connected to air quality. They have found a correlation between exposure to toxic mold microbiomes and the experiencing of paranormal activity induced through mental or neurological symptoms. It is well known that some fungi, like rye ergot fungus, can also cause psychosis in humans. It is worth remembering that reported hauntings have stereotypically appeared in older structures, like disused factories, old hotels, cemeteries, castles, and creepy basements... all containing poor air quality.

I wanted to achieve the verification of my psychic work via the equipment, so I turned on the ghost box and started to ask the same questions.

"What room are we currently in?" I asked.

The word "kitchen" was uttered four times in a female voice in quick succession, in the same way I had heard the name Jo presented to me. Everyone on the vigil heard the clear response. I followed this by asking how many days it had taken to travel here from her own home. Once again the ghost box responded perfectly to my question by clearly stating the number "Ten." Previously I had only received a sense of how long the journey had taken; this time I had received a definitive answer.

I accessed an online map on my cell phone after this vigil to ascertain the distance between Rushford (where Johanna had lived) and Canby. With modern roads and infrastructures, the distance between the two was just over three hundred miles. It would not be unreasonable during her era to cover around thirty miles a day by using a horse and carriage. Thus the simplest of math would suggest that this journey did take ten days as Johanna had stated.

I continued to interview Johanna. I wanted to know what era she thought it was, due to her belief that we were in the kitchen and not in the bathroom. I asked who she thought the current president was, and again the ghost box clearly delivered a definitive response when she said the name "Taft." It was once more spoken quickly in a multiple of three, as if to clarify the answer, "Taft... Taft... Taft."

This was an interesting development, as I recalled that President Taft only served a single term in office from 1910-14. So President Taft would have started his tenure twelve years after Johanna died. This meant that Johanna had an awareness of events in the physical realm after she had passed, but only up to a point when that knowledge and sentience strangely stopped; otherwise she would have mentioned a more contemporary president. Perhaps she had chosen to stay within a timeframe she felt happiest in, creating a reality around herself that allowed her to access the house and how it looked when she was alive. I wanted to see if this theory was possible, so I then asked her if the house looked like it did when she was alive. The ghost box replied "Yes."

As I have said, I have often wondered about the effects of energy dissipating over time. This would make sense if one were to embrace the reasonable idea that ghosts and spirits require energy to move things around and to be physical. It is known that high levels of EMF are recorded during contact. Was it possible that Jo's inability to have a further awareness of the house and current affairs past this timeframe was linked to a slow dissipation of energy?

It would make sense that Jo would want to remain in the house in spirit after her passing to keep an eye on her family and grandchildren. Jo had provided a very interesting set of circumstances and in more depth and detail than the usual pleasantries and surface responses that one often hears during such sessions.

Conclusion

The investigation at the Lund-Hoel House stands out for me in many ways. I want to prove through my work and writing that beyond all reasonable doubt an afterlife exists. I believe this was achieved when one considers the responses and interactions I had with Johanna. I had no previous knowledge of who this lady was when I first entered the property and made contact with her. I then corroborated the psychic information by recording the same audible responses via my equipment. I was then required to research deeply into historical archives to ascertain her identity, which then also proved to be successful. This is verifiable evidence through three separate sources.

We gained a glimpse of what it might be like to be in spirit as Johanna presented a knowledge and sentience of current affairs beyond her passing, suggesting that we can still see and access the physical world and continue to gain knowledge after death. I believe Johanna feels a responsibility or obligation to the family home as the strong matriarchal figure to oversee the property and how it is run. I believe based on the work and dedication of Jan, the board, the volunteers, and the citizens of Canby, she can have no complaints.

THE CANBY THEATER

CANBY, MINNESOTA

Where the spirit of a previous owner still wants a say in how the theater is run.

I was introduced to Mike, the manager of the Canby Theater, by Jan from the Lund-Hoel House. The theater had been closed for many years but was now being renovated back to its former glory by a dedicated, nonprofit board of volunteers. This restoration period created an ideal window of opportunity for my team, as we would not be interfering with the running of the theater, and refurbishment disturbances are often a catalyst for paranormal activity.

Mike had been involved with the theater for many years and had an extensive knowledge of the building's history. He also provided me with historical documentation. I supplemented this information with online research.

History

The first soil was broken for the theater by the local highway contractor J. J. Govercki. Canby hardware store owner Gordon Victor then began the construction from the architectural plans of Mr. Crosier. The building was then completed by the Swedberg Brothers of Wheaton in 1937 and called the New Canby Theater, as other theaters had previously occupied various sites around the town. It stood resplendently in blond brick and had a seating capacity of six hundred. A swamp cooler was then installed that accessed the underground well, keeping the auditorium filled with wet cold air.

The Canby Theater 1939

Finishing touches were then placed on the interior under the supervision of Minneapolis designer and decorator Otto Nielsen. Swanky, post-modernistic decorations were added to the lounge with late Art Deco influences. This area allowed sharply dressed individuals to enjoy their pre-screening drinks, with ladies sporting bright red lipstick discussing the latest fashions and town gossip. All sat comfortably in low, square, modernist couches, next to elegant, narrow floor lamps.

The cinema also benefitted from a small soundproof booth that was located towards the back of the balcony, called a *cry room*, for those nursing children. It had a glass window and an accompanying speaker, allowing distraught parents to retire from the auditorium without missing the film. The theater then added a second screen to the basement in 1982.

The Canby Theater photographed during the Second World War

Investigation

Mike firmly believed that the theater was haunted and recounted several tales from his experiences of the last twenty years. On one occasion he was in the lobby alone when the lid of a flip-top garbage can began to rattle, swinging back and forth. This action was then repeated on a second garbage can that was positioned on the other side of the concessions counter. Back and forth the interaction went until this action was punctuated by the sound of a child's maniacal laughter. Mike left the building with some alacrity and only came back later when accompanied to lock up. But this was not the only incident to chill his blood. One evening after a film had finished he was walking between the rows of seating using a leaf blower (a common device used in theaters to push the litter towards the front of the auditorium in order to collect it quicker). He was then surprised and shocked to feel the cold breath of a spirit on his face. He said that after his initial walkthrough several weeks previously, the theater's auditorium lighting had malfunctioned. The lights had flashed on and off for no apparent reason and could not be stopped. It was difficult to provide a reasonable explanation for this event.

During my baseline tests of the theater it became noticeable how much EMF energy was emanating throughout the building.

Almost every wall, pipe, and fixture appeared to be generating significant electromagnetic fields. I wondered if the old copper water piping was being used to ground the electrical currents in the building. Any prolonged length of time spent in this location resulted in receiving a debilitating headache and nausea. The current renovation work should resolve many of these issues.

This did however allow for the possibility of ghosts and spirits to access the energy in order to manifest themselves. It may be that one location is not more haunted than any other, but may have the right environmental parameters to make us more aware of the paranormal activity. Naturally occurring EMF, the presence of water or dampness, and the right air pressure, would all have to be considered. There is certainly a good argument to suggest that the basement of the Canby Theater was fulfilling those criteria. I have found damp atmospheres to be very conducive to paranormal activity, and you could argue that electromagnetic fields operate better in those environments, especially when we acknowledge that paranormal activity appears more prevalent in graveyards, castles, and basements.

Armed with the knowledge the walkthrough and baseline tests had provided, I positioned the team in the furnace room under the lobby. Mike said he was always reluctant to venture into this area during his duties. He had often felt a sense of foreboding and energy there and our equipment verified this. I started the vigil and stood at the back of the room looking towards the open door and the corridor beyond. The smallest amount of light was noticeable bleeding from the left-hand side of the corridor, as a faint illumination bounced down the stairs from the lobby and crept along the floor. It was just the merest hint of a glow that allowed me to see the dim outline of the K2 meter that I had positioned on the floor outside the open door.

Ten minutes into the vigil I startled to see a break in the weak glow that seeped into the blackout, a momentary flicker of a shadow. I believed this to be a figure walking along the corridor towards us out of sight, a phenomenon witnessed by all members of the team. We sat in anticipation wondering who or what might present itself by coming around the corner at any minute. Suddenly the K2 meter lit up from its neutral position. Whatever walked down the corridor was now standing in the doorway and looking directly at us. The K2 meter started to dance with an array of green and amber lights that blinked and flashed in front of us. I asked the entity to continue to illuminate the lights if it was male. The reading remained constant. After a minute I asked the spirit to keep the lights flashing if it was female. The lights stopped and I felt a coldness enter the room. The spirit had now joined us, leaving the readings it had registered on the K2 meter behind. I believed this action signified a male presence.

As the room flooded with an icy chill I turned on the ghost box and the familiar popping of looped scanning crackled into the frosty EMF-infused air.

"Thank you for joining us," I said. "Did you work here?"

"No," was the reply in a very quick and firm manner.

"Were you born in Canby?" I enquired further.

"No," was the response once more.

I considered his replies and deduced that he might be the spirit of a person who had built or owned the theater, so I jumped to the following question.

"Did you own or build the theater?"

"Yes," the spirit answered—my psychic hunch had proved to be correct.

"What is your name?" I enquired.

"Bill," he retorted in a loud and clear voice that was heard by all.

"Do you prefer Bill or William?" I asked further.

"William," he responded.

This was a vital piece of evidence as one could argue that a series of "yes" or "no" responses could be random. Yet here was a definitive answer to the question, "do you prefer being called Bill or William?" to which there are only two possible answers—and I had received one of them.

"Do you like how the restorations are going?" I continued.

"Yes!"

"Is there anything you would like to mention or bring up in terms of how the theater should be run?" I asked.

"Seven," was his mysterious response.

I did not understand this reply, but I made a note of his answer.

"Is there anything else you would like to say?" I asked, to allow William to add anything to the conversation.

"No, thank you," he said.

This seemed like a good time to end the dialogue and I thanked him for his time and input.

When the teams reunited back in the lobby, I told Mike about the conversation that had taken place in the furnace room. I asked him if the response of seven had any significance for him. Mike proceeded to tell me that the board of the Canby Theater had met just days previously and discussed how much they should charge for admission when they reopened. They had settled on the sum of seven dollars. This would suggest that William had an awareness of those discussions and was in fact giving his approval to their decision.

Mike then informed me that one of the two brothers that built the theater was called William Flieder. The census record for 1940 lists William as being born in Minnesota on July 24, 1895. During this time, he was residing on Oscar Avenue in Canby with his wife Edna, thirteen years his junior. He died on February 1, 1983 at the age of 87.

Conclusion

It was remarkable to think that William had an awareness of how the theater was being run and still wanted a say in those affairs thirty-three years after his passing. I suspect his spirit was present during the board meetings and I would encourage the members to leave a chair out for him. What is abundantly clear is that both Johanna from the Lund-Hoel House and William appear to be happy with the legacy both buildings are achieving, and both spirits are proud to witness this evolution. I believe our humanity requires us to help those in spirit as much as those in the physical realm. It could now be suggested that those in spirit also feel a duty to oversee and help us *on earth as it is in heaven.*

THE SS METEOR

SUPERIOR, WISCONSIN

Does a ghost crew haunt the hull of the only remaining whaleback freighter?

The SS *Meteor* did not have a history of documented hauntings, but the energy from repetitive manual labor over a prolonged period of time in confined and exacting conditions with moments of fear and worry should have left a residual energy in every rivet, bolt, hand-rail, and square inch of sheet metal.

Team leader Scott resides in Superior and made the necessary arrangements for the team to investigate this last remaining whale-back cargo freighter. Mikhael was our guide and kindly gave the team an informative and knowledgeable tour, allowing us to access every part of the vessel. He provided me with an extensive history of the ship that I supplemented with my own online historical research and handwritten notes I had taken from the information provided by the ship's museum.

History

The SS *Meteor* was designed by Captain Alexander McDougall and was built in Superior, Wisconsin at a cost of $181,573 in 1896. It was called a whaleback freighter due to its innovative tubular steel hull, which floated low in the water. The *Meteor* weighed 5,200 tons and was 380 feet long with a depth of 26 feet. It was also one of the first ships on the Great Lakes to have its accommodations aft, with only a small room for the anchor windlass at the bow. She was originally called the *Frank Rockefeller* and was used to move iron ore from Lake Superior to the steel mills of Lake Erie. She was then laden with coal for the return journey. Throughout her service she carried a variety of other cargos including grain, sand, gravel, cars, gasoline, and oil.

The ship was involved in many maritime incidents throughout her career. At Isle Royale, on November 2, 1905, the ship became lost during a thick snow storm and she was grounded. The majority of the damage came from the barge she was towing that crashed into the stern of the now stationary ship. In 1942 she was wrecked at Manistique and would have been scrapped if not for the increased demand for tonnage during the Second World War. Then in 1969 she ran aground once more on Gull Island Shoal at Marquette, Michigan. It was decided not to repair the aging steamer's single hull due to the extent of the damage. So in 1972 the last remaining whaleback freighter was finally brought back to Barker's Island, Superior and converted into a museum ship.

The SS Meteor

Investigation

The monolithic vessel loomed large against the threatening slate grey sky on a wet evening in May. The drizzle-infused wind would make this a difficult and dangerous location to investigate. All manner of mishaps and accidents were awaiting to befall those who were less than vigilant. A curved slippery deck, rusting distressed walkways, low pipework, and treacherously steep wet ladders all had to be traversed with care.

My team started in the boiler room. This was a giant, cold, cave-like vastness that dripped water into the echoing darkness. We sat at the bottom of this cigar tube in a pit littered with the detritus of rust, peeling paint, and a prismatic slick of oil. It had no redeeming features and was only marginally better than when the stokers were shoveling lung-clogging coal into the searing open furnaces where temperatures could reach 130 degrees. This area of the ship had seen the least amount of change, and it still housed its original triple expansion steam engine, capable of generating 1195 horsepower at 75 rpm for a speed of 12 knots.

We started the vigil and noted that every small noise was distorted to loud reverberating proportions. The slightest innocuous movement of the second investigation team on the upper deck sent down exaggerated bellowing base notes like a badly dented tuba. I could also hear the ship's cables distantly groaning and shuddering in the wind. The inky darkness rendered vision redundant and senses heightened.

I heard several footsteps walking between Scott and me. We sat no more than eight feet apart, both facing the giant, awe-inspiring steam boilers. This was followed by scuffling sounds. I believed that an entity was circling us in observation. I tried my best in difficult conditions to psychically focus. I managed to receive a two-syllable word that ended in *"boy"*, like *tallboy*—but it was hard to make out. I believed this to be a name, and I wondered if it belonged to the individual who was now with us. I turned on the ghost box.

"Is anyone down here?" I asked, as we continued to hear footsteps.

"Run!" someone shouted in a male voice.

"What's your name?" I enquired. I then heard a faint murmur.

"Say that again." I responded.

"I can't." His tone was very somber and sad.

"How old are you?"

"Twenty," he said.

"You sound unhappy. Why are you unhappy?"

"I don't know," he replied. Then we could hear what sounded like crying coming through the equipment.

"Are you unhappy?" I asked.

"Yeah," we now heard in a female voice.

"Why are you unhappy?" I continued.

"I am dead!" she said. Then we heard more crying and sobbing coming through the ghost box.

"Why are you here?" I enquired.

"That is what we do. We are all dead," was her response.

"So how many of you are down here?"

"Seven!" she said.

"Do you work here?" I continued.

"Mate, mate, I'm a mate," came the male voice again.

A mate is a deck officer aboard a merchant vessel, such as the chief mate (first mate), second mate, or third mate. One of the mates is always the watch-keeping officer unless the master takes that responsibility. Each mate also has other duties including making the passage planning, overseeing the loading and unloading of the ship, and personnel management.

"I'm dead!" the woman randomly responded once more, followed by "Adrian!"

"Yes, you have my attention, what would you like to say?"

"Run away!" came the reply, and she continued by contradictorily saying, "We are not dead!"

From a biblical perspective spirits are not dead. The Bible tells us in forty-six separate places that when we enter the spiritual realm we will have eternal life in God's embrace. It tells us further that the punishment for going to hell is having your spirit destroyed. So those who are not in hell are alive eternally in spirit. We would certainly not be able to engage in this present dialogue if the individuals we were talking to were dead in spirit.

"So do you have a message for me?" I asked.

"Get out, get out, get out!" was her brisk reply.

"Why do you want me to get out?" I enquired.

"It's dangerous!" she said.

I was not about to disagree; this was a heavily industrialized area and distressed in every aspect. This would also have been a very dangerous vocation for the crew members. The history of deaths and shipwrecks on the Great Lakes is well documented.

I wanted to increase the strength of our evidence by receiving the same information through a second piece of equipment. I asked Scott to continue the conversation with the P-SB7. He began scanning at 250 MHz in a reverse sweep on the FM waveband.

"Are there seven of you here?" he asked, to confirm the facts we had already received.

"Yes," came the same answer I had obtained earlier.

"Do you like us being down here?" Scott continued.

"Get out... go!" Once more the response corroborated our previous answers but now through a second device.

"Do you want us to leave?"

"Yes, get out!" it persisted.

"Can you see us?" Scott enquired.

"No," she responded.

I did not know whether her lack of being able to see my team was due to the ways different dimensions overlap, or because it was so dark.

The device then shouted out a series of words in a female voice that sounded like the woman's name Elena or Helena. It repeated this several times and was difficult to make out, but I assumed this to be the name of the female spirit with whom we were engaging.

"Are you an officer's wife?" I questioned.

"Yes," came her reply.

"Is your husband with you?" I asked.

"Yes, he is dead!" she responded.

Captains and officers were allowed to bring their wives and families with them if they so wished. Many of the traditions surrounding the unlucky omen of having women onboard were not reflected on the Great Lakes. The vigil was now drawing to a close, and I asked if there was anything they wanted to tell me.

"Help me!" was the chilling reply.

"Go!" was then shouted out, now in a male voice. This was obviously a series of conflicting requests, with the man asking us to leave and the woman asking for help.

"What help do you need?" I continued.

"I want to go home," she said.

"Leave us alone!" was then interjected, as the male voice once again interrupted and contradicted the woman. I wondered if they were married.

I then spoke directly to the woman and explained that it should be possible for her to *think* herself wherever she wanted to be. I told her that she did not have to feel a sense of duty to the ship, as it was now safe and used as a museum. I continued to tell her that she did not need to feel imprisoned by a loyalty to any other individual who she felt was perhaps keeping her there against her will. I continued to say that she had a right to be happy—even in spirit. I added that she could use any of the power in our batteries and equipment if that helped her to go where she needed to go. I asked if she had a final message for me.

"Adrian… yes," she replied.

"What?" I enquired.

"Thank you!" she said. I finished the vigil.

The Crew's Quarters

Heather's team was investigating the crew's quarters and the mess area during my vigil in the boiler room. Heather was in the process of setting up the equipment when a voice suddenly said, "Heather... erm!" Heather turned to Caroline and asked what she had said. Caroline replied that no one had said anything! Heather then used her DVR in real time with her earbuds and heard two very distinct moans coming from a disembodied voice.

The crew's quarters

Heather started the vigil, and her team instantly witnessed poltergeist activity. The flashlight trigger object rolled across the floor on its own, and then a food storage cupboard in the galley flew open by itself. Heather said that the voice of a woman had come through on the ghost box and said "Hello," followed by the word "Ghosts." I wondered if in these moments the female spirit whom I had made contact with in the boiler room was traveling between decks.

The Captain's Cabin

Based on the information Heather had shared with me, we decided the crew's quarters were worthy of a second vigil, so we extended the team into the captain's cabin and the officers' sleeping quarters. I positioned myself on the guest bunk in the captain's sleeping area opposite his own personal bathroom. Despite being the captain's quarters, this area was still an example of function over form. Necessity over comfort was the design brief here. It looked uninviting with its white, cold, metal walls and sparse furnishings.

The captain's quarters dated from 1942 and had a separate office. This was where the captain checked logs, prepared paperwork, and organized paychecks. There was also an alarm that could be activated from the pilot house to alert the captain of emergencies. To my left was a porthole, and I could clearly see the lights of Superior and Duluth dancing on the rippling water under the night sky. The officers' quarters were also added in 1942. Before this the crew was accommodated in mixed ranks. Limited sleeping quarters were also found under the windlass machinery at the front of the ship. Labels above each door delineated the living quarters by rank and responsibility.

As we settled into the quietness of the vigil, Scott heard a sigh close to where he was sitting in the corridor. Minutes later Kris, who was listening through his headphones on his DVR in the captain's office, heard a male voice suddenly say, "Hello, Scott!" Scott then started a dialogue as the spirit had acknowledged him.

"Did you know me before tonight?" Scott enquired.

"No," came the response.

Then without warning the flashlight Scott had placed in the corridor of the officers' quarters came on and pierced the blackness with a blinding beam. This startled the team as the whole location jumped violently in contrast from dark to light. The flashlight blinked and strobed in a regimented fashion for several minutes. The team agreed that it looked like somebody trying to communicate via Morse code. Our skillset is great and expansive but it does not cover a working knowledge of Morse code, so we continued with the vigil.

Greg now noted with his thermal imaging camera that a transient, colder mass was moving around us. It was at least four degrees colder than the ambient interior temperature. It passed across the floor and up the walls. Scott confirmed this by following Greg's guidance in tracking the anomaly with a laser thermometer. This device also registered a colder temperature than the surroundings. I then turned on the ghost box in order to communicate with whatever was there. The first words out of this device came through loud and clear—"Get Out!"

"Who wants us to get out?" I asked.

"First mate, first mate," he responded twice in a male voice. This was the entity that I had spoken with in the boiler room.

"Two Harbors," he then said.

"What is that?" I asked.

"Lakes," he said.

Two Harbors is a location just twenty-seven miles northeast of Duluth on the Minnesota shore of Lake Superior.

"Were there shipping incidents at Two Harbors?" I enquired.

"Yes," came the reply.

"Did you run into difficulties?" I continued.

"Yes," he said.

"Before or after you worked on this ship?"

"Before," he replied.

"Did anyone die in those incidents?" I asked.

"Definitely!" he said.

"So to confirm, at least one person died?" I continued.

"Yes!"

No more contact or dialogue was forthcoming despite further questioning. The spirits had either grown tired of our probing or were unable to respond due to a lack of energy or unknown aspect.

After I reviewed the paranormal evidence we had gathered in both the boiler room and the crew's quarters, I realized I had a long road ahead of me in terms of historical research. I decided to start by looking into the wrecks that were located around the area of Two Harbors on Lake Superior, as one of the spirits had clearly said, "Two Harbors" and "lakes." I found many shipwrecks in this location but one stood out for me—it was called the Amboy. I recalled that psychically at the very beginning of our first vigil in the boiler room I was given a two-syllable word ending in *boy* that I believed to be a name.

The *Amboy* was a single-decked, wooden-hulled, full-rigged, three-mast schooner-barge designed by Quayle and Murphy of Cleveland, Ohio in 1874 for the Cleveland Transporting Company. She was 205 feet long and carried 1,500 tons of cargo for the Ohio and Michigan iron ore trade. I investigated the *Amboy* further and was astonished to discover that she was originally called the *Helena*. This was a name that had come through several times on the ghost box during the same vigil when I thought the spirit was trying to say Elena or Helena. I then wanted to historically research whether she had run into difficulties in the Two Harbors area and if this was before the *Meteor*, as suggested by our spirit conversation.

Further research suggested that the *Helena* was cursed, as tragic incidents and accidents appeared to follow one after another. On September 14, 1882 the *Helena* veered off course and sunk the Canadian steamer *Asia* in the St. Mary's River at Georgian Bay, Ontario. The *Helena* only received minor damage, but she caused the *Asia* to sink with the loss of one hundred lives. A report in *The Dominion Annual Register and Review* of 1882 gives the verdict of the jury in an inquest held in Collingwood, Ontario, on September 20:

> That the deceased came to their death through the wreck of the steamer Asia and undue exposure in open boats and nothing with which to bail out the boats; that the aforesaid insufficient equipment was the result of gross and culpable negligence on the part of some person or persons unknown to this jury, and that those persons are therefore guilty of manslaughter.[29]

Then in July 1891 the *Helena* was struck and sunk by a steel steamer called the *Mariska* in the same location. She went down fully laden with coal in thirty feet of water. The *Helena* was then raised two weeks later and removed to Milwaukee for extensive repairs. An article written in the *Milwaukee Sentinel* of September 18, 1891 highlights her plight:

Underwriters decided to accept the wrecked barge *Helena* as a total loss and she will be sold to the highest bidder as she lies at the shipyard.[30]

The highest bidder was the Milwaukee Tug Boat Company which renamed her the *Amboy*. Then in 1899 she was sold once more to the Tonawanda Iron & Steel Company of North Tonawanda, New York. She was employed to sail between Two Harbors, Ashland, Duluth, and the steel mills of Tonawanda, towed by a larger wooden steamer called the *George Spencer*. Tragedy struck for a final time when the two ships were bound for Duluth on the night of November 28, 1905, in what was to be known as the Mataafa Storm. Twenty-nine other ships were lost or disabled in the storm with the loss of thirty-six lives on Lake Superior alone. The *Duluth Evening Herald* of December 1, 1905 describes the night the *Amboy* and *George Spencer* hit the rocks:

> Both boats lost their bearings in the snowstorm and landed on a sandy beach. As soon as they struck, buoys with lines were thrown over the side. When they floated ashore they were caught by fishermen and made fast. With an improvised life buoy rigged in the hawsers the entire crew were taken safely to shore preceded by Mrs. Harry Lawe, wife of the mate, who was acting as steward. The vessels ran on the rocks Tuesday morning, and for thirteen hours the situation of the crew on the battered hulks was desperate. Fishermen rushed into the surf almost to their necks and aided the sailors to escape. The Spencer's cargo can be lightered but there is little hope for saving the boat. The vessels were coming up without cargo to load ore. Capt. Frank Conland sailed the Spencer and Fred Watson was master of the Amboy. The Spencer was valued at $35,000 and the Amboy at $10,000.[31]

The *Duluth News Tribune* of December 6, 1905 stated that:

> Captain C. O. Flynn returned last evening from an
> inspection of the stranded steamer George Spencer
> and schooner Amboy. He said the schooner Amboy
> is a total wreck... the steamer Spencer is still in good
> shape. Her hatches are intact, and she does not ap-
> pear to be seriously damaged. As to the condition of
> her bottom that cannot be told at present.[32]

What I instantly recognized from this historical documentation
was that the ship had sunk near Two Harbors, as the spirits had informed me. I was then intrigued to read that Mrs. Lawe was a stew-
ard on the ship that night and was the wife of the first mate—the two
spirits in the *Meteor* said they were married, and he informed me he
was the first mate. They also told me the two names given to the ship
that sank that night, the *Helena* and the *Amboy*. Although I did not
know this at the time, I now believe the husband and wife team that
haunts the *Meteor* to be Mr. and Mrs. Lawe.

Mr. and Mrs. Lawe would certainly be coming through in spirit
if they felt a duty and a responsibility in the afterlife for the sinking
of the *Amboy* and the *George Spencer*. It was incumbent upon the
first mate to be the officer of the watch. He would have been responsible for the positioning of the ships in relation to each other and the
shore. We were also informed by the Lawes that many lives were
lost on Lake Superior that night—thirty-six were recorded. They
may still feel they need to warn people to evacuate the ship before
it is too late.

I then wondered why they would haunt the *Meteor* when the
ship that sunk was the *Amboy*. I considered that the wreck of the
Amboy was less than thirty nautical miles away from the *Meteor*
and the Lawes would have lived in the surrounding area. As the
last remaining vessel of its type they would have remembered from
their own lifetime, it makes sense they would haunt it. You can only
think you want to be somewhere in spirit if you know and remember
where it is you want to be. I would not be able to haunt a property I

have never visited or had no knowledge of in my lifetime, as I would have no memory of it to be able to place myself there.

I also recalled that the Lawes told me they had worked on the *Meteor* sometime after the *Amboy* sank. So this could also account for their presence. The *Meteor* ran into difficulties in 1905, so their pleas for help and forceful directions to leave the ship due to the danger could actually apply to both the *Amboy* and the *Meteor*.

Conclusion

In 2001, numerous organizations, including the Great Lakes Shipwreck Preservation Society, the Wisconsin Underwater Archeology Association, the Lake Superior Maritime Museum Association, and the Superior Public Museums started the SS *Meteor* Preservation and Stabilization Project, due to the ship's decay compounded by the harsh weather conditions. The *Meteor* was also listed by the Wisconsin Trust for Historical Preservation as one of the most endangered historical properties in Wisconsin. The wreck was listed in 1994 on the National Register of Historic Places.

I hope I can implement a follow-up investigation to verify my thoughts and to find out who the other spirits are, as the Lawes stated on several occasions that seven entities were present. The *Meteor* may not be a ghost ship, but it apparently has a ghost crew. It was also interesting to note that the Lawes seemed unsure as to whether they were dead or alive. It must be confusing when you spend your whole life knowing that you are going to die, only to then experience a life in spirit. Perhaps our definition of the word *dead* needs to be challenged, as this is not the finite ending many believe it to be. It is not a full stop; merely a semi-colon.

THE MASONIC TEMPLE

SUPERIOR, WISCONSIN

Does poltergeist activity reside in the secret and historic world of the freemasons?

I have investigated many Masonic temples in the past, including the historic lodge in Pipestone, Minnesota and the Old Sessions House in Clerkenwell, London—the center for the British Freemasons. They always bring a sense of awe, reverence, secrecy, ritual repetition, and the energy of collective thought. In my experience, these qualities are the perfect catalyst for paranormal activity. Masonic Temple #236 has been owned by the Elks Lodge since 1982 and has never been investigated.

The Masonic Temple, Superior, Wisconsin

There have been many strange events recorded in the building that could be described as paranormal. One staff member named Janet remembers a chilling incident where a glass slid out from a shelf vertically and smashed to the floor. It has also been noted that napkins would be pulled from their holders by themselves. Other staff members have found random pennies lying around the building, and the game machines were known to turn themselves on and off. I was also informed by a local dignitary of a tale she was told as a small girl that spoke of human bones buried at the front of the temple. Children would subsequently cross over the street and run past the building, terrified at the thought of seeing a ghost.

The staff of the Elks Lodge was open and accommodating and provided me with extensive historical information on both the building and the lodge. I supplemented this with online research and data supplied by the Douglas County Historical Society.

History

This grand structure was built in 1908 and is a dichotomy of architectural orders and styles. Its red sandstone façade entertains the harmony and symmetry of the Neo-Classical Greek order, with a triangular pediment supported impressively by four sturdy Corinthian columns detailed with finely carved capitals. The architrave has the chiseled words "Masonic Temple" displayed in large Roman serif letters. Long, curved, Queen Anne styled elongated windows stretch all the way down the walls to the balcony and complete the look. The interior now boasts a club with a dance floor, billiard room, large banquet hall, and a spectacular lodge room.

The Benevolent and Protective Order of Elks, often known as the Elks Lodge, or simply the Elks, is an American fraternal order and social club founded in 1868. It is one of the leading fraternal orders in America claiming nearly one million members. The Elks had modest beginnings as a social club for theatrical show performers called the *Jolly Corks*. It was established as a private club to elude the New York City laws governing the opening hours of public taverns.

The Elks originally borrowed a number of rituals, traditions, and regalia from the Freemasons. However, by the first decade of the twentieth century much of this had been abandoned as the Elks sought to establish their own identity. The original two degrees required for membership were consolidated into one degree in 1890, the apron was discontinued in 1895, the secret password was gone by 1899, and the badges and secret handshake were abandoned by 1904. Initiation and funeral rituals still exist but they are not considered to be secret. The initiation ceremony involves an altar with a Bible placed upon it with a chaplain leading the brethren in prayers and psalms. Another tradition of the order is the number of communal cemetery plots favored by the group. These are marked with impressive statuary.

Previous famous members of the Elks include: General Dwight D. Eisenhower, Franklin D. Roosevelt, Harry S. Truman, John F. Kennedy, Gerald R. Ford, Jack Benny, Clint Eastwood, Buster Keaton, Babe Ruth, and William F. Cody (Buffalo Bill). Also, in the novel *Babbitt* by Sinclair Lewis of Sauk Centre the main protagonist George Babbitt was an active member of the Elks.

The Lodge Room

I entered through the large, heavy, wooden double doors and penetrated the once secretive and ritualized environment of the Freemasons and Elks. This area looked like a cross between a courtroom and a throne room. The royal blue patterned carpet and deep brown, solid furniture, with dusty blue velvet upholstery, gave an air of authority, history, and heavy thinking. The central altar was lit from above and displayed a Bible and the sculpture of an Elk's head. An impressive balcony presented the whole auditorium with double rows of benched seating running around the walls and what looked like a throne at the opposite end on a raised floor. There was a lectern in front of the chair and a taxidermy Elk's head on the wall behind it. The antlers threw a long shadow that spread itself across the wall. Religious and unknown ceremonial regalia set throughout the room also caught my eye and piqued my interest.

We decided to start our first vigil in this most dominating and impressive room. We had brought with us a comprehensive array of equipment, and we spent the first hour setting up these devices and meters. We used the billiard room next door as a control area where we placed our equipment cases, batteries, and supplies. Scott then noticed that a K2 meter he had left in this area suddenly jumped to the highest reading whenever we returned to the control room to access equipment during the setting up stage. It would then dissipate back into its neutral setting as we left, suggesting that we were actually being followed around. During our evidence review, Scott discovered a perfect EVP from the DVR he was running during our whole time in the building. In the recording of the billiard room you can hear Scott say to Heather, "Something appears to be following us," and a loud, clear disembodied voice then asks, "Are you worried?"

Without realizing what he had recorded at the time, Scott went about the task of placing an infrared static camera on a podium pointing towards the throne-like seat. We also positioned two independent, infrared slave lights to illuminate the area, allowing the camera to record more detail in this dark, windowless environment. As the team began the first vigil, we were shocked to see one of the infrared lights leap off the podium onto the floor. We went to check and reposition the device. This was the first physical sign of paranormal activity, and our hopes were raised as we continued.

We were then treated to an epic light show as two flashlights left on the throne and altar suddenly turned on and off randomly, blinking, oscillating, and splitting the darkness with intermittent beams of illumination. The K2 meters we had placed around the room also joined in by tracking up and down like malfunctioning traffic lights. They ran from green to amber to red and back again, producing the kind of reading only reserved for fuse boxes and electric poles. The static meter was also displaying the presence of electrical energy and was weaving its lights back and forth in a rainbow array of colors. Due to this visual information I knew contact would be imminent.

Psychically, I started to see an older, greying gentleman who had a fatherly aura, a non-threatening paternal air of authority and leadership. Just then my focus was broken by a visible light anomaly that started to circle itself around a large desk in the far corner. Every team member saw the orb. Using the thermal imaging camera from his position on the balcony, Greg informed me that a considerable temperature drop had just occurred in this same area. I turned on the ghost box.

"Would you like to talk to me?" I asked.

"Thank you," a female voice said.

I was a little surprised that the man I saw psychically did not respond first.

"Are you married?" I enquired.

"Yes!" came through in the male voice. I assumed the two were together.

"So is that your wife with you?" I continued.

"Yes," said the woman this time.

"Thirty-two years," she continued.

"Were you married thirty-two years?" I asked.

"This week," came her reply.

I was informed by Janet, our guide, that the voice of the female spirit sounded like her late friend and former lodge member Nancy, who had recently joined her husband Don in spirit.

"Nancy, is that you?" I asked, based on this new information.

"Yes," she replied.

"Did you work here?" I continued.

"Yes," she responded once more.

I asked Janet what Nancy used to do and was informed she worked in the kitchen.

"Did you used to cook?"

"Yes, that was work," she said.

"Are you happy to talk to me?"

"Yes!" she replied.

"Are you together with Don?" I enquired.

"I'm happy!" she responded.

"Is there a message?"

"Friend, friend," she replied twice.

"Will you be part of my team?" I then asked, with the idea of having Nancy help me from beyond the veil to contact further spirits in the next vigil.

"Yes, sir!"

"Do you leave pennies around?" I continued, remembering the story Janet had told me about finding coins laying around in unusual places.

"Yes," came her response once more.

"Left around for the ladies to find?" I added.

"Yes, sir!" she said again.

"Do you need help with anything?" I asked.

"Nothing."

No more contact was made with Nancy or Don, despite our best efforts to coax a further dialogue. We finished the vigil.

After the investigation I searched for, and found, Don's obituary. Donald Seidlitz died at the age of seventy-eight and was a long-time Superior resident. He died on March 29, 2015 at St. Mary's Hospital in Duluth. He was born on December 24, 1936 in Cornell, Wisconsin. He graduated from Cornell High School in 1954 and joined the United States Army, serving his country until 1956. He then attended the University of Wisconsin in Eau Claire from 1956 to 1958, and then Madison from 1958 to 1960, earning a degree in economics. Don was employed by the Social Security Administration from 1960 to 1995 as a claims representative. Don was a member of the Elks Lodge for over thirty years, and there was a photograph of him accompanying the text. He was the gentleman I had seen psychically in the lodge room.

I was interested to read that Don had married Nancy in September 1979. So when Nancy told me their wedding anniversary was that week, and they had been married for thirty-two years, she must have thought in spirit it was September of 2011. Perhaps this was a period of their lives where they had fond memories, so they had chosen to be in spirit during that era.

Janet added that most of the paranormal activity she had experienced in the lodge had quieted down ever since Nancy had passed. She believed that Nancy was keeping the spirits in line from the other side, perhaps stifling their ability to be active in this location. Now the mysterious placing of pennies around the building was accounted for.

Basement

The basement had a mechanical room, a kitchen area, and a large banquet room that housed rows of tables and chairs with a fully stocked bar. Poltergeist activity had been observed in this area. We started by taking baseline readings in the mechanical room at the front of the building. We agreed that this was not the best environment for a vigil due to the noise and cramped conditions. This decision was reinforced by an EVP Scott recorded as we walked through this location that said, "I'm working here, there's nothing." In that brief sentence a spirit had suggested that he felt an obligation to continue laboring in this location. He did not want us to disturb his task.

We started the vigil in the banqueting and bar area when I was suddenly struck by a terrible headache, a sick nauseating feeling that left me on the verge of passing out. I kicked off my shoes and tried to ground myself quickly with a meditation exercise. I asked Janet if anything strange or bizarre had happened in the area in which I was sitting. She told me that a gentleman had died in that exact location. He had stood up as a guest speaker to give a speech at a bowling banquet and literally collapsed. I told Scott and Heather to continue with the vigil as I relocated to another part of the room. Within minutes I began to feel normal again. I had never experienced such a strong, painful, residual psychic energy before. It was an intriguing but painful experience.

Halfway through the vigil Heather said she could psychically hear the words "ka nee wana." She assumed this to be Native

American in origin and phonetically documented the phrase in her notebook. After the vigil we searched for the words using the Internet and discovered that "ka knee wana" meant "the alive ones" in Lakota Sioux. We thought that Heather may have been catching a brief moment of conversation between several Sioux Indians in spirit. We found historical research that described many settlements and Native American activity in the area. I wondered if any ancient skeletal remains were discovered during the original basement excavation, like at the St. James Hotel in Red Wing, Minnesota. It would also make sense that Native American Sioux spirits would refer to any members of my team as "the alive ones."

Conclusion

It would have once been unimaginable to have access to the inner sanctum and workings of the Freemasons and Elks Lodge. Yet as their changing policies and attitudes became more overt I was able to interact with their resident spirits. I found it remarkable to witness two deceased lodge members providing me with a wealth of researchable information, especially as they were also recognized by the staff and members of the lodge who had joined us. It was also unique to feel so much residual energy during the basement vigil, despite becoming unwell. How remarkable to have this sensation corroborated when we were told a death had occurred in that very space.

I was left to ponder the old children's tale that claimed bones were buried at the front of the building. Could there actually be some truth to the story that may have been forgotten over time, especially when considering the briefest of evidence that we had received in the Lakota Sioux language. It may of course have been a creepy bedtime story told to frighten Catholic children. The Catholic Church has historically criticized Freemasonry and banned church members from joining the organization as far back as 1738, as illustrated in the papal bull charter *In Eminenti Apostolatus*. It has continued to uphold this ban with the threat of excommunication as recently as Pope Benedict XVI (serving as Pope from 2005 to 2013), who wrote in a letter that those who enroll in Masonic associations are "in a grave sin and may not receive Holy Communion." Whether a true story or one used only to frighten children, I suspect the tale of the skeletal remains will remain a mystery.

FAIRLAWN MANSION

SUPERIOR, WISCONSIN

Many have wondered what kind of paranormal activity exists in Fairlawn. My team would now be the first to find out.

The investigation at Fairlawn is one of my own personal highlights of this book and my journey across the Midwest. Scott had worked diligently with the board members to allow us this unique opportunity since Fairlawn had never opened its doors to a paranormal team before, and we felt privileged to be given the opportunity.

Several Fairlawn board members and staff have experienced paranormal activity throughout this Victorian mansion, from the phenomenon of smelling cigar smoke coming from the card room next to the billiard room, to the experience of feeling followed. Legends exist surrounding the drowning of several children in the basement swimming pool and the presence of a restless murdered servant. Tragedy is also interwoven throughout the Pattison family history, losing two children from two separate sets of twins.

Accompanying us on our investigation were three knowledgeable board members who provided me with extensive historical information. I augmented this research through online sites, books, and the exhibits in the building.

Fairlawn Mansion, Superior, Wisconsin

History

This grand, forty-two-room, Queen Anne styled Victorian house was the family home for the lumber and mining baron Martin Pattison. It was constructed in 1891 from locally quarried Amnicon red sandstone and cost $150,000 to complete—a considerable sum of money at the end of the nineteenth century. Martin Pattison was born on January 17, 1841 in Ontario, Canada, and was first employed as a common laborer in the lumber business. In 1879 he married Grace E. Frink in Marquette, Michigan, and they had six children together. The Pattisons came to Wisconsin and settled in Superior where Martin established a logging business along the banks of the Black River. He then sold his interests and entered into the iron ore trade on the Vermillion Range, locating the famous Chandler and Pioneer mines. Pattison had also served the local community as three-time mayor and local sheriff. He died in his bed at Fairlawn in 1918.

With its ornate rooms and ostentatious furnishings, Fairlawn became a testament to the Pattison's success, financial position, and standing within the local community. Its most prominent feature is the four-story turret, complete with a widow's walk that overlooks the bay. In the summer, bedding gardens dot the expansive lawns with traditional flower varieties of peony, rose, hydrangea, and lily. It was during our walkthrough of these grounds that Gloria took several baseline photographs of the house using her thermal imaging camera. During the evidence review she noticed a humanoid outlined in shades of orange and yellow standing at the widow's walk behind the railings at the top of the turret. Every team member had looked up at the house and turret as those photographs were taken, and not one of us saw a figure. The widow's walk has been a local source of folklore, with many residents claiming to see a haunting spectral apparition looking out over the bay. Then during the interior walkthrough and baseline tests we discovered that access to the widow's walk area had been blocked and prohibited due to safety concerns. Only the team and our guides were present at this location for the investigation, and we were all standing outside looking back at the house and the widow's walk.

A ghostly figure captured by a thermal imaging camera in the top left corner of the widow's watch

After Martin Pattison died, the house was turned into a children's home. It remained a residence for orphaned and fostered children from 1920 to 1962, with forty-five to fifty children present at any given time. Over two thousand infants passed through its doors and a small supportive community has now evolved of ex-residents that reaches deep into the town of Superior. Grace moved to Los Angeles, California after Martin's passing and died in 1934.

Investigation

Every aspect and design of this building was considered in the finest detail. Even crescent shaped door handles were fitted to allow the servants to open the doors with their elbows when carrying linen or trays. The house was conceived with a hidden series of stairs and corridors for the domestic staff to use. They could then access each part of the house without being seen. Several board members had actually experienced an uneasy and uncomfortable sensation when traversing the servant's stairs that weave innocuously through the building. We were able to verify that this area was thick with EMF energy on our walkthrough.

Grace's Bedroom

I had brought a large team to Fairlawn on a stiflingly warm, sticky, late spring evening in the hope of covering as much ground as possible in this sprawling house. I decided to take my first team to Grace's bedroom, as Scott had photographed some unusual light anomalies in the mirror during the walkthrough.

As we started the evening, automobile traffic became instantly noticeable for its light and noise pollution. Every passing vehicle sent the flash of its headlight beams racing across the walls of the darkened bedroom, and the engine sounds soiled my audio recordings. I positioned myself so I could see the mirror and fireplace opposite, with a line of sight into two further rooms. To my left was a small bathroom (now used as a display area for period fashions), and beyond that was the bedroom where Martin Pattison had died. I turned on the ghost box.

"Will you say hello?" I started.

"Get out!" came the brash response in a male voice.

"Why?" I enquired.

"I find it offensive," was the odd reply.

I considered that the etiquette of the late nineteenth century may dictate that a strange foreign man should not be frequenting a married lady's bed chamber. Then the K2 meter I had placed on the bed flickered into life for the first time. Was a spirit now sitting on the bed?

"Do you like my bedroom?" was then uttered as a full sentence through the device in the same male voice. This statement instantly suggested a sense of ownership, so I responded by asking, "Is that Martin?"

"Hello!" he said, followed by, "You're not allowed on this floor!"

"No?" I asked. He then replied by saying, "George."

"George!" he repeated for a second time.

It now sounded like the original statement of not being allowed in the room was not directed at me, but to a second spirit. This was a dialogue taking place between two spirits in which Martin made the statements "Get out" and "You are not allowed on this floor" to a spirit named George. In between that recorded dialogue, Martin had asked me if I liked the room. He would not have engaged me with such pleasantries if he did not want me there.

"I'm not a ghost," was then called out in a child's voice, followed by the number "Eleven." I now believed George to be the spirit of a former resident of the children's home, and he was expressing his age as eleven. Perhaps his claim of not being a ghost illustrated a lack of understanding as to what had happened to him.

During the children's home era the girls occupied and slept on the second floor, and the boys resided on the floor above. Was it possible that Martin was chastising one of the boys for being on the wrong floor? This would suggest that both Martin and George's spirits were together in the same room, but both came from different eras during their lifetimes.

"Did you come from upstairs?" I asked George in the hope of finding some evidence to back up my theory.

"Yes!" was his clipped reply. He then said, "Haunt!"

"So you haunt the house?" I asked, thinking that just moments earlier he had claimed not to be a ghost.

"Yes, upstairs," he replied.

This confirmed my theory that George had come from the floor above and was probably a child in the era of the care home. I then wondered if George had informed me he was not a ghost as he did not wish to scare me. I believed that he may have scared several living people and caused distress by appearing or by making contact with them. Once he knew how accepting I was of his circumstances he may have relaxed this stance.

"Do you like school?" I asked in a bid to try and engage the eleven-year-old in conversation.

"It's very boring," he said in a very stereotypical childlike fashion.

"Do you have any brothers and sisters?" I continued.

"Two brothers," he replied.

I then wanted to establish the year George thought it was.

"Who is president?" I asked.

"Ted," was then shouted out in an adult male voice that sounded like Martin again.

The only president that was affectionately known as 'Ted' was Theodore Roosevelt, whose term in office ran from September 14, 1901, to March 4, 1909. Martin's lifetime would have overlapped this term between the ages of sixty to sixty-eight—Martin died in 1918 at the age of seventy-seven. I believed this to be further proof that spirits can present themselves in any era and age they wish, in the same way George presented himself as an eleven-year-old boy. This entire dialogue and vigil suggested that spirits can see other spirits from other periods in exactly the same way I was able to access both George and Martin from our own physical realm.

I presented my findings and the notes I had made when my teams reassembled after this vigil. I was then informed by one of the board members that a little boy visited the home with his mother whenever she was employed by Grace Pattison to help them with entertaining. His name was also George. Whether or not George was from the Pattison's era or the children's home era, he would not have been allowed in that room. Mischievous children appeared to be part and parcel of this magnificent house. I recalled from my notes that the carriage house was destroyed in 1952 by fire due to children playing with matches. This building would certainly provide the best playground, with its hidden passages and secret stairways.

The Swimming Pool

To use the term swimming pool for this area would be a serious misrepresentation. It resembled more a plunge pool, and any individual would only need to stand up in the shallow water to avoid drowning. A few long strides in any direction would also see the swimmer reach the edge. It was a rough-finished concrete construction that had not held water since the 1920s. It was now used for the storage of carpeting and lumber.

Local legend states that when the house played host to the children's home several residents drowned in this location. Based on the visual evidence, and the knowledge that the basement was out of bounds and the pool had been drained, I found this myth to be unlikely. I believe the story stems from the fact that local authorities have sealed the information in relation to the history of the children's home due to the non-disclosure of documents relating to the orphans and their original families, rather than any clandestine cover-up of misadventure. The local historical society had no record of such a misadventure, and the accidental drowning of children in care would have been widely reported and remembered.

Scott had taken a team into this location for the first vigil. He described what had happened during the sharing of information between each vigil. When he and the other team members started the investigation they began experiencing the physical sensation of having their hair pulled. Then a female voice via the ghost box asked them to leave. Scott then cut the vigil short as the nauseating pressure created by the paranormal energy had rendered several members of his team physically sick.

I ventured down into the basement with trepidation based on Scott's report. I instantly noted on my arrival that my ears popped due to a change in air pressure. I could feel the electrically charged atmosphere and asked myself whether the energy was attracting the paranormal activity like a catalyst, or was the paranormal activity creating the energy.

There was no easy way into the swimming pool and the team had to scramble over the high-sided walls and carefully step down into the pool via the boxes and furniture that filled the area. There was definitely a heavy feeling in this location, and as I went about preparing to start I began to cough, a sign that a spirit wanted to talk through me. Greg then told me he could see a cold area moving around the team on his thermal imaging camera, perhaps observing us. I turned on the ghost box in a quest to solve once and for all the legend of the Fairlawn swimming pool. I soon heard the conversation of several spirits talking and engaging with one another over the familiar hiss and pop of the white noise and scanning.

"Every time I see you," a male voice then said.

"When do you see me?" I asked.

"When I'm talking," he said.

This was a baffling opening sentence, but my thoughts were then taken by one of the most remarkable pieces of paranormal evidence I have ever encountered. Suddenly the entire area of the pool was filled with the sound of water splashing about and children playing. We sat in the dark in bewilderment as two minutes of a real-time haunting unraveled for our aural experience. We could barely comprehend the sounds we were experiencing, those of children messing around in the pool, with the physical reality that we were sitting in the empty pool that had been drained for over ninety-five years. All of our audio devices recorded this event. I now believe that the spirit at the beginning of this interaction was actually referring to other spirits. Was it possible that an adult spirit was saying to spirit children, "Every time I see you!" responding to them as they sneaked into the pool to play, believing they had been unseen.

"I'm dead. He said I am dead!" the same male spirit uttered.

"Who said you are dead?" I enquired.

"There are little kids—he said I'm dead!" He continued, "The little kids."

I wondered who had told him he was dead.

"Who are you?" I asked in a bid to try and have a question answered.

"I'm sick of all the questions."

"So there are kids down here?" I asked.

"It's important," he continued.

"Will they get into trouble?" I pressed.

"No," he responded.

"So they do as you say?" I continued.

"Yes."

"Do you know who I am?" I asked, wondering if he had been following us around and listening to our earlier conversations as we progressed through the house.

"Send you home," he replied.

"Would you like me to go back to London?" I asked but received no reply.

"Did you work here?" I continued.

"Yes."

"When did you work here?"

"Wednesday mornings."

"So you worked here on Wednesday mornings?" I tried to confirm.

"Yes," he said once more.

"What did you do?"

"Grass," he replied.

I assumed that he was perhaps working on the grounds and may have been tasked with cutting the grass every Wednesday morning.

"Ghost!" he then interjected.

"Are you afraid of ghosts?" I enquired.

"Ghosts—lost," he then said.

"What are you? Are you a ghost?" I continued.

"Yes," he said.

"Are you bothered by ghosts?" I asked.

"Yes spirit, spirit," he replied.

"Why, what do they do to you?"

"It gets cold and they talk," he said.

I could not disagree with the ghost. In my experience they are cold and talk a lot. Could it be that his peace and quiet was being ruined by noisy children in spirit?

"It's so quiet," he now interjected without having been asked a question.

"What would you like us to do then?" I asked.

"Pray," he said.

"Shall we pray for you?" I asked.

"Bring God," he pleaded.

We sat in the surreal darkness of a drained Victorian swimming pool having had a spirit tell us to pray for him. What else could I do but gather my team together and verbalize a prayer into the echoing void. I asked God to come into this place and to embrace the spirit to give him peace. No more contact was made. As I walked back to the control area clutching my equipment, I wondered how I was going to tell the rest of the teams what had just happened.

The Sitting Room

The fully restored first floor of the mansion features gilded murals on the ceilings and a frieze, a grand entrance hall and open staircase, marble and tiled fireplaces, and the original leaded and stained glass windows. It was an opulent, visual feast of craftsmanship. Cost was irrelevant. Even the hallway was designed to be wide and spacious as a sign that the family could afford to waste space.

I had taken photographs extensively throughout the building during the walkthrough and baseline tests. I placed the camera tripod in the hallway and photographed Martin Pattison's study from numerous positions. Next to the study was the sitting room. This was used as a visiting area for the children during its time as an orphanage and as a waiting room for those looking to see the visiting doctor. This was an important fact as I began to feel a cramp in my lower stomach, perhaps a troubled appendix or similar condition. I started the third vigil in this location by using the ghost box, as this had been a very successful tool during the previous vigils. It is good practice to stick with the techniques and equipment that are working.

"Why are you here?" I asked.

"I have nowhere else to go," came the quick reply in a girl's voice.

"How many others are here?"

"Only me," she said.

"No others?"

"No."

I believed she was referring to the room we were currently investigating, rather than to the whole house. I then psychically had a name come through to me beginning with J.

"Are you called Jill or Jen?" I asked.

"Jen," she replied.

"Do you prefer Jen or Jennifer?" I enquired further.

"Jen," was her response.

"Did you live in the house?"

"Yes," she said.

"Did you work here?"

"Yes," she said once more, and then bizarrely exclaimed, "I'm losing time!"

"Did you work on the clocks?" I asked.

"Yes," she said, followed by the word "Time."

Just then a boy joined us in spirit. He shouted his name out over the ghost box for all to hear. "Luke!"

I engaged with this new spirit. "Did you work here, Luke?"

"Yes," he said, "I grew up here."

"So you grew up here?" I tried to confirm.

"Yes," he replied.

"Does your stomach hurt?" I asked, in relation to the pain I was feeling once more in my abdomen.

"Yes," he said.

"Have you had an operation?"

"Yes," he said once more.

"Have you seen a doctor?" I continued.

"Yes," he said.

Scott then asked me if I could see him psychically. I focused and could make out what looked like an eleven or twelve-year-old boy standing next to me.

"He looks about eleven," I replied to Scott.

"How old are you?" I then asked via the ghost box.

"Ten," he said.

"What's going on?" he then asked.

I explained why we were there and who we were.

"Do you like the way the house is run?" I added.

"No!"

"Why?"

"It does not look like how I remember it," he replied.

"And why is that?"

"The furniture is different," he said.

Then as previously discussed in this book, the contact just abruptly finished and no further contact was made.

The young female spirit who first came through had claimed to work and live in the house. Domestic servants would have resided in the building during the Pattison's era. Regular chores would have included the upkeep and regular winding of the numerous house clocks. I was also informed that the Fairlawn board had recently refurbished one of the building's clocks. Perhaps her statement of losing time also referred to the conversation we were having, and perhaps she felt we were keeping her from her ghostly duties.

Time would be a very different concept for Jen in spirit, so it would perhaps be out of dutiful loyalty that she still haunted the house. During my psychic sessions with clients, the deceased have given me the impression that time does not exist for them, and they are experiencing eternity. This may be alarming and difficult to initially experience when freshly in spirit. Perhaps this could best be described as dreamlike time, when we believe our dreams to be experienced in a longer time period than they actually are—most dreams only last between five and twenty minutes. Remember, physical aging is made redundant if a ghost can present itself in any way it wishes from its own linear timeline. The idea of losing energy would perhaps have an impact on a ghost's ability to access our physical realm but would not necessarily be detrimental to its own environment and dimension.

I believe the boy arrived from the era of the children's home. It could be suggested that the pain of his stomach ailment had left his spirit wandering around this room waiting to be seen by the doctor. A residual, intelligent haunting brought about by the experience of pain and suffering is a common set of circumstances.

The Phantom of the Office

After the investigation, I looked in detail at the walkthrough photographs. It was then I saw a strange and chilling floating phantom head hovering at waist height by the office desk. The head was featureless other than for what looked like two eye-holes and a mouth. It resembled some sort of mask or material covering and was a blueish-green color.

I had not seen a photograph of an entity like this before and I wondered about its origin and whether I had captured some sort of elemental from another dimension, especially as it appeared so jarringly out of context to the room.

The phantom face in Martin Pattison's office

I tried to debunk the image by thinking about the way the photograph was taken. Yet it could not have been anything caused by the flash, as I had disabled this feature when I took the picture. I also considered that the laser that measures the focal length of the subject matter may have reflected in some way back to the camera, but there was little for it to be reflected by. I had also taken several photographs from the same position, as is good practice for a paranormal investigator, using a tripod and a cable release. In the four other photographs the phantom anomaly did not appear, suggesting that the phenomenon was transient, allowing me to only capture its image once as it passed through the space in that millisecond.

A close-up of the phantom face

Conclusion

The contact made in the basement swimming pool at Fairlawn was unique. The prolonged sound of water splashing as an audible residual haunting was exceptional, and to then experience an extended ghost box dialogue with a male spirit that concluded in a prayer was unprecedented. Fairlawn was also interesting for the way we recorded two sets of ghosts in two different locations communicating with one another. We found Martin addressing the child spirit George in the bedroom and the male spirit in the basement talking to the children in the swimming pool. That male spirit also complained that the ghost children were disturbing him. It is remarkable to think that this is the same complaint many of the living make.

THE MAXFIELD HOUSE

MANKATO, MINNESOTA

Does a devastating fire still distress the resident spirits?

The Maxfield House is the oldest building in Mankato, yet its unassuming nature leaves the majority of passing traffic unaware of its age and historical importance. Its current occupant is the Save Mor Jewelry store owned and operated by Jackie. She was very supportive of my work and allowed me to conduct two separate investigations. This presented a unique opportunity to review the evidence from the first investigation and to then apply that knowledge to the second.

Jackie provided me with a documented history of the building that I supplemented with obituaries and newspaper articles obtained from the Blue Earth County Historical Society.

History

Mankato is located at the confluence of the Minnesota and Blue Earth Rivers and was chosen as a settlement due to its river traffic access. Its name derives from *Mahkato,* which means *greenish-blue earth* in the Dakota Sioux language. It is now the fourth largest city in Minnesota with a population of 40,000 spread across Blue Earth, Le Sueur, and Nicollet Counties.

Parsons King Johnson became the first white European Ameri-can to settle permanently in this area during February 1852 as part of the migration across the Midwest. He was quickly joined by Henry Jackson who gave his name to the town and county of Jackson, Min-nesota. Both Johnson and Jackson staked claims along both rivers. On May 11, 1858 a small number of residents organized the city of Mankato, three years before the construction of the Maxfield House. The city was established on land purchased in a treaty between the United States government and the Dakota Sioux. The breaking of this treaty led to the Dakota Indian War of 1862.

George Maxfield was born in Monongalia County, West Vir-ginia, on October 20, 1810. In 1829, he moved to Ohio and became a wagon maker. He then married Sarah Boden in November 1831. Sarah was born in Pennsylvania on July 5, 1812. The 1840 cen-sus documents the family living in Etna Township, Licking County, Ohio. It included George, Sarah, and their four children at that time. I found information that showed George was active within local pol-itics, having represented Licking County at the Democratic State Convention in Columbus on July 4, 1850.

In the spring of 1853 George Maxfield and his family moved to Mankato to join a small group of families. Emily Jane Maxfield, the third child of George and Sarah, documented the following de-scription of their arduous journey. She was seventeen years old at the time. She later married and went by the name Belle Hanna.

> They took the train from Columbus to Cincinnati. The ride on the train was a thrilling experience to the women and children, as none had ever ridden on a train before. At Cincinnati they took a large steam-boat up the Mississippi to St. Paul. They brought a cow along. On the way, she broke loose and swam ashore on an island. They stopped the boat while the men were catching the cow; the children went ashore and played games. For more than a year, this was the only cow in Mankato.

At St. Paul they tried to buy furnishings to replace those left behind, but there was very, very little to buy. There had been such an influx of newcomers everything had been sold. James Hanna and his daughter Lee and George Maxfield and Emily decided to go up to Mankato and prepare a place for their families. They took a steamboat up the Minnesota to Mankato where they arrived in May, 1853. When their boat arrived there were only 15 white people in Blue Earth County. There were quite a number on the boat.[33]

Another account described in the book *Old Rail Fence Post* was written by Laura Elizabeth Maxfield, the fifth child of the family. She was twelve years old when the family moved across the country. Laura became Mrs. J. R. Beatty through marriage.

Landed in Mankato May 26, 1853.

George bought the only set of dishes and clock to be found in the whole of St. Paul when they arrived. There were only a few houses in Mankato and the only thing we could find to live in was the frame of a warehouse that Minard Mills had just begun to build on the south end of the levee.[34]

During the latter part of 1853 the family moved into the first timber-framed building in Blue Earth County as described above. It was roughly built from lumber intended for a warehouse by the river where the end of Walnut Street is now located. After working in a store for several years, George began quarrying limestone and running a lime kiln. He realized the potential in providing building materials in this flourishing settlement. He continued with this operation for the remainder of his active life.

By 1856 this small pioneer town had reached a population of two hundred and continued to grow with the introduction of a sawmill in the same year. In 1861 George built a home on North Second Street; it was a single floor construction and consisted of two large rooms with a dugout cellar. A year later George joined the Blue Earth militia and witnessed the infamous execution of thirty-eight Dakota Sioux Indians on December 28, 1862. This incident remains the largest mass execution in American history.

The Maxfield family supported the Union's cause fully during the Civil War, and George and his four sons volunteered to fight. Minnesota only became the thirty-second state on May 11, 1858, so Minnesotans wanted to support the Union and thus provided a large number of soldiers despite its limited population. Approximately 170,000 Minnesotan men were involved in the war from 1861-1865.

George enlisted on October 7, 1863 as a private in Company E of the 9th Infantry Regiment, Minnesota. He was wounded on December 16, 1864 at Nashville, Tennessee and was mustered out on August 24, 1865 at Fort Snelling. George and Sarah's son Kinsey accompanied his parents on their journey to Mankato when he was just eleven years old and grew up in the house. As a young man of nineteen years he enlisted on August 10, 1862 in the same regiment as his father. Kinsey documents his incredible army career in a letter dated August 28, 1915 that was printed by the *Daily Review*. It gives a detailed account of one of the most historic military incidents of Minnesota's past:

> Having recently read a story in one of the Minne-
> apolis dailies headed, 'Indian Gazes Upon Grand-
> sire's Skull,' which although a good story, contains
> too much fiction for good history, I thought I would
> venture to give the facts as I know them. Company
> E, Ninth Minnesota Volunteer Infantry, was stationed
> at Hutchinson, Minnesota, during part of the summer
> of 1863, of which I was a member. Near midnight on
> the night of July 3, Chauncy Lampson came to our
> quarters out of breath and nearly naked with his skin
> scratched with briers so that he was blood all over,

and asked us to go to a place near their farm to get
the body of his father, who he said had been killed by
the Indians.

A number of our company, I think about nine, including myself, started from Hutchinson as soon as possible in our government wagon with young Lampson
as guide and reached the farm shortly before daylight,
but the fog was so thick that we could not see the lead
mules and thought it best to wait until the fog lifted
before going farther. As soon as we could see a reasonable distance, we started again, but Lampson refused to go any farther, telling us that his father's body
was about a mile farther on near a little lake where
they were hunting for deer, which were very plentiful,
so we went forward without him with scouts ahead to
prevent surprise. Upon going over a little hill we came
upon a dead Indian in the wagon road near a bunch of
hazel brush and raspberry bushes, and after scouting
around we found tracks of one Indian leading to where
a pony had been tied, and we trailed him for several
miles through the heavy grass and sloughs until we
lost the trail on the high ground. We then loaded the
body on the wagon and returned to Hutchinson, where
it was recognized by a number of old settlers as being
that of Little Crow, the identification being positive
because of his extremely fine hair for an Indian, and
having both wrists broken and out of place and his
breast being badly scarred in a fight with a bear near
Hutchinson a number of years before.

Our assistant surgeon, Dr. R. W. Twitchell, who was
from Hastings, I think, was at Hutchinson at the time
and wanted the body, so we gave it to him. He put
the body in an Indian canoe with a lot of strong lye

and after the bones were bleached, wired the skeleton together and kept it for a number of years. I heard some time afterwards that he had sold the skull to someone in New York City, but I never heard what disposition was made of the balance of the anatomy. The facts of the fight by the elder Lampson and his son Chauncy with Little Crow and his son were substantially as follows: Lampson had a farm about six miles from Hutchinson in the edge of the Big Woods, on which Lampson and his son were working on July 3, 1863, and about four o'clock in the afternoon they thought they would kill a deer to take home with them. In going up a small hill on the wagon road they heard voices, and crawling carefully up to the tip saw two Indians picking and eating wild raspberries. After talking it over Mr. Lampson said he would crawl down through the grass to a tree near where the Indians were and rest his gun against the tree and make a sure shot at the larger Indian, while Chauncy was to fire at the smaller Indian. So Lampson got to his position, and aiming steadily at the big Indian's heart, fired and hit him through the hips. Both Indians dropped immediately and Lampson crawled back to where Chauncy was and as he was going over the top of the hill the big Indian fired at him, the bullet cutting the skin on his back. Chauncy at the same time fired at the Indian, hitting him just below the heart. Lampson then told Chauncy that he had a mortal wound through the body, and for him to go to Hutchinson as quick as he could and get the soldiers to bring his body.

After Chauncy left, Lampson crawled into a thick patch of hazel brush near the road, and soon after Little Crow's son carried his father to a wide place in

the road within ten feet of where Lampson was hiding, and talked with his father until after midnight,
when Little Crow died. The son after putting new
moccasins on his father and straightening him out,
took the pony and started north. Little Crow's son
was some time later captured near Devils Lake and
brought back to Fort Snelling. Lampson later told
us that he had a large sized Colt's revolver and had
aimed over a dozen times at the young Indian, but
before he could pull the trigger the revolver wiggled
so bad that he was afraid to shoot, so he let the young
Indian go. Lampson afterward received three or four
hundred dollars bounty from the state and the thanks
of the legislature for killing Little Crow. If the skull
of Little Crow, in the State Historical rooms, is bullet
shattered, it is a pure fake."[35]

Kinsey served for three years and four months; he participated
in eleven battles and twenty-three skirmishes.

Wesley Maxfield enlisted as a corporal in the same regiment as
his brother and father on August 19, 1862 at the age of twenty-sev-
en. He gained promotion to full sergeant and was wounded on June
10, 1864, at Brice's Cross Roads, Mississippi. George's oldest son,
James Maxfield, stayed behind in Ohio when his father took the
family to Mankato. He fought in the 47th Regiment Massachusetts
Volunteer Infantry, Company K, and with Company D of the 12th
Cavalry Regiment of Ohio. George Jr. also wanted to participate
with his father and three older brothers but was too young to enlist,
so he ran away from home and became a drummer boy. He was
wounded three times during the course of the conflict.

George Maxfield sold his property to Henry Shaubut in the early 1880s. Henry Shaubut arrived from Seattle in 1854 and built the
first stone building in Mankato in 1855. This was considered to be
the only secure property during the Sioux uprising and many local
residents sought shelter there.

In 1892, the Maxfield House was enlarged to include a four bedroom second floor with an extension added to the kitchen area at the back of the building. The construction materials were all sourced locally with the bricks coming from north Mankato. The twenty-one-inch-thick, original limestone walls were separated by an air-space with wooden planks between the walls, enabling the plastering of the exterior walls. The back of house still had the original roofline. Henry then sold the house to Lawrence Henline in 1896.

George and Sarah both died in 1893. Sarah died on June 14, and George followed just six months later on December 21. His death was reported in the *Saint Paul Daily News* the following day:

> George Maxfield Dead. Mankato, Minn., Dec 21. George Maxfield died today, aged eighty-five years. He came to Mankato in 1853, and has resided here since that time. He held the offices of mayor, councilman and city treasurer. His wife died in June at the age of eighty-two, since which time he has been very melancholy. They had lived together sixty-two years. He leaves eight children. Kinzie and Charles Maxfield of Minneapolis are sons of deceased. He instituted the Masonic lodge of Mankato in the fifties, and was a Knight Templar. The Masons will have charge of the funeral.[36]

An obituary written in the *Mankato Daily Free Press* on Tuesday, December 26 noted that "there was a downpouring of rain—making the graveside service brief."

Investigation

One does not often receive the opportunity to paranormally explore the oldest building in any city and I was excited to start. I interviewed several long-serving members of the Save Mor Jewelry staff who had witnessed paranormal activity in the building. They had experienced the phenomena of being watched and the feeling of an unexplained presence in the room with them. This sensation was solely restricted to the shop floor and the office area. Storage boxes had also mysteriously fallen to the floor in the back of the shop in the room that houses the safe. I noted that this area was very active with EMF energy.

Perhaps the most prominent and intriguing paranormal contact came when Jackie was helping a client to choose a ring on the shop floor. During this interaction they were interrupted by the sound of a faucet being turned on, coming from the kitchen area at the back of the shop. Jackie went to see what had taken place and found the faucet fully on—no one else was in the building. Jackie turned the flowing water off and went back to the client. They were then inter-rupted for a second time by the same faucet; once more Jackie had to turn the faucet off. It did not come on for a third time. This makes me believe that a spirit was seeking her attention—or desperate for water.

We conducted a walkthrough looking to record baseline data. As we entered the building, a staircase was presented directly oppo-site. This ascended to the bedrooms upstairs that were being used for offices. Directly left was a second door that led onto the shop floor with a linear row of jewelry display cases and a wall that present-ed chains and earrings. Beyond this room was a second shop area and a beautiful, curved, wooden spiral staircase that descended into the old river rock basement. The kitchen behind the second display room was the last area and the carriage house could be seen in the yard behind the property through the kitchen window.

The Front Basement

Several staff members said they felt the presence of a spirit in the basement towards the front of the building, so I decided this would be a good place to start the first vigil. This area was a small work-room that was utilized as a smoking area. I had often considered that spirits would want to reside in areas like this if they had smoked when they were alive. I wondered if they could experience the same favorable sensations that smoking gave them if they now congregated with smokers in the physical realm. Greg set up a static infrared camera in the corner of the room and ran cabling through the building to a monitor on the shop floor. I arranged the chairs in a semi-circle so the team could observe the corridor outside as well as the area we were investigating.

The basement of the Maxfield House where the fire was lit

I turned off the lights, plunged the team into darkness, and started the vigil. Before we were more than a minute into the silence there was a very distinctive knock that was not the sound of the building moving. As the team listened intently for a further sound, a second noise was heard. There were three distinct footsteps, as if someone had started to walk and then stopped. I then heard the footsteps once more, this time behind me; somebody was definitely creeping around the room. I wanted to know who was observing us so I turned on the ghost box.

"What is your name?" I asked.

"Charles," came the response in a child's voice.

"Is your name Charles?" I asked for clarification.

"Danger!" The voice said loudly.

"Adrian!" It then shouted to gain my attention. He must have been listening when the group introduced itself at the beginning of the vigil.

"Why is there danger?" I enquired.

"Death!"

"Why did you say death? Is there something I should be concerned about?" I pressed. Silence prevailed so I asked once more.

"Is your name Charles? Yes or no."

"Yes."

"Did you used to live here?" I continued.

"Yes."

"When were you here... a hundred years ago... ninety years ago?"

"Stop!" it shouted as I got to ninety.

"You are a smart guy," it then said.

"Is there a woman with you?" I asked.

"Beth," was the reply, now in a female voice.

"Is your full name Elizabeth?" I questioned.

"Beth!" she reinforced.

"Danger!" once more was spat out into the cold, damp darkness.

"George, are you here?"

"Go ahead," he said, now bringing the number of spirits to three.

"Do you like us being here?"

"I can't breathe!" he exclaimed.

"Why can't you breathe?" I asked.

"George," he said once more.

"What state where you born in, George?" I continued to try to gain as much researchable evidence as possible.

"George... it's in our house!" was the reply.

Remarkably, George then asked me a question. This is a rare occurrence and I do not recall many times when a spirit has taken the lead on a ghost box session.

"How did you get here?" he enquired. I now felt like I was intruding on his property.

"We were invited by Jackie, the owner, to talk with you," I said.

"We built the house," he replied.

"And it is a fabulous house," I stated.

"Exhausted," he then expressed without me prompting him with a question.

"Why do you hang around here?" I asked.

"Fire!" came the answer.

"When was the fire?" I questioned. No reply was forthcoming.

"Was it 1880... 1890... 1900..." He shouted "Yes" when I got to 1900.

"Nineteen hundred and what?"

"Four," was the answer.

"Do you like what Jackie has done with the house?"

"Tired," was the seemingly random response for a second time.

"Charles," it then said once more.

We then experienced a considerable amount of silence before I decided to finish the vigil.

"Will you say goodbye?" I asked.

"I'll say goodbye," a male voice replied.

I had been given a lot of information from the spirits to work with. Jackie said that she was unaware of any history of a fire on the property, but I remembered how one spirit was desperate to turn the faucet on. I spent the following week at the Blue Earth Historical Society in the hope of uncovering a documented fire in the building. I also wanted to verify the existence of the individuals I had spoken to. I knew who George was, but I did not know if Beth or Charles were part of the Maxfield family.

I then discovered through the census records of 1860 that Charles Flandreau Maxfield was one of George Maxfield's sons.

Born in 1855, his profession was listed in the 1870 census as a bookkeeper, and he was residing in the Maxfield House during this time. I was told through the ghost box though that the fire happened in 1904, and Charles had a child's voice (Charles Flandreau would have been forty-nine in 1904). I am aware that spirits can present themselves in any form they wish, so a middle-aged Charles could certainly have come through as a small child—if that is how he wanted to look. The census of 1895 places Charles in a boarding house in Minneapolis where he was working as a grain inspector, and the 1910 census lists him as residing in Duluth. Therefore, after my initial excitement of finding Charles, I did not believe he was the individual I was looking for—since he was not residing in Mankato in 1904.

I did see from the census of 1880 that several grandchildren were living with George and Sarah Maxfield in the house. I wondered if another boy named Charles could be part of the family around the date of 1904. I then found that Charles was the name of the eldest son of George Jr. and Bertha Born, who were married in 1888; George Jr. was the sixth child of George and Sarah. My research showed that this Charles would have been around fourteen years of age in 1904. I then realized that the George who came through during the vigil was probably George Maxfield Jr. and noted further that his wife was named Bertha. I then wondered if she had been known as Beth, or perhaps I had misheard her trying to say Bertha. I went back and listened to the audio recording of the vigil and found it difficult to distinguish whether *Beth* or *Bertha* was being said. If my interpretation of the research was correct, I had the father, mother, and son, all come through together in spirit.

I then realized that the Maxfield family had sold the property to Henry Shaubut in the 1880s and so would not have been residing in the house during 1904. I could also find no historical proof that a fire had started on the property. So fearing that I may have come to a historical dead-end, I went about the meticulous task of turning every page of the *Mankato Free Press* newspaper for the year 1904 in the hope of finding a clue. To my astonishment I found an article with a headline from May 27 that turned the blood in my veins cold: "George Maxfield's House goes up in Flames."

> Residence Burns: George Maxfield's House goes up in Flames. The residence of George Maxfield, part way up the Franklin street hill, burned to the ground last evening, together with all of the contents that were on the second floor. The house was a story and a half frame dwelling.
>
> It is not known just how the fire started, but it is thought to have started from the chimney. Mrs. Maxfield had been out all day and returning made supper and the family and just sat down to the table when a neighbor ran in and told them that the roof was on fire. The flames made rapid headway, but the contents of the first floor were saved.
>
> An alarm was turned in from box 13 at about six o'clock, but the house was located up the steep hill. The chemicals were carried up, but did not avail against the fire.
>
> Mrs. Maxfield carried $300 insurance in the property with H.F. Leonard, but this will not nearly cover her loss. As the family are not in very good circumstances, the loss falls heavily upon them.[37]

It definitely sounded during aspects of the vigil that the spirits were very much in the historical moment and were warning my team of the fire.

I had historically found a boy named Charles that was a Maxfield who would have been a child in 1904. I had also found his father, George Jr. and a person I believed to be his mother, Bertha. I remarkably found a document that stated there was a fire in the family home and on the exact year the spirits had told me. Unfortunately, it was the wrong house. The property that caught fire was where

George Jr. and Bertha had lived with their children just a short walk from the Maxfield House. The property I was investigating had new owners before Charles had even been born.

This was an interesting aspect of the investigation, as I believe the 1904 fire was understandably a traumatic experience for the family, with the loss of their home and possessions. Is it then possible that an imprint of their emotional turmoil could be left in a moment of time like an "intelligent residual" haunting—a phenomenon I had never experienced before? It is also worth mentioning that this interaction confirms that you have the ability to coexist with your departed family members in spirit. I also considered that I had asked repeatedly for George Maxfield to come through and communicate with me. Should it then come as a surprise if George Maxfield Jr. heard and presented himself to me and brought his family with him—especially as they once had lived in the house and lived close by?

I also pondered why George Jr. said he couldn't breathe. The article clearly states that nobody had died in the fire, but I considered the possibility that the smoke may have affected him, since he had probably strived to remove as many possessions as possible. I then went to look for George Jr.'s obituary in the hope of shedding more light on his verbal evidence. I found an article dated January 2, 1913 in the Blue Earth County Historical Society, with an opening paragraph:

> Geo. Maxfield, Pioneer Resident, Passed Away Early Last Evening. George Maxfield passed away at Immanuel hospital last evening after a month of illness. He had been a sufferer from asthma for years, and his death was due to chronic bronchitis and asthma.[38]

George Jr. had died through an inability to breathe! So was George Jr. expressing to me his final moments in the physical realm, or was he overcome with the choking fumes and smoke because of the fire? Perhaps the fire was the catalyst for the lung problems he had suffered with in later life.

I then arranged a follow-up investigation with many unanswered questions and facts needing to be verified. I had obtained a copy of a photograph of George Maxfield at the historical society archives, and I showed Jackie and her family his portrait. Jackie's sister went white when she saw the image and exclaimed that she had seen that very gentleman in the family home when she was growing up. George Maxfield and his extended family had obviously kept a close eye in spirit on their property and the new family that owned it.

George Maxfield

The first place I was eager to reinvestigate was the basement. I was excited to be going back into this location armed with the historical facts I had discovered. It was instantly noticeable that a smell of burning was now strangely evident in this area. A smoky, woody, burnt ash-like aroma was not from cigarettes. As the vigil started, the whole team agreed that there was a sensation of not being able to breathe, and our lungs felt heavy. I was very much aware of how George Jr. had died, but I did not believe this to be a group psychosomatic response. I wanted to make contact with the spirit of Charles once more to try to confirm his place in the Maxfield family.

"Is Charles there?" I asked.

"Yes," came the reply in the now familiar child's voice.

"I know you," it then responded.

This indicated to me that the spirit had a sentient memory of my previous visit.

"Is your mother here?" I enquired, with the idea of wanting to confirm that the Charles I was once more engaging with was the son of George Jr. and Bertha.

"Yes, I think so," he said.

I thought this to be a slightly odd reply in that he did not seem sure whether his mother was present or not. Perhaps he was unsure whether his mother was with us in the room or back in the spirit realm where he had just come from. Then without any prompting the ghost box shouted out the name "Bertha." This short, six-letter name instantly corroborated all of my historical research.

"What year was the fire? Nineteen what?" I asked.

"Four," was the response. I knew the fire had happened in 1904, so once more I had cross-corroborated my historical research with the evidence I had received from the previous investigation.

"Blue Earth veteran," it then exclaimed, without any prompting.

I was aware that the Maxfield family had participated fully in the Civil War and that George and his four sons had all fought with distinction as veterans of Blue Earth County.

"Why are you here?" I continued.

"Legacy, legacy," I heard twice in a male voice.

"So are you here because this is the only property left to be in?" I asked.

I have considered for some time that spirits may only be able to reside in places they remember from when they were alive, because they have to be able to remember them to haunt them—as mentioned in the SS *Meteor* chapter. If their bones are buried in the graveyard, then they must undertake a process that requires them to *think they want to be somewhere so they are,* with physical geography appearing to be an irrelevance. But for this concept to work you must know where you want to be in order to think yourself there. Thus, if the Maxfield House is the only property still remaining that they knew from their own time, then it might be the only property they can actually visit. Other houses in Mankato were built in their lifetime and are still standing, but perhaps they did not go into them or have knowledge of the interior and layout. It would be like me asking you to imagine the furnishings and interior of a random house that you have never visited.

This theory would appear to answer the question I have often pondered as to why we never see the ghosts of cavemen, when you consider that we have been roaming the planet as a species for hundreds of thousands of years. Thus in theory we should see more ghosts and spirits from our earliest ancestors than we do of the recently departed. Yet most hauntings of an intelligent nature only appear to go back to a period of history that can be measured in just centuries. Could we now consider that after several hundred years, if nothing remains from that period that is familiar to deceased beings, then they cannot maintain an awareness of a place to be able to haunt? The spirits of ancient English kings and queens, for example, can still haunt their archaic castles because those castles are still there and they resided in them. With this concept in mind I asked the following question.

"So do you come here because this is the only building left that you remember that is still standing?"

"That's pretty much it, yes," he said. The whole team sat in the darkness and fully processed this answer and what it might mean for the theory of paranormal investigating.

Due to the strong response I received from the spirits regarding the fire, I decided to try an experiment. I had brought with me a small, cast-iron campfire cauldron, and with Jackie's permission I wanted to light a small controlled fire in the basement to see what effect this might have on the spirits. We took every precaution and made sure a bucket of water was standing by. I did not intend to destroy the oldest building in Mankato.

"Shall I light a fire down here?" I asked.

"That's offensive!" he shouted. I presumed this to be George Jr.

"So what if I just do it now?" I asked.

"You bastard!" came the loud and aggressive response. It was certainly not my intention to agitate the spirits and be disrespectful. Therefore, I emphasized the nature of my experiment further.

"I promise to put it out again," I explained.

"We are sorry," came the reply.

"So is it okay if I light a fire?"

"No problem, yes," they said.

I lit the fire and we sat in the basement and watched the flames lick around the paper that now illuminated the vigil. It was very surreal to light a fire in the middle of a basement floor. But the experiment had worked by eliciting a strong response from the spirits before I had even struck a match. The fire died out a minute later, and I asked the team if I should light a second one.

"Don't do it!" shouted the same spirit from the ghost box. Out of respect for those who had lost their home and still appeared to be suffering from the trauma, I decided there would be no benefit in continuing.

"So you forgive me for lighting a fire?" I asked.

"Of course," came the response. We ended the vigil and cleared the basement.

The Carriage House

Due to the harsh coldness of the Minnesota weather we were unable to investigate the old carriage house at the back of the property during our first investigation. This time the weather was hot and humid, with sporadic lightning that crackled and fizzed all around us. I was quietly optimistic when we started the vigil on the top floor of this old wooden construction.

We sat in the darkness for fifteen minutes without anything happening, just listening to the sound of the rain lashing against the roof. There were no EMF readings, and I was strongly considering moving the vigil to another part of the building. I then turned on the ghost box in a bid to gain a communication, as this device seemed to be providing the best results at this property.

"Watch out!" it instantly shouted in a male voice.

"Watch out for what?" I asked.

"Ghost!" it said.

"Do ghosts exist?" I responded.

"Yes."

"So why do I need to watch out?" I continued.

"You need to understand," he said.

"Understand what?" I asked.

"Death!"

"You need to get this," he continued. "The afterlife."

"So what do I need to know about the afterlife?"

"It's real you know."

I agreed with him and told him that I had spoken with many ghosts and spirits.

"Can you see us?" I asked.

"Yes, yes." he said twice.

"Who am I talking to?"

"Frank, Frank," he said.

"Hi, Frank. Do you hang out with your friends here in Mankato?"

"Community."

"So you all live in a community?" I continued.

"Yes."

"Can you see the jewelry store?"

"No," came his reply.

"So does the building look like it did when you were alive?"

"Yes," he said.

The dialogue ended abruptly as is now the convention with this process. After an hour of prolonged silence with no further contact I ended the vigil.

"Will you say goodbye?" I asked.

"Goodbye," the spirit said, indicating that he was still with me but unable to continue the stimulus and response dialogue we had started with such energy.

Heather had led a team in the carriage house at the same time I was working in the basement earlier. She told my team between the vigils that she had also received the name *Frank* from the ghost box.

She had asked what Frank did for a living and he replied, "Trees."

She then responded by asking if this was how he made his money and he said, "The lumber business."

I thought it was a remarkable piece of evidence that, unbeknown to each team, both had received the same name, in the same location, at different times, with different equipment. All I had to do now was find Frank. The following week I revisited the Blue Earth County Historical Society.

I knew that Lawrence Henline had purchased the house in 1896, and the carriage house was then built to the rear of the property. This would suggest, based on my previous theory, that a Maxfield could not be haunting this location as it had not been erected during their stay in the house. I found that the Henline family had made its money from the lumber business just as Frank suggested. An article written in the *Mankato Free Press* in 1921 entitled "Early Lumber Day Prices" discusses the Henline family and how they emigrated from Austria to Mankato in 1855.

There was a great demand for lumber during the era the Henline family had arrived in Mankato, and they quickly established a sawmill on the Minnesota River that they operated from 1866 to 1870. A plot of land could easily be jumped by another pioneer if a building was not quickly erected on the lot. I then discovered that Lawrence Henline had a son named Frank; Frank Henline had died in the house under tragic circumstances—his obituary was printed in the *Mankato Free Press* in 1914:

> Death of a Young Man: Frank J. Henline, Son of
> former Councilman Lawrence Henline, Victim of

MYSTERIOUS MIDWEST   271

Tuberculosis. Frank J. Henline died at the home of
his father, former Councilman Lawrence Henline,
816 North Second street, at 11:45 p.m., yesterday of
tuberculosis. He had been ill with the disease for a
year. The young man was born in Mankato on May
7, 1892 and always lived here. He attended the city
schools and at the time he was taken ill was at the
Commercial College. He was a bright young man
and well liked by all who knew him. He leaves two
brothers and two sisters, John, Henry, Zita and Mary.
The funeral will be held at nine o'clock Thursday
morning from St. Peter and Paul's Catholic Church.[39]

The *Mankato Review* also documents the tragic demise of
Frank Henline. "A very sad death occurred last night at 11:30 when
Frank Joseph Henline, the twenty-one-year-old son of Mr. Henline
died." It continued to outline the cause of his death in more detail.
"About a year ago he was attacked with a severe cough that stuck
with him to the end and ultimately caused his death." The Henline
family eventually sold the Maxfield House to Samuel Gieske in
1929. The Gieske family lived in the house until the early 1970s.

Conclusion

It became a complex task just to unravel the individual aspects
of paranormal evidence presented in this chapter. It also required
the greatest amount of historical research. Just delivering the facts
and details in an accessible way proved demanding. The Maxfield
House certainly provided some of the greatest evidence I have ever
experienced from the spirit world and it helped to feed my theories
concerning the afterlife.

Many incredible paranormal incidents occurred on this property, starting with the photograph I discovered of George Maxfield—
the apparition that Jackie's family said they had seen in their home.
It was also remarkable to hear Charles say that he could only haunt
the property because he remembered it—and because it was still

there. This poses the question of what happens in spirit when there is nothing left from the life they remember. Could every old building that is destroyed leave a number of spirits unable to return? Frank said that the afterlife was real and that he was residing in the community he once grew up in and remembered. He could not see the new environment, but he could see me.

I believe that the greatest evidence presented by the spirits of the Maxfield House was in the detailed and extensive facts they presented to me as names, dates, and events, which after painstaking and comprehensive research proved to be historically correct. This is especially true when you consider that these details and facts have long since been forgotten.

My greatest thanks are extended to Jackie and her family for allowing my team to access their property. If it were not for those open-minded, non-judgmental, welcoming folk of the Midwest, this book would be nothing more than a collection of unproven theories interspersed with second-hand regurgitated facts. Now it is a document that delivers primary evidence straight from the very mouths of the dead—those who have experienced our history!

EPILOGUE

It is normally considered good practice within academic circles to outline, formulate, and write a conclusion or epilogue before you start your book. This gives you a sense of your goals and what you are looking to achieve in the text. In my initial epilogue I wanted to highlight any evidence that I captured in my planned investigations in order to illustrate that an afterlife exists. Yet, as I now look back at a finished manuscript, I realize that rather than scattered highlights, the evidence is actually running through every sentence, paragraph, and chapter. The book you are holding only exists because of the contact I had with the dead.

What came as a further surprise was the strength and frequency of how the psychic evidence was corroborated with the equipment responses, and to then have that duality reinforced by historical research, allowing me to reconstruct the past when in most cases dates, names, facts, and details were lost or forgotten. Examples of such evidence includes the fire in Mankato, Mary Jane's death at Loon Lake Cemetery, Vaclav Soukup's nationality, and the simple acknowledgement of a bell positioned on the dining room floor of the Christie House—the incident that started this journey.

To embrace the concepts and philosophies presented in this book requires an acceptance that science cannot prove everything and a leap of abstract thinking that encompasses what it is like to be

in spirit. We live in a society in which the majority would show con-
tempt or disbelief at what is presented here (a Gallup poll conducted
in June 2005 showed that only 37 percent of Americans believed in
haunted houses; a further survey by The Associated Press and Ipsos
in October 2007 found that only 34 percent of Americans believe in
ghosts), so our faith in these concepts shines out like a symbol of
thoughts and ideas, a beacon that can set our minds free in a restric-
tive, science-reliant society. Yet before the dawn of modernity, just
a few generations ago, our very own ancestors would have received
this evidence as perfectly reasonable. To dispute the content of this
text suggests that this is a work of fiction, that I fabricated it, or
entered into some sort of deceit. Yet every audio recording, every
piece of video footage, and every photograph is available to access
via my lectures, book signings, websites, media work, and events.

In attendance at each location were property board members, volunteers, local residents, and staff. These are professional,
well-educated individuals who can now independently tell you that
they were there when contact was made and can verify each and
every sentence. They had no opinion or agenda towards the paranormal and the afterlife, but all shared an enquiring mind. They came
away from those vigils as witnesses to the astonishing events that
transpired.

Only history can now decide whether we are at the dawn of a
new way of thinking and exploration, a renaissance and an awak-
ening of what is to be found beyond the veil, or whether we will
have derision placed upon us for believing that an exploration of a
basement with electrician's tools and a broken radio would provide
contact. But a drive, a passion, a commitment to finding new ways,
new technologies, new locations, and new experiences is what it
is to be human. As the British poet Robert Browning (1812-1889)
once put it, "Ah, but a man's reach should extend his grasp. Or what
is heaven for?"

This book explores what happens when we die and whether an
afterlife exists. But you will have to form your own opinion based
on the facts presented here. I also hope that this book goes some way

to increasing the profile and importance of many of the sites I have investigated. I would like it to help diminish the continuing threat many face from redevelopment or closure, so that the dead and the living can enjoy them and frequent them in the years to come. This journey was not just an exercise in writing about history—it was living it.

ACKNOWLEDGEMENTS

To my mother, I am sorry I tried to hide my broccoli in a glass of milk when I was a young. To my father, who took me to every museum in London throughout the duration of my childhood—I'm sure knowing how a triple-expansion steam engine works will be useful one day. He kept the family amused with his dancing at weddings—his impression of a man standing in a minefield. To my sister Joanne, regardless of what the hospital said, I still think daring you to come down the stairs on a space hopper in 1977 was very funny. And finally to Heather, Lorna, Jyeton, Kathy, Nathan, Scott, Kim and Greg, and all at the The International Paranormal Society. I would like to thank those, deceased or living, who have contributed and made possible this historical, paranormal adventure through the Midwest.

Deceased

The Christie House maid, Dr. George Christie, Edith Christie, Henry W. Schroeder, John Sheets, Bea, Mary Jane Terwillegar, Vaclav Soukup, Hoxie Rathbun, Michael, Matthew, Lawrence Buhler, Robert Underwood, George Le Tourneau, Lucy, Doug Davidson, Jeff, Edward, Stacy Bradshaw, Adelaide Bradshaw, Peter Peters, Emanuel Dvorak, Johanna Huseby Lund, William Flieder, Frank, Red, Mr. and Mrs. Harry Lawe, Captain of the SS Meteor, Donald and Nancy Seidlitz, Martin Pattison, George, Luke, Jennifer, Mary, Wade, Jim, Mark, Charles Maxfield, George Maxfield Jr., Bertha Born Maxfield, Frank Henline, Monique, Doris.

Living

The following also supported me, kept me focused, and were there for me in various ways when I needed them: Paul, Karen, Ashley, Jordon, Caroline, Gloria, Kris, Dave, Sarah, Adam, S.E.E. Paranormal, Theresa, Denise, BryAnna, Dee, Rob, Cathy, Nick, Dawn, Julie, Scott H., Susan, Janet, Diane, Mikhael, Susie, Jan, Mike, Jo, Barbara, Jackie, Shelley, Mandy, Gary, Ian, and all at Calumet Editions, Mum, Dad, Joanne, and to all the small local historical societies that are reliant on the good will and charity of their members and volunteers to remain open and functioning as non-profit organizations. We all have a duty to make sure these buildings are still around for future generations to enjoy, long after we have departed ourselves.

All photographs (unless stated on the copyright page) are by Adrian Lee.

To all the negative spirits and energies out there: I have read to the end of the good book, and we win!

The Christie House
15 First Street South
Long Prairie, MN 56347

The First National Bank
239 Central Avenue
Long Prairie, MN 56247

The Kemp Block Opera House
144/150 Central Avenue
Long Prairie, MN 56247

The Pioneer Village
78748 550th Avenue
Jackson, MN 56143

Loon Lake Cemetery
Intersection of County Road 75 and County Highway 4
48804 715th Street
Middletown, MN 56143

The Rathbun Dugout
85907 510th Avenue
Jackson, MN 56907-3109

State Theater
926 Fourth Avenue
Windom, MN 56101

Windom Public Library
904 Fourth Avenue
Windom, MN 56101

Business, Arts and Recreation Center
1012 Fifth Avenue
Windom, MN 56101

The Bradshaw House Hotel
640 Main Street
Baldwin, WI 54002

The Wieting Opera House
101 South Church Street
Toledo, IA 52342

The Railroad Crossing
Main Street
Sanborn, MN 56083

Forepaugh's Restaurant
276 South Exchange Street
St. Paul, MN 55102

The Lund-Hoel House
401 St. Olaf Avenue North
Canby, MN 56220

Canby Theater
109 St. Olaf Avenue North
Canby, MN 56220

SS Meteor Maritime Museum
300 Marina Drive
Barker's Island
Superior, WI 54880

Fairlawn Mansion
906 East Second Street
Superior, WI 54880

The Masonic Temple
1503 Belknap Street
Superior, WI 54880

The Maxfield House
Save Mor Jewelry
816 North Second Street
Mankato, MN 56001

BIBLIOGRAPHY

Newspapers and Periodicals

"Building Gone," Cottonwood County Citizen, Volume. LXXXIX, Windom, Minnesota. May 18, 1971, p. 1.

Canby News, Canby, Minnesota, August 18, 1893.

"Cottonwood County Bank Building Spring 1895 for $5000," *Windom Reporter*, Vol. XXIV Number 29, Windom, Minnesota. March 21, 1896. p. 1.

Cottonwood County Citizen, Windom, Minnesota, October 13, 1883.

Cottonwood County Citizen, Windom, Minnesota, July 8, 1911.

Cottonwood County Citizen, Windom, Minnesota, October 18, 1931, p. 4.

Cottonwood County Citizen, Volume XLVII, Number 46, Windom, Minnesota, October 18, 1931, p. 1.

Cottonwood County Citizen, Special School Edition, Volume LXXII, Number 16, Windom, Minnesota, April 24, 1954, p. 1.

Cottonwood County Citizen, Windom, Minnesota, January 4, 1978, p. 2b.

Duluth Evening Herald, Duluth, Minnesota, December 1, 1905.

Duluth News Tribune, Duluth, Minnesota, December 6, 1905.

"Fire Fiend Visits Windom," *Windom Reporter*, Windom, Minnesota, February, 1911, p. 1.

"Geo. Maxfield, Pioneer Resident, Passed Away Early Last Evening," *Mankato Free Press*, Mankato, Minnesota, January 2, 1913.

"George Maxfield's House Goes Up in Flames," *Mankato Free Press*, Mankato, Minnesota, May 27, 1904.

Glaser, Alvin, "History of the Jackson County Fair," *Tri County News,* June 25, 2007.

Henline, Frank, "Early Day Lumber Prices Related," *Mankato Free Press*, Mankato, Minnesota, September 30, 1921.

"High School History Begins in 1889," *Cottonwood County Citizen*, Windom, Minnesota, June 6 1990, p. 8.

"John H. Sheets Called by Death: Died Suddenly Last Friday After a Short Illness with the Flu," *The Todd County Leader*, Long Prairie, Minnesota, July 5, 1928. p. 1.

"Judges Find 8,067 Wads of Gum Under State Theatre Seats," *Cottonwood County Citizen*, Windom, Minnesota, December 21, 1955. p. 1.

Krueger, Coralee, "State Theater Tradition of Entertainment Spans 78 Years, *Cottonwood County Citizen*, Windom, Minnesota, November 28, 1992, p. 13.

Long Prairie Leader, Long Prairie, Minnesota, July 5, 1928, p. 1.

Long Prairie Leader, Long Prairie, Minnesota, September 9, 1932, p. 1.

Mankato Free Press, Mankato, Minnesota, January 13, 1914.

Maxfield, Kinsey, *Daily Review*, Mankato, Minnesota, August 28, 1915.

Meissner, Susan, "Historic State Theater," *Cottonwood County Citizen*, Windom, Minnesota, August 16, 1995, p. 2.

Milwaukee Sentinel, Milwaukee, Wisconsin, September 18, 1891.

"Owe Debt to School House," *Cottonwood County Citizen*, Centennial Edition, Windom, Minnesota, June 4, 1970.

Peters, Rosalie, Staff Writer. *The Daily Globe*, Minnesota.

Ross, Jenna, "Towns Shell Out to Save Screen Gems Created Windom Theater Inc.," *Star Tribune*, Minnesota, September 8, 1913.

Redwood Gazette, Number 34, Redwood Falls, Minnesota, March 3, 1910.

Redwood Gazette, Number 32, Redwood Falls, Minnesota, March 9, 1910.

Redwood Gazette, Redwood Falls, Minnesota, June, 1910.

Redwood Reveille, Number 23, Redwood Falls, Minnesota, March 15, 1910, p. 10.

Redwood Reveille, Number 24, Redwood Falls, Minnesota, March 22, 1910, p. 1.

Saint Paul Daily News, Saint Paul, Minnesota, December 22, 1893. p. 3.

Spirit Lake Beacon, Spirit Lake, Iowa, March 18, 1880.

"The Move in 85," *Cottonwood County Citizen*, Windom, Minnesota, March 20, 1986.

"The Sad Death of Frank Joseph Henline, Son of Mr. and Mrs. Lawrence Henline Passes Away," *Mankato Review*, Mankato, Minnesota, January 13, 1914.

"Vaclav Soukup of Hunter Passes to Long Rest December 18," *Lakefield Standard*, Lakefield, Jackson County, Minnesota, January 2, 1919. p. 1.

Van De Walle, Kelly, "Village People Needed," *Jackson County Pilot*, Jackson, Minnesota, March 16, 2006.

"Was it Murder? Death of Lewis Miller at Sanborn Still a Mystery," *Redwood Reveille*, Redwood Falls, Minnesota, March, 1910.

Windom Reporter, Windom, Minnesota, September 7, 1893.

Windom Reporter, Windom, Minnesota, September 11, 1914. p. 1.

Windom Reporter, Windom, Minnesota, October 2, 1914. p. 1.

Windom Reporter, Volume 60, No. 11, Windom, Cottonwood County, Minnesota, November 13, 1931, p. 1.

"Windom's Fine New High School Building," *Windom Reporter*, Windom, Minnesota, December 12, 1911.

"Windom's New High School is Modern in Every Detail," *Cottonwood County Citizen*, Windom, Minnesota, November 18, 1931.

"Worthington Men Buy Wonderland Theatre," *Cottonwood County Citizen*, Number 41, Windom, Minnesota, October 20, 1937. p. 1.

Books

Baldwin, P. *How Night Air Became Good Air. Environmental History.* Vol. 8, No. 3. Forest History Society, Forest History Society and the American Society for Environmental History, American Society for Environmental History, Oxford University Press, 2003. 412-429.

Beecher, Catherine E. and Professor Harriet Beecher Stowe, *The American Woman's Home.* Rutgers University Press, 2002.

Burleigh, Sandy. Pioneers Peek Out from the Past: On Baldwin Wisconsin and Surrounding Areas. Hiawatha Design, 2001. 104.

Chapman, Samuel, D. History of Tama County, Iowa. Its cities, towns and villages, with early reminiscences, personal incidents and anecdotes and a complete business directory of the county. Nabu Press, 2010.

Curtiss-Wedge, Franklin. *History of Redwood County, Minnesota.* Vol. 1. Chicago Jr. and Co. 1916. 309.

Hodge, Frederick Webb. *Handbook of American Indians North of Mexico.* Vol 1. U.S. Govt. Printing Office; 4th printing, edition, 1912. p. 801.

Leavenworth Wilder Morris, Lucy. *Old Rail Fence Corners: The A.B.C.'s of Minnesota History.* Scholar Choice Edition, 2015.

Old Rail Fence Corners: Frontier Tales Told By Minnesota Pioneers. Borealis Books, 1976.

Pipestone County Historical Society. *Pipestone County History Minnesota*. Dallas, TX: Taylor Publishing Company, 1984.

Richter, Gary and Arthur L. Finnell, Sanborn Centennial History 1881-1981 Inc. Townships of Charlestown and Germantown. Sanborn Centennial book Committee, 1981.

Shepherd, Sylvia Elizabeth. The Mystery of Murder Hill: The Serial Killings of Belle Gunness. 1st Book Library, 2001.

Shutter, Rev. Marion Daniel. History of Minneapolis, Gateway to the Northwest, Chicago-Minneapolis. The S J Clarke Publishing Co, 1923.

The Dominion Annual Register and Review, 1882. Facsimile Publisher, 2005. Pp. 204-205.

Websites

The following sites were accessed between February 2012 and July 2016.

American Ancestors, by New England Historical Genealogical Society. www.newenglandancestors.org.

American Civil War Soldiers. Ancestry.com.

Civil War Veterans Buried in Tama County, Iowa. http://iagenweb.org/tama/military/Civil-War-Burials.html.

Descendants of Hezekiah Maxfield of Maryland, Second Generation. http://maxfield5.tripod.com/maxfieldhe2d1.html.

Find a Grave. http://image2.findagrave.com/photos/2011/310/67012768_132071525181.jpg

Find a Grave. Research on Emmanuel Hepner. http://www.findagrave.com/cgi-bin/fg.cgi?page=gr&GRid=67012768.

Geni Family tree. *My Heritage Company*. Family tree information on the Lund family. www.geni.com/people/Johanna-Lund/6000000013514444730.

Hesseltine, Jeff. "Descendants of John Hesseltine" Updated September 28, 2000. Ancestry World Tree. http://awt.ancestry.com.

History of the Minnesota Valley, including the Explorers and Pioneers of Minnesota (1882), p. 563. Ancestry.com.

IA GenWeb Project. Research on Emmanuel Dvorak. http://iagenweb.org/boards/tama/biographies/index.cgi?read=157844

Idaho Death Certificates, 1911-1937. familysearch.org.

Illinois State Archives. Illinois Statewide Marriage Index, 1763-1900. www.cyberdriveillinois.com/departments/archives/genealogy/marrsrch.html.

International Genealogical Index. www.familysearch.org.

Iowa Gravestone Photograph Project. http://iowagravestones.org/gs_view.php?id=345778

Iowa Trails, a project of genealogy trails. http://genealogytrails.com/iowa/1886pennsylvaniasoldiers.htm.

Iowa Gravestone Photograph Project. http://iowagravestones.org/search.php?cfield=last&ctype=1&ctxt=PETERS&cfield2=first&ctype2=1&ctxt2=&pg=34.

Maryland Marriages, 1655-1850. Accessed November 2004. Ancestry.com. Also found at Baltimore County (Maryland) Marriage Licenses, 1777-1846. Baltimore County (Maryland) Clerk of Circuit Court. International Genealogical Index. www.familysearch.org.

"Memorial Day Program Information." *Star Online, Pipestone County.* http://www.pipestonestar.com/Stories/Story.cfm?SID=49942.

Minnesota Territorial and State Censuses 1849-1905: 1885 Census. Ancestry.com.

Minnesota Death Index 1908-2002. Ancestry.com.

NBC 24. Research on deceased Toledo, Iowa, residents. http://nbc24.com/news/local/police-man-killed-in-apparent-drunken-driving-crash-in-south-toledo?id=1081865.

Nineteenth Century U. S. Newspapers. Accessed through New England Historic Genealogical Society. www.newenglandancestors.org.

One-Third of Americans Believe Dearly May not have Departed. Research on polls taken on what percentage of Americans believe in haunted houses. http://www.gallup.com/poll/17275/OneThird-Americans-Believe-Dearly-May-Departed.aspx

People Search, find relatives and locate ancestors. Research on Emmanuel Dvorak. http://www.locateancestors.com/dvorak-born-in-1896/#ixzz3iZyEQZKq.

People Search, find relatives and locate ancestors. Research on William Flieder. http://www.faqs.org/people-search/flieder/#ixzz3CCZbtSSL.

Poll: One-Third of Americans Believe in Ghosts, UFOs. Research on polls taken on what percentage of Americans believe in ghosts. http://www.foxnews.com/story/2007/10/25/poll-one-third-americans-believe-in-ghosts-ufos.html

Rose, Arthur P. *An Illustrated History of Jackson County, Minnesota.* 1910. http://www.archive.org/stream/anillustratedhi-00rosegoog#page/n32/mode/2up.

Tama Co., Iowa USGENWEB Project, History of Tama County Iowa. http://iagenweb.org/tama/history/toc2.html.

Vital Records, ca. 1865-1927. Minnesota District Court (Blue Earth County*). International Genealogical Index.* www.familysearch.org.

Zinn, Melba Pendler, ed. *Monongalia County [West] Virginia, Records of the District, Superior Courts,* 2:111. Westminster, MD: Heritage Books, 2000. googlebooks.com.

Letters

Grover Fuller, Anna K. "The Unfortunate Letter Carrier." Letter. 1934.

Rathbun Funk, Margaret. Letter, February 24, 1922.

Census Records

Sanborn Census. 1895. Accessed at the Redwood Falls Public Library, August 4, 2015.

NOTES

(ENDNOTES)

1   *Long Prairie Leader*, Long Prairie, Minnesota. July 5, 1928. p. 1.

2   *Long Prairie Leader*, Long Prairie, Minnesota. September 9, 1932, p. 1.

3   *Spirit Lake Beacon*, Spirit Lake, Iowa. March 18, 1880.

4   Glaser, Alvin. "History of the Jackson County Fair." *Tri County News*. June 25, 2007.

5   Glaser, Alvin. "History of the Jackson County Fair." *Tri County News*. June 25, 2007.

6   Van De Walle, Kelly. *Jackson County Pilot*, Jackson, Minnesota. March 16, 2006.

7   Van De Walle, Kelly. "Village People Needed." *Jackson County Pilot*, Jackson, Minnesota. March 16, 2006.

8   Peters, Rosalie. Staff Writer. *The Daily Globe*, Minnesota.

9   "Vaclav Soukup of Hunter Passes to Long Rest December 18." *Lakefield Standard*, Lakefield, Jackson County, Minnesota. January 2, 1919. p. 1.

10 Grover Fuller, Anna K. "The Unfortunate Letter Carrier." 1934.

11 Rathbun Funk, Margaret. Letter written, February 24, 1922.

12 *Windom Recorder*, Windom, Minnesota. September 11, 1914.

13 *Windom Recorder*, Windom, Minnesota. October 2, 1914.

14 *Cottonwood County Courier*, Windom, Minnesota. October 13, 1883.

15 Burleigh, Sandy. Pioneers Peek Out from the Past: On Baldwin Wisconsin and Surrounding Areas. 2001. p. 104.

16 Burleigh, Sandy. Pioneers Peek Out from the Past: On Baldwin Wisconsin and Surrounding Areas. 2001. p. 105.

17 Burleigh, Sandy. Pioneers Peek Out from the Past: On Baldwin Wisconsin and Surrounding Areas. 2001. p. 105.

18 Burleigh, Sandy. Pioneers Peek Out from the Past: On Baldwin Wisconsin and Surrounding Areas. 2001. p. 105.

19 Chapman, Samuel, D. History of Tama County, Iowa. Its cities, towns and villages, with early reminiscences, personal incidents and anecdotes and a complete business directory of the county: Nabu Press. 2010. p. 897.

20 Richter, Gary, and Arthur Louis Finnell, Sanborn, Minnesota, including the townships of Charlestown and Germantown: Centennial History, 1881-1981, 1981. p. 3.

21 "Was it Murder? Death of Lewis Miller at Sanborn Still a Mystery," *Redwood Reveille*, Redwood Falls, Minnesota, March, 1910.

22 *Redwood Gazette*, Redwood Falls, Minnesota, June, 1910.

23 *The St. Paul Daily Globe*, St. Paul, Minnesota. July 10, 1892. p. 2.

24 *The St. Paul Daily Globe*, St. Paul, Minnesota. May 1, 1890. p. 2.

25 *The St. Paul Daily Globe*, St. Paul, Minnesota. July 12, 1892. p. 8.

26 *The St. Paul Daily Globe*, St. Paul, Minnesota. February 15, 1891. p. 1.

27 *Canby News*, Canby, Minnesota. August 18, 1893.

28 Beecher, Catherine E. and Beecher Stowe, Professor Harriet. *The American Woman's Home*: Rutgers University Press. 2002.

29 *The Dominion Annual Register and Review, 1882.* 1883, Pp. 204-205.

30 *Milwaukee Sentinel*, Milwaukee, Wisconsin. September 18, 1891.

31 *Duluth Evening Herald*, Duluth, Minnesota. December 1, 1905.

32 *Duluth News Tribune*, Duluth, Minnesota. December 6, 1905.

33 Leavenworth Wilder Morris, Lucy. *Old Rail Fence Corners: The A.B.C.'s of Minnesota History*: Scholar Choice Edition. 2015.

34 Leavenworth Wilder Morris, Lucy. *Old Rail Fence Corners: The A.B.C.'s of Minnesota History*: Scholar Choice Edition. 2015.

35 Maxfield, Kinsey. *Daily Review*, Mankato, Minnesota. August 28, 1915.

36 *Saint Paul Daily News*, Saint Paul, Minnesota. December 22, 1893. p. 3.

37 "George Maxfield's House goes up in Flames." *Mankato Free Press*, Mankato, Minnesota. May 27, 1904.

38 "Geo. Maxfield, Pioneer Resident, Passed Away Early Last Evening." *Mankato Free Press*, Mankato, Minnesota. January 2, 1913.

39 *Mankato Free Press*, Mankato, Minnesota. January 13, 1914.

Made in the USA
Middletown, DE
12 February 2019